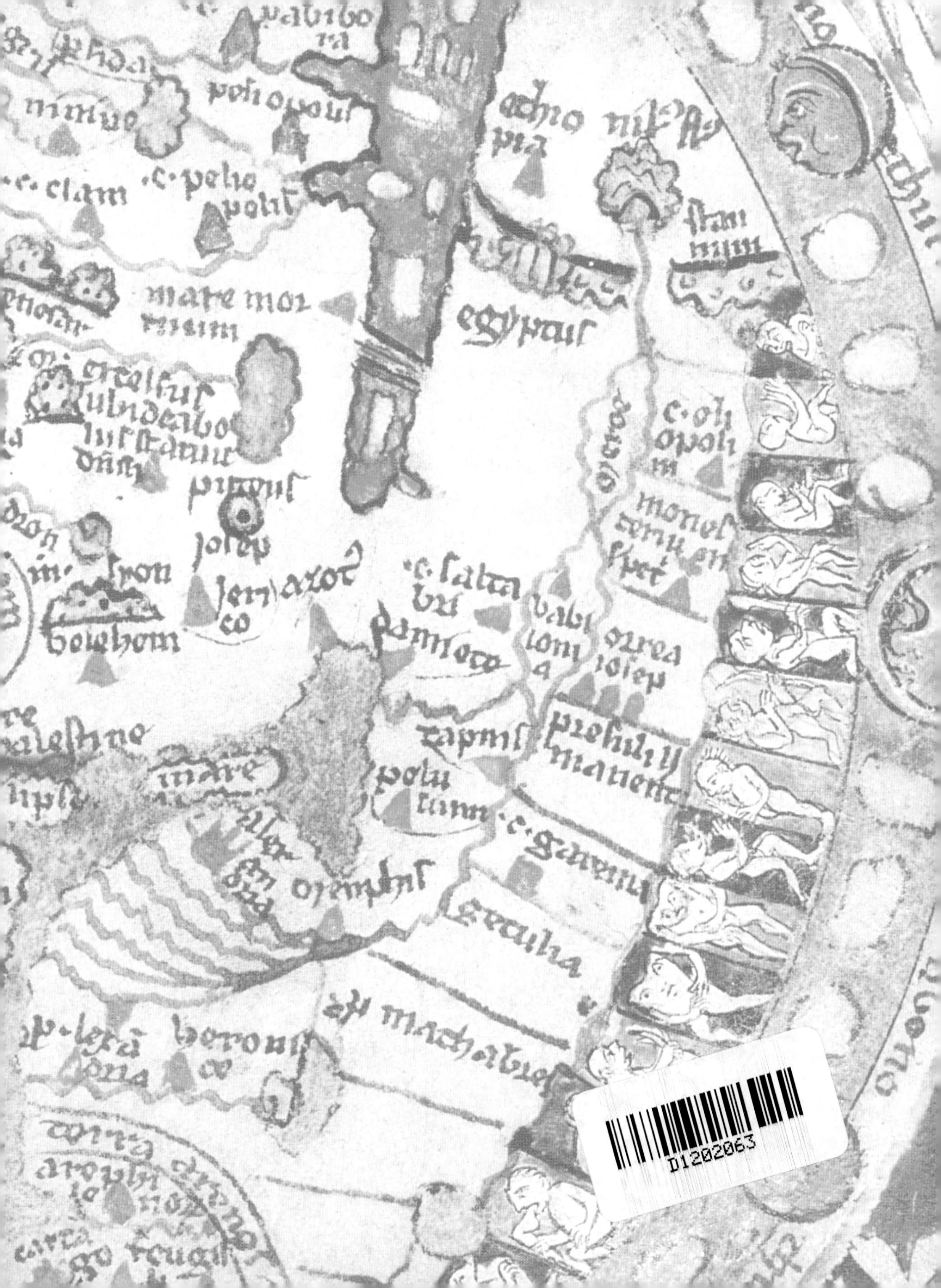

The Normans

The Normans

Christopher Gravett & David Nicolle

First published in Great Britain in 2006 by Osprey Publishing,
Midland House, West Way, Botley, Oxford OX2 0PH, United Kingdom.
443 Park Avenue South, New York, NY 10016, USA.

Email: info@ospreypublishing.com

Previously published as David Nicolle, Elite 9: *The Normans*; Chris Gravett, Fortress 13: *Norman Stone Castles (1) The British Isles 1066–1216*, Chris Gravett, Fortress 18: *Norman Stone Castles (2) Europe 950–1204*; and Chris Gravett, Warrior 1: *Norman Knight AD 950–1204*.

A CIP catalogue record for this book is available from the British Library

ISBN 1 84603 088 9

Page layout by Ken Vail Graphic Design, Cambridge, UK
Index by Alison Worthington
Maps by The Map Studio
Originated by The Electronic Page Company, Cwmbran, UK
Printed in China through Bookbuilders

06 07 08 09 10   10 9 8 7 6 5 4 3 2 1

For a catalogue of all books published by Osprey please contact:

NORTH AMERICA
Osprey Direct, c/o Random House Distribution Center, 400 Hahn Road, Westminster, MD 21157
Email: info@ospreydirect.com

ALL OTHER REGIONS
Osprey Direct UK, P.O. Box 140, Wellingborough, Northants, NN8 2FA, UK
E-mail: info@ospreydirect.co.uk

www.ospreypublishing.com
Front cover image: Topfoto / British Library / HIP
Title page image: Topfoto / British Library / HIP
Endpapers image: British Library

Contents

Introduction

The importance of the Normans in British and European history is denigrated, or at least accepted only grudgingly, by the English-speaking world. It is as if the English still could not come to terms with defeat by an army of supposed Frenchmen at the battle of Hastings in 1066. European scholars have generally taken a more objective view of the Normans and their spectacular two centuries of conquest. While the Anglo-Saxons created England, many would argue that the Normans at least began the creation of the United Kingdom of England, Wales, Scotland, the Channel Islands, the Isle of Man and, even to this day, part of Ireland.

The Norman contribution to French history is important, though less clear-cut, while the state they established in southern Italy and Sicily survived under successor dynasties until the unification of Italy in the 19th century. The last 'Norman state', that of the principality of Antioch in northern Syria, has received far less attention. It was clearly not so important in world history; yet its role in the story of the Crusades was in many respects as central as that of the Kingdom of Jerusalem itself.

PREVIOUS PAGE
St Edmund routs the
Danes, a manuscript of
1125–1150. Here the
lances are shown couched
in the prevalent 12th-
century fashion. The
rider at lower left has
horizontal ties across
his saddle bows which
may be to secure an
overblanket. Notice also
the figure at lower right
who wears a coif and
tunic as well as a long
underskirt. (© Photo
Scala Florence, Pierpont
Morgan Library 2004,
M.736 f7v)

Who were the medieval Normans? Were they tamed Vikings or provincial Frenchmen? Xenophobic English historians have argued that they never were a distinct people; but the fact remains that the Normans themselves and many of their contemporaries believed in a *Gens Normannorum* ('the Norman people'). Ethnic origins are irrelevant: if a group thinks that they are a separate entity, then they are one – even if only for a limited period. These *Normanni* certainly cultivated a sense of identity and common characteristics which, in the case of the Normans, tended to be of a military and political type. Ferocity, boundless energy, cunning and a capacity for leadership were their heritage, to which modern scholars would add supreme adaptability and a simple piety. This sense of *Normannitas* ('Normanness') survived into the 13th century, but was by then being submerged beneath new national identities which survive to this day – French, English, Scots and Irish. The situation in Italy was obviously different; while in Antioch, personal identity remained largely religious to the end.

In the early days similarities between the Normans and their Viking predecessors were clear enough. Amazing military successes resulted from careful planning, speed of movement, decisiveness, daring and sheer ruthlessness. Added to this was a strong business sense and an appreciation of the value of money. Yet it was the Normans' adaptability that set them apart from the Vikings. Both dominated their age militarily, but the Normans soon adopted Carolingian feudalism, cavalry warfare and castles to build archetypal feudal states in Normandy and England. They also adopted Christianity and became the strong sword-arm of a reforming church hierarchy.

In Italy they adopted advanced Byzantine or Islamic bureaucratic and financial structures, to build not only the most efficient but also perhaps the richest state in western Europe. In England they took over Anglo-Saxon political and legal institutions. By adding strong leadership and improved financial organization they guided the kingdom towards that fusion of democracy and law, strong government and individual freedom that was to become England's main contribution to European history. To differing degrees similar processes occurred in Scotland and the other Celtic states.

A vital key to such successes, military and political, was the Normans' characteristic toleration. If obedience and taxation were forthcoming they generally left their subjects alone. In Italy and Sicily this resulted in one of the great flowerings of culture in European history. Elsewhere the result was relative stability in which economic, political and cultural advances could take place.

The actual origins of the Normans lie in the Viking incursions of the 9th and 10th centuries into England and north-western France. In or about 911, Charles III (the Simple), King of the West Franks, was forced to allow a chieftain called Rollo, operating in the Seine valley, to settle his men on territory in what is now Upper or eastern Normandy bounded by the rivers

Bresle, Epte, Avre and Dives. The Treaty of St-Clair-sur-Epte has come down in a semi-legendary form. In return for the gift of land the king would be a nominal overlord, possibly recognizing Rollo's conversion to Christianity and receiving military aid. The new state would also act as a buffer against further raiding. Rollo soon expanded his territories into Lower or western Normandy. In 924 the Bessin and districts of Sées and Exmes were granted to him, whilst his son and successor, William Longsword, gained the Cotentin and Avranchin in 933.

The newly defined boundaries fitted less those of the Carolingian province of Neustria than the old Roman province of the Second Lyonnaise. From this, Rouen had become the metropolitan head of the province and remained as the most important city of the new Norman duchy. The new settlers spoke Scandinavian and had come to a country in which the native population was Gallo-Roman with an overculture of Germanic Frankish lords. Rollo at least seems to have been Norwegian, but the settlement of Vikings soon saw the new creation given the name of Normandy – land of the Northmen. It was not long before the Normans in Upper Normandy, their ducal base at Rouen, began to adapt themselves to French custom and largely adopted what is now termed the Old French tongue. In Lower Normandy Scandinavian customs tended to linger and for a time the two areas lived uneasily with one another. This state was ended after a revolt of lords, largely in Lower Normandy, was crushed at

The Bayeux Tapestry was probably worked within 20 years of the battle of Hastings. Here Count Guy of Ponthieu appears to wear a sleeveless coat of scale armour when receiving Duke William's messengers. (Bayeux Tapestry, Ancient Art and Architecture)

9

Val-ès-Dunes in 1047 by the youthful Duke William II and King Henry I of France. Thereafter William set about establishing a ducal presence in the west at Caen and tied his lords more closely, assisted by the old unifying boundaries of metropolitan Rouen.

The Norman dukes had always had an uneasy relationship with the French king. As nominal overlord they owed him feudal fealty and whilst Normandy was in formation the king was content. After Duke William's victory at Val-ès-Dunes the new stability disturbed the monarch who decided the duchy was becoming too powerful for comfort. He therefore allied himself with the Angevins on the southern borders of Normandy. Anjou would always be a rival for the land along the southern marches and here lay perhaps the most contested border. In 1054 and again in 1057 King Henry, allied with Count Geoffrey of Anjou, led forces into Normandy. He was beaten off both at Mortemer and Varaville, leaving William in a strong position.

When William's second cousin, Edward of England, died in 1066 the duke swore he had been named as heir during that king's previous exile in Normandy. The Angevin count and the French king had both died in 1060; the new king was a minor in the wardship of William's father-in-law; the Bretons to the west had been given a show of strength. Under these auspicious circumstances the duke made his bid for the English crown. Harold, the new

William raises his helmet to scotch rumours of his death at the crisis of the battle of Hastings. He seems to wear separate mail sleeves on the forearms. The angle of the helmet suggests it is actually held by its chin straps. On Eustace of Boulogne the square on the chest is visible, as if the ventail has been loosened to aid identification. (Bayeux Tapestry, Ancient Art and Architecture)

king, was beaten near Hastings and William at a stroke had brought a new and rich kingdom under the sway of Normandy. As King of England he now increased his power enormously. Unfortunately the cohesion of this situation was never strong. His sons squabbled as each wished to control all. William Rufus succeeded his father in 1087 but died whilst hunting in the New Forest in 1100. His young brother, Henry, took the throne and imprisoned his elder brother, Robert of Normandy. Tragedy robbed Henry of a male heir when his own son drowned in the White Ship disaster in the Channel. Consequently civil war broke out on Henry's death in 1135 between his daughter, Matilda, and his nephew, Stephen, who had been made king by barons hostile to a woman's rule.

The war made the lords aware of how difficult it was to owe fealty both to a duke of Normandy and an English king. On Stephen's death in 1154 Matilda's son, Henry, took the crown. Henry, who had inherited the county of Anjou from his father, marked the beginning of the Plantagenet line of kings; England was now part of an Angevin empire that stretched from the borders of Scotland to the Pyrenees. The country, of course, was still essentially an Anglo-Norman realm. However, now lords were forced to renounce dual control of cross-Channel possessions, settling either in England or Normandy.

It was the French king, Philip II Augustus, who finally wrested the duchy from the control of the English crown. His most obvious target was Normandy, an area which also isolated Paris from the Channel. Disputes about the possession of the Vexin area in the Seine valley were serious in themselves, but they also led to the final showdown. Richard I, known as the Lionhearted, who ascended to the throne in 1189, defended Normandy successfully, though he might also have squandered his military and financial resources. In 1199 his brother John inherited a far more difficult situation. Angevin power was scattered across an enormous empire. Nor was John as respected by the Norman warrior class as his Crusading brother had been. The aristocracy of Normandy was also attracted by the increasingly brilliant culture of Paris, with its cult of chivalry, poetry and Courtly Love. Many still resented the Angevin takeover, and John found himself deserted by some leading barons. The Angevin cause also suffered from the brutality of both Richard's and John's mercenaries, particularly as much of the fighting took place on Norman soil. The French king was even able to use the Norman duke's right to enter castles by claiming that he, as the duke's legitimate sovereign, should also be permitted to enter any fortress he wished. The war dragged on sporadically until, in 1202, Philip launched a series of major campaigns. Brittany, part of Poitou, Touraine, Anjou, Maine and finally, in the spring of 1204, Normandy itself, fell.

The area would again be dominated by the English during the Hundred Years War but, in 1204, one could say that for the first time in over 300 years Normandy had returned to the French fold. The consequences were less clear-cut for those involved. Many Anglo-Norman barons held lands on both sides of the Channel. Some did homage to both kings, but most remained in England. Normandy thus lost the bulk of its leading aristocracy and was quite easily absorbed into France. Nevertheless, Norman knights still sought employment in the remaining Angevin areas for many years.

The energy of the Normans carried them beyond Normandy and England. At the same time as adventurers were conquering England, other Normans were carving out kingdoms in southern Italy and Sicily. Mercenaries had fought in a revolt against the Byzantines in Italy as early as 1017 and began settling in about 1029, but it was not until 1041 that Robert Guiscard and his followers began to seize land for themselves. The Pope recognized their possessions around Apulia and Calabria in 1059, hoping to use the Normans as a counter to pressures from the emperor in the German lands to the north. By 1071 they had taken Bari, effectively ending Byzantine control. The invasion of Sicily began in 1060 and was not completed for 31 years. Initially ruled separately, the states came under one authority in 1127, being recognized as a kingdom three years later. In about 1134 a successful invasion of Tunisia was under way, taking advantage of internal feuding between the Zirid rulers. From 1148 until its collapse by 1160 the Normans ruled an area from Tunis to the Gulf of Sirte. Despite attempts to attack the Greek mainland

A painted marriage chest, probably Breton, 1150–70, depicting a knight mounting his horse and two others at full gallop. The front rider carries a lance with pennant, and both carry kite shields. (Photo12.com, Oasis)

and the capture of Thessaloniki, the Siculo-Norman kingdom was riven by discord which ended in 1194 with the invasion by the German Hohenstaufen Emperor, Henry VI.

Normans were also very much in evidence in the First Crusade. Two of the leaders were Duke Robert of Normandy and Bohemond of Taranto with his contingent of south Italian fighters. Bohemond went on to set up the principality of Antioch in Syria. Situated on a trade route and the richest Crusader state, the port of Lattakieh was the final town of the principality to fall to the Muslims in 1287.

An ivory altar back shows southern Italian warriors wearing what appears to be scale armour. Their helmets seem to have either early attached neck-guards, or simply a deep helmet over a coif. (Salerno, Cathedral Museum, David Nicolle)

Chronology

	25 Dec. William is crowned King William I of England in Westminster Abbey.
1068	Siege of Exeter.
1068–71	Siege of Bari in southern Italy
1070	Final major revolts in England put down.
1071	Capture of Bari by the Normans.
1071–72	Siege and capture of Palermo. Roger I is made Great Count of Sicily.
1073	Siege of Amalfi.
1076–77	Siege of Salerno.
1077	First attack on Normandy by Fulk le Rechin of Anjou and siege of La Flèche.
1078	First revolt of Robert, William's eldest son.
1079	William defeated at Gerberoi by his son, Robert.
1081	Battle of Durazzo. Italo-Norman army of Robert Guiscard and son, Bohemond of Taranto, defeats Byzantine army and takes Corfu.
1081	Second attack on Normandy by Fulk le Rechin and second siege of La Flèche.
1081	Sea battle off Durazzo (Dyrrachium).
1081–82	Siege of Durazzo.
1082	Normans capture Damascus.
1083	Second revolt of Robert against King William I.
1085	Death of Robert Guiscard.
1087	Death of King William I. William Rufus succeeds as William II. Robert becomes Duke of Normandy.
1088	Sieges of Tonbridge, Pevensey and Rochester.
1090	Normans capture Malta and Gozo.
1091	Norman conquest of Sicily completed.
1095	Preaching of First Crusade.
1097	Battle of Dorylaeum. Forces of First Crusade, including Italo-Normans of Bohemond, hard pressed until second column surprises and defeats Turks.
1098	Bohemond captures Antioch.
1100	Bohemond becomes Prince of Antioch. William II killed in New Forest. Younger brother Henry becomes King Henry I of England.

1101	Death of Roger I of Sicily.
1106	Battle of Tinchebrai. Henry I defeats and imprisons his brother, Duke Robert of Normandy.
1107–08	Siege of Durazzo by Bohemond. A treaty is forced on him and he leaves for Italy.
1111	Death of Bohemond of Taranto.
1118	Battle of Alençon. Henry I defeated by Geoffrey of Anjou whilst trying to relieve the castle.
1119	Battle of Brémule. Henry I defeats invading force of Louis VI of France.
1124	Battle of Bourgthéroulde. Household knights of Henry I defeat rebel Waleran of Meulan.
1130	Election of Roger d'Hauteville as King Roger II of Sicily.
1132	Battle of Nocera. Roger II of Sicily defeated by Apulian Norman rebels.
1134	Death of Duke Robert II. Normans invade Tunisia.
1135	Death of Henry I. Accession of King Stephen. Civil war breaks out in England over disputed succession between Henry's nephew, Stephen, and his daughter, Matilda.
1136	Siege of Exeter.
1138	Battle of the Standard (Northallerton). Army of Stephen defeats David I of Scotland.
1139	Siege of Devizes. Siege of Ludlow.
1141	Battle of Lincoln. Robert of Gloucester and rebel forces come to relief of city, defeat and capture Stephen. Exchange of Stephen for Robert when the latter captured trying to break out of Winchester later that year.
1142	Siege of Oxford. Matilda escapes Stephen's siege lines.
1144	Geoffrey of Anjou conquers Normandy during civil war.
1148	Norman province in North Africa established.
1154	Death of Stephen. Accession of Henry II, son of Matilda and Geoffrey, Count of Anjou. Death of Roger II of Sicily. Accession of William I, the Bad.
1158–65	Henry II invades Wales
1160	End of Norman province in North Africa.
1166	Death of William I, the Bad. Accession of William II, the Good.
1169–71	Henry II invades Ireland.
1173–74	Revolt of Henry's sons, and attacks of Louis VII of France. Scots invade northern England and besiege Carlisle, Brough and Prudhoe.

1184	Papal forces capture Rome supported by Guiscard.
1188–89	Second revolt of sons of King Henry II.
1189	Death of Henry II and accession of his son, Richard I (Lionheart). Death of William the Good of Sicily.
1190	King Richard leads the Third Crusade to the Holy Land. Capture of Richard. Accession of Tancred of Lecce.
1192–94	Philip II captures Norman border castles.
1194	Richard ransomed and returns. Norman kingdom of Italy and Sicily falls to Emperor Henry VI. Death of Tancred – accession and death of William III.
1194–98	Recapture of fortresses by Richard.
1199	Death of Richard I at siege of Châlus castle in France. Accession of brother, John.
1203–04	Siege of Château-Gaillard.
1204	Loss of Normandy to Philip II of France.
1215	Magna Carta is sealed. Civil war sees rebels and Prince Louis of France besiege Rochester.
1216	Prince Louis besieges Dover. Death of John. Accession of Henry III.
1287	Port of Lattakieh, last possession of principality of Antioch, falls to Muslims.

History of the Normans

The Normans were both a militaristic and a hierarchical people. Ducal authority was ascendant during the 11th century, although tensions with barons always remained present, and a periodic source of conflict. Under the dukes developed an increasingly feudal Norman society, and feudalism in turn generated the ranks of cavalry, infantry, archers and crossbowmen. When the feudal army did not suffice for a campaign, as it often didn't, mercenaries were employed in large numbers. From the Normans' hierarchical military arrangements, the knight also emerged with an almost aristocratic status by the mid-12th century, accompanied by the introduction of heraldry and the Chivalric Code. This part examines not only the military, political and social structures of Norman society and its attendant ideologies, but also the distinct variations in these structures across the Norman territories, from Ireland to Antioch. It also assesses the power and limitations of Norman weaponry – the lance, the crossbow and bow, swords and javelins – and how tactics and equipment were modified according to local cultural traditions. In so doing, this part helps explain why the Normans were a major power across Europe for over two centuries.

Feudalism

Until the early 11th century the Normans were still Viking in character, welcoming Scandinavian raiding fleets as allies. On the other hand one important Viking institution, the democratic assembly or *thing*, was never seen among the Normans. Early Normandy was also militarily weak compared to its neighbours, Norman forces being smaller than those of Anjou as well as having inferior discipline.

As the feudalization of Normandy progressed during the 11th century, however, so Norman strength grew. Feudalism has often been described in misleadingly simplified terms. Essentially, however, it was a means of unifying a state by binding together ruler and ruled, king with duke, local lord with humble knight, through solemn oaths of vassalage, fealty or homage. This was considered an 'honourable' arrangement, and it formed a contract under which the strong agreed to defend the weak, the weak to support the strong. The more favoured a vassal, the more likely he was to be awarded a piece of land or fief, plus its inhabitants. This he held as the tenant of his lord. Such an estate was to help a vassal, usually a knight, to afford the increasingly expensive military equipment of the day. This was the archetypal *fief de haubert* – the hauberk being a mail shirt which supposedly distinguished an elite armoured cavalryman from the rest of the army. The fief also freed the warrior from manual work so that he could concentrate on his military skills.

Medieval terminology is notoriously imprecise, but it does seem that the *milites* were true vassals, though not necessarily holding land, while the *stipendiarii* swore lesser oaths and fought primarily for pay. Each could, however, be regarded as an early form of knight. Comparable bonds linked the peasants with the enfiefed vassal, but were decreasingly 'honourable', which in turn reflected the declining military status of the general peasant levy. Not that foot soldiers as such were disappearing from the scene. In fact infantry seem to have grown more specialized, and were no longer simply drawn from an untrained peasantry. Deep-rooted as Norman feudalism was by the mid-11th century, it was never as neat as the system imposed upon England after 1066. One Norman peculiarity was the *vavassor*, an unclear military status and form of land tenure between knight and peasant which was probably left over from pre-feudal times.

Duke, Lords and Church

The south door of the cathedral at Bari in southern Italy possesses early 12th-century carvings which portray mailed knights wearing armour similar in style to that seen used by the Normans elsewhere. The left-hand figure appears to be about to throw his lance or strike overarm. (David Nicolle)

In many parts of Europe the growing effectiveness of the military class led to private war and near anarchy, but in Normandy it was accompanied by a growth in the power of the duke. This was not a smooth process, as ducal authority – particularly over castle-building – suffered a setback in the 1030s and 1040s. A breakthrough came in the reign of Duke William – later William the Conqueror – before his invasion of England in 1066. At first William cooperated with his military aristocracy; then in 1047, he crushed those who still defied him in the decisive battle of Val-ès-Dunes. During the following years the duke's government was aggressive, warlike and much to the taste of his knights and nobles. He was, in fact, a fine general, calm but decisive and able to win the respect of ordinary soldiers. William's exceptional organizational ability was well illustrated in his gathering of an army and a fleet in 1066. The

duke's own large estates (*domain*) enabled him to enfief and enrich loyal supporters, who were then placed in command of key castles and forces. Duke William did not, however, have such control over castle-building, and so had to take a more persuasive, cooperative line with his barons. Yet he did win the right to enter any castle, so stopping local lords from falsely seizing additional fortifications in his name. Neither were economic measures ignored, the development of William's favourite city of Caen being encouraged in an effort to strengthen ducal authority in Lower Normandy.

Powerful as William might have grown by 1066, the duke still had to consult his barons and win their sometimes grudging support for his great invasion of England. Diplomatic preparations were also vital. Duke William remained a vassal of France, virtually independent though he now seemed. Yet he convinced most European rulers of his right to the English crown, and above all he won Papal support, symbolized by a banner which was flown at Hastings.

The warlike aristocracy Duke William came to dominate was a new class of men compared to the old aristocracy of France. These latter often claimed descent from Carolingian times, but few Norman families could trace their ancestry back before 1010. The military class had also bred with remarkable speed. Most knights remained poor and land-hungry, land-hunger being simply a matter of survival, and by 1066 Normandy had been exporting warriors for more than a generation.

The alliance between Duke William and the Papacy reflected a long-standing cooperation between the Norman leadership and the Church. The Church helped unify Normandy; many ecclesiastical leaders came from the Norman aristocracy, while others were retired warriors. The secular aristocracy enthusiastically founded monasteries, many of which then owed military service for their lands. In fact it seems as if many of the earliest landed knights were linked to such abbeys, particularly those near exposed frontiers. Not that there was yet any great social distinction between landed and landless knights. Knighthood itself held little status, and merely indicated that a man was a professional warrior. He often appeared as a mere statistic, as in a pre-1066 charter of the Abbey of St Père de Chartres which described one village as having 'a church, land for three plough teams, twelve peasants, five free knights and a mill'. Nor did knighthood yet involve much pomp or display: rather, it consisted of hard training and harder knocks.

Norman Warriors

Cavalry training was undertaken in groups of five to ten. Standards of discipline were clearly higher than most critics of medieval warfare have allowed, and the same was probably true of command and control at this basic unit level. It might also be fair to say that medieval generalship was as good – or as inadequate – as in any other age.

The basic fighting unit was the *conroi* of 20 to 30 men in two or three ranks. This would have been identified by its own small spear-mounted flag or *gonfanon*. While shield devices were probably only decorative at this time, flags were essential for command and control. The evidence suggests that the Norman *conroi*, or the larger *bataille* to which it contributed, was well able to make controlled charges, to wheel, to turn, and even to retreat in 'feigned flight' – a difficult manoeuvre demanding discipline and adequate signalling procedures.

The whole question of the feigned retreat by 11th-century Norman cavalry is still hotly debated. It seems to have been employed against the French at St Aubin in 1053 and against the Sicilian Arabs at Messina in 1060. The Normans might have learned it from their Breton neighbours, or from men returning from service in southern Italy or Spain. Breton cavalry seem to have known of the feigned retreat even in the 10th century. It is worth noting that the Breton left wing at Hastings was the first part of Duke William's army apparently to retreat. This is normally considered to have been a genuine flight, whereas the second retreat by the duke's own men is widely regarded as a feigned flight. Literary descriptions of the battle of Hastings also concentrate on swords rather than spears: perhaps the latter were soon broken against Saxon shields, or had been hurled at the foe. Cavalry training certainly included the throwing of javelins from horseback.

In wider strategic terms the supposedly impetuous Normans were notably cautious in warfare, often adopting a patient wait-and-see attitude. Careful reconnaissance was normal, and winter campaigns common. On the other hand battles involving only cavalry were rare, at least in France. The role of infantry remained important, and 11th-century knights were both trained and willing to fight on foot. References to *milites pedites* – 'footknights' – are, however, few in relation to the total of ordinary *milites*.

Archery was certainly important among the Normans, Duke William himself being a renowned bowman. Their conquest of England led to a great increase in the use of the bow in the British Isles. Two distinct classes of archers are shown on the Bayeux Tapestry, those in the main picture being well dressed or even armoured, while those in the lower panel are a ragged band. Perhaps the former are professionals, the latter representatives of a general levy

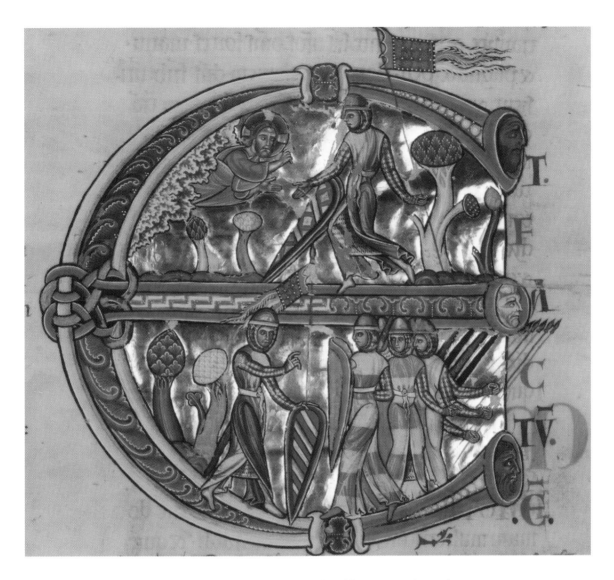

or *arrière ban* – a rarely used and shadowy remnant of the old Germanic levy of all free men. At the end of the Bayeux Tapestry one Norman archer pursues the defeated Saxons on horseback. He wears spurs; and while this might be an artistic error, it has been used as evidence either for the unlikely existence of Norman horse-archers, or to indicate that professional bowmen were mobile mounted infantry. The Norman archers at Hastings were skilled and disciplined enough to drop flights of arrows on their foes in a form of zone-shooting normally associated with Byzantines or Turks. It is even possible that some of the shorter bows in the Bayeux Tapestry were of southern European composite construction: perhaps these were used by mercenaries enrolled by Duke William? Other evidence suggests that crossbows were employed, though none

An initial from the Winchester Bible of c. 1170 shows knights in flowing surcoats with simple decoration. Their mailcoats have the sleeves extended to cover their hands while leaving the fingers exposed. (Reproduction by permission of the Dean and Chapter of Winchester Cathedral)

William of Normandy killing Harold at the battle of Hastings in a miscellaneous chronicle, probably of the late 13th century. (Topfoto/British Library/HIP)

are illustrated on the Tapestry. They were clearly already known in France, and would become common among the Normans soon afterwards.

By the end of the 10th century the increasing power of the military aristocracy had already given rise to the Peace of God movement in southern and central France. In this the Church and common people tried to curb the violence of lesser barons and knights. Local rulers often supported the movement, as they had an interest in stability if not in actual peace. Duke Richard II of Normandy at first rejected the Peace of God, trusting in his own ability to keep the peace. Near-anarchy followed his death, and Duke William was happy to proclaim his own Truce of God in 1047, the year of Val-ès-Dunes. This truce laid down the days when fighting was banned and also listed those people who could not be harmed in 'private warfare'. The duke himself and his armies were, of course, exempt from such restrictions.

As a virtually independent prince, the Duke of Normandy had political relationships with neighbouring rulers, the most important of whom was his nominal suzerain, the King of France. After defeating the last French attempt to destroy the duchy in 987 the Norman dukes followed a relatively consistent policy of support for the French crown. Tensions remained, and even as late as 1054 and 1058 the king invaded. Anjou and Flanders were, however, normally the main threats to Normandy.

Norman relations with Anglo-Saxon England were more straightforward. In the year 1000 an Anglo-Saxon fleet may even have attacked western Normandy to forestall Viking raiders based there; but as Normandy became Christian in religion and French in speech, so its dukes found a common interest with the rulers of southern Britain in closing the English Channel to Viking fleets. This alliance broke up when the Normans supported Edward and the House of Wessex against Cnut of Denmark in their struggle for the English throne. When Edward (the Confessor) returned from exile in Normandy to take the English crown he was, understandably, pro-Norman in his sympathies. As a man of southern England, Edward feared the Scandinavian threat and knew that a Norman succession after his death would finally close the Channel to the Vikings. The paucity and tendentious character of surviving evidence also means that Duke William's claim to the English throne should perhaps be given more credibility than it normally is.

The Norman duke's comparable fear of Scandinavian intervention contributed to William's alliance with his erstwhile rivals in Flanders in 1066. Other perennial victims of Viking raiders had been the Channel Islands or Îles Normandes. These are not, nor have they ever been, part of England; nor, contrary to popular opinion, were they part of the duchy of Normandy in 1066. The islands were instead a personal dependency of Duke William, as were the counties of Brittany and Maine. Like these areas, they contributed men and ships to the great expedition of 1066.

Many Norman warriors, administrators and churchmen had served in England under Edward the Confessor. Some were responsible for reorganizing English defences along the Welsh borders around 1055, though their attempts to introduce Norman-French styles of cavalry ultimately failed in battle. Not until 1066 was English military tradition really changed.

The Norman Conquest of England was perhaps the single most dramatic event in British history, but it was less important in the history of Normandy itself. During the early post-Conquest years the wealth and strength of England helped the dukes strengthen their position. This can be seen in the *Consuetudines* of 1091, which gave the ruler greater control over castle-building as well as the right to occupy any fortification whenever he wanted to. It stated that a man might not attack an enemy if this foe was on his way to or from the

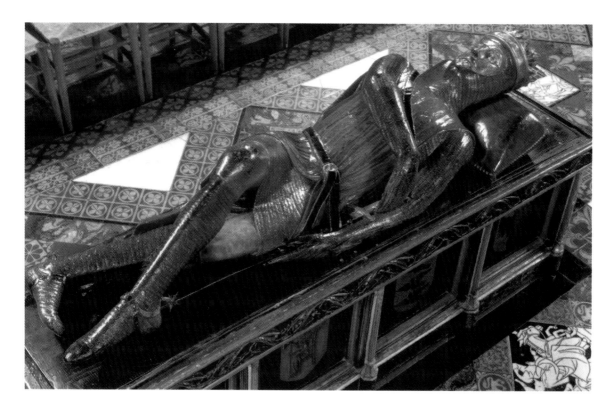

The late 13th-century wooden effigy of Robert 'Curthose', Duke of Normandy, eldest son of William the Conqueror, in Gloucester Cathedral. (Topfoto/Woodmansterne)

duke's court or army. Pilgrims and merchants were similarly protected. Pillaging was banned, as was the burning of houses and mills and damage to agricultural tools. Such efforts to control endemic violence were limited to what was practically possible, but this Norman Peace did go beyond the earlier Peace of God by banning fighting on Wednesdays and Monday mornings...

As before, the development of government power went in fits and starts. After William the Conqueror died in 1087 his realm was divided between William II, who became King of England, and Robert 'Curthose', who ruled Normandy somewhat ineffectively. The duchy consequently fell into anarchy, with the aristocracy recovering much of its lost independence. Not until 1106 were the two areas reunited under Henry I, who went on to demolish most of the unauthorized 'adulterine' castles recently erected.

Meanwhile the status of the knights continued to rise, until, by the mid-12th century, they had become a true minor aristocracy. With this went the development of heraldry and the passing on of motifs – though not as yet true coats-of-arms – from father to son. This preceded the adoption of closed helmets which hid the wearer's face, and was probably unconnected with it. The first certain reference to undoubted Norman heraldry was in 1127, when Henry I knighted his son-in-law Geoffrey of Anjou and gave him the badge of gold lions on a blue ground. A lion might already have been Henry's own badge.

Two lions were used by Henry II, and two lions or leopards on red remain the arms of Normandy to this day. A third beast was subsequently added by Richard I to distinguish the arms of England. King Stephen is sometimes credited with arms of three gold centaurs on red: this was probably a later invention, though he might have had a centaur or 'sagittary' as a badge.

The military demands made upon knights in Normandy were actually less than those seen in Anglo-Norman England, but whereas the rural knights of England were largely demilitarized in the late Norman and Angevin periods, the knights of Normandy remained a warrior class for longer. In England a tax called *scutage* (shield money) was paid in preference to military service, and the idea eventually spread to Normandy, where it was adopted earlier than in the rest of France.

Shaken by a rebellion in 1173–74, Henry II set about regularizing the military situation. The first result was the Assize of Northampton (1176) which investigated the duties of castle guard in England. Four years later these were reformed, and in the same year the Ordnance of Le Mans did the same for the king's French provinces. In 1181 the Assize of Arms sorted out the question of personal and government weaponry, as well as prohibiting the export of military stores and equipment. These Assizes stated that a knight should have at least a hauberk, helmet, shield and lance, an ordinary freeman a smaller mail *haubergeon*, an iron cap and a lance. The urban burgess class was permitted a padded gambeson as armour, an iron cap and a lance but no more. Military equipment was, in fact, growing more expensive, and the best was consequently limited to a professional elite. In 1080 a mail hauberk cost 100 *sous*, from two to five times as much as a horse. A horse itself was worth five times as much as a bull, and by the 13th century a warhorse or *destrier* was no less than seven times as valuable as an ordinary horse. The best destriers came from Spain, northern Italy or Sicily.

One way to obtain this expensive equipment was to win it in a tournament; but Henry II had banned tournaments in England. Those who sought fame, fortune and adventure in this field had to travel to France, Flanders, Burgundy or Champagne. The warrior class was inevitably becoming stratified between knights, *bachelers*, *pueri*, *armigeri* (squires), *vavassors*, *serviens*, *serjeants* and others. By 1133 *vavassor* service in Normandy was expected only of men holding 50 to 60 acres, and they were later regarded as being worth from one quarter to one half of a full knight. The exact meaning of *bacheler* is still uncertain, but it probably referred to youthful enthusiasm and perhaps inexperience rather than to a strict military status.

One group of warriors who were clearly rising in importance were the mercenaries. They proved themselves not only to be better trained and equipped than most feudal warriors, but also more reliable. Various groups are recorded, including the highly respected Brabançons from present-day Belgium, and the fearsome Cottereaux and Routiers. The Brabançons appear mostly to have been serjeants, probably crossbowmen and spearmen of urban burgess background led by knights, but by 1202 they and other Flemish mercenaries included fully armoured cavalry on armoured horses. The Cottereaux may have been infantry of lower class or even outlaw origins, the Routiers perhaps being horsemen. Nevertheless, crossbowmen remained the mercenaries most in demand through this period. Mercenaries were employed not only for major campaigns but also to garrison castles. Aragonese from northern Spain are recorded under Henry II, while Richard I apparently introduced a few Muslim troops, either enslaved PoWs from the Crusader States or more probably men from Norman Sicily. (A relic of their brief service in Normandy might have been the two 'Turkish bows' of presumed composite construction listed among William Marshal's effects in 1246.) After Normandy and Anjou were lost to the French, men from these areas were still recruited as mercenaries by King John of England, who particularly welcomed skilled engineers.

A third group of warriors were the men from various vassal states. Some Welsh and Scottish contingents could be seen in this light, while troops from Brittany and Maine were clearly vassals. Even as late as 1120 Bretons were regarded as supreme cavalry but far less effective on foot. In the battle of Tinchebrai (1106) all of Henry I's army dismounted except the men of Brittany and Maine. At Lincoln (1141) the Bretons similarly refused to fight on foot.

The motte is erected at Hastings. These artificial mounds topped with timber palisades and a wooden tower were quick to build. They were served by a bailey or courtyard protected by earthen bank and palisades. The whole castle would be surrounded by a ditch. Some castles consisted of a simple ringwork without a motte. Such structures continued in use throughout this period. (Bayeux Tapestry, Ancient Art and Architecture)

During the 12th century, however, the government, the administration and to a lesser extent the military styles of Brittany were remoulded in the Norman image, and traditional Celtic systems finally disappeared.

Norman warfare became more organized and sophisticated during the later 11th and 12th centuries, but there were few fundamental changes. Sieges were central features of almost all conflicts and most battles resulted from attempts to relieve a garrison. Battles were also regarded as unpredictable and potentially disastrous, so that set-piece confrontations tended to be a last resort or a result of miscalculation. In fact many battles were avoided by truces or negotiations or by one side backing down. Unnecessary bloodshed within the military elite was similarly avoided. Knights disliked fighting their previous comrades, while even humbler infantry were often able to restrain knightly aggression against their fellows.

Norman infantry were not yet organized in such recognizable units as were the cavalry – yet they were no rabble. Where possible they protected their flanks with natural obstacles such as rivers, woods, hills or marshes. In open country round or rectangular formations were adopted, the shape being a matter of local

The second great seal of Richard I, struck in 1194 on his release from captivity. Despite popular opinion, the king is not shown wearing a surcoat. A long undergarment issues from beneath his mail. The shield now carries the three lions of England for the first time. His helm is quite advanced, almost fully covering the head and provided with a fan crest, presumably of metal, on which are echoed the lions of the shield. (Public Records Office, London)

31

Siege of Jerusalem 'portrayed upon a tile' (Ezek.4.1.), showing wheeled battering rams, and some of the earlier representations of crossbows; from a manuscript from Auxerre, c. 1000. (*Commentaries of Hayman on Ezekiel*, Ms.Lat.12302, Bib.Nat., Paris)

tradition. At Rouen in 1174 a defensive ditch had to be filled so that a formation of infantrymen 200 wide could advance; they seem to have totalled 5,000 to 6,000 men in three corps 12 ranks deep. Light infantry with bows, spears or javelins reappeared in certain areas; their role was skirmishing, or protecting the flanks of the main force. Sometimes they acted as almost autonomous units.

Improvements in crossbow design were a vital feature of warfare in the 11th to 13th centuries. This weapon became very popular in the Norman areas from the reign of Henry I onwards. Compared with simple European handbows, crossbows were easy to shoot accurately, had more range, a flatter trajectory and considerably greater penetrating power. Their only disadvantage was in loading time. Even this was more characteristic of later and more powerful crossbows, which had to be 'spanned' by using a windlass or crank: earlier types were basically spanned manually. Lock mechanisms were at first all of wood, but some parts were soon being made of horn, with a still unsprung trigger of iron. The loading stirrup fastened with sinew or rope appeared late in the 11th century, a belt with a loading hook sometime in the late 12th. Early crossbows were also

large and heavy. The actual string still had to be pulled back up to 90cm (35in), whereas 15th-century steel crossbows only had a draw of some 20cm (8in). The incorporation of composite bows of mixed horn, wood, whalebone and sinew made for a smaller yet more powerful weapon. This was almost certainly a result of experience in southern Italy, Sicily or the Middle East.

Normandy had few naturally defensible frontiers; defence was consequently organized in depth. Walled towns like Verneuil, Tillières and Nonancourt along the River Avre were created primarily as defensive bases. Elsewhere numerous castles, strongly garrisoned and fully supplied, overlooked fords and other vulnerable points (see 'Norman Stone Castles').

The interior of the donjon at Brionne. The castle sits in a small, arc-shaped enceinte; this may be one of two siege castle earthworks constructed by William the Bastard in 1047. A similar earthwork is found north-west of the town, on the edge of the opposite hill. In 1124 Henry I besieged Robert's son Galeran here. The lower part contains blocked small windows and the upper embrasures, suggesting two building periods. (Chris Gravett)

The Normans in Britain

In Normandy the years following 1066 saw a steady development of existing military styles, but in Britain they witnessed a military revolution. Duke William's invasion and the conquest of England were among the most astonishing feats of medieval arms, but the expedition was not a solely Norman affair. It attracted volunteers from all over France and beyond, many of whom subsequently settled in England. The planning was not particularly detailed, but the duke's strategy showed a real grasp of the geopolitical situation. William was clearly also capable of seizing an opportunity when it was offered.

Harold and his army were lured into an exhausting march south and then into a premature defensive battle. William's army then demonstrated – not without difficulty – the superiority of Norman-French mixed cavalry and infantry tactics over the Germanic-Scandinavian infantry traditions of the Anglo-Saxons. Clearly the couched lance was still being evolved, for spears were used in various other ways at Hastings. The throwing of such weapons was rare, but downward thrusts and other techniques were common. Most evidence relies on the Bayeux Tapestry, which may have been made, if not actually

During the battle of Hastings, Duke William rode among his men with his helmet raised to quell a panicky rumour that he had been killed. (Angus McBride © Osprey Publishing)

designed, by English seamstresses. The Tapestry might, in fact, be a more reliable representation of Anglo-Saxon than of Norman warriors.

The degree of continuity in English military systems after 1066 is still debated, but the military organization of Anglo-Norman England was not uniform. Cavalry, for example, were drawn from more than just the ranks of the land-holding knightly class. Nor was the imposition of feudalism the same in all areas. Military burdens were unevenly spread, falling hardest on the earliest areas to be conquered. At first landless 'household' knights were the most immediately available force. Only after the Conquest was secure were most knights settled on the land and given *fees* or fiefs. Even as late as the mid-12th century landless knights were a common feature of vulnerable frontier zones.

One of the most noticeable changes in the English military system was a steady emigration by the old Anglo-Saxon military elite, particularly by the generation following that defeated at Hastings. Younger warriors saw little hope of advancement in an England dominated by their conquerors. Although resistance had crumbled these men remained a threat to Norman security, and so their departure was welcomed by William the Conqueror and his son, William II. Some Anglo-Saxons left in the late 1060s, mostly to Denmark, and this emigration continued through the 1070s and 1080s. Large numbers moved on from Scandinavia in the wake of the famous Varangians, through Russia and down to Constantinople. Here the English became a major, perhaps even the main, element within the Byzantine Emperor's Guard. It has recently been suggested that one large group sailed directly to the eastern Mediterranean under Earl Sigurd in around 1075. The bulk then refused to serve as mere guardsmen and were sent northwards to retake the lost Byzantine province of Cherson in the Crimea. Here they are supposed to have merged with a Goth community surviving from the great age of Germanic migrations and, according to legend, to have created another *Nova Anglia* (New England) in southern Russia!

Back in Britain the departure of the old aristocracy did not mean the demilitarization of the Anglo-Saxons as a whole. The military power of England was large, from 5,000 to 7,000 men if necessary, and the Normans made good use of it. English infantry often needed training by Norman professionals, particularly when called upon to fight against cavalry, but they seem to have been quick to learn. It was here that the strongest military continuity between Anglo-Saxon and Norman times can be seen. The rank-and-file of Anglo-Norman armies was of mixed origins, including men of noble blood, assimilated Englishmen and adventurers from many parts.

The Norman Conquest raised the prestige of the bow as a war weapon, and by the 12th century it had become perhaps the most effective tool in the defence of northern England against Scottish raiders. English influence on cavalry seems unlikely. The fact that the Anglo-Saxon word *cniht* (knight) was adopted in preference to the French *chevalier* as the term for a professional horse-warrior

Although crudely executed, weathered by the centuries, and photographed in shadow, these two carvings of Anglo-Norman warriors, c. 1180, from the south door of St Mary's Barfreston church in Kent can still be seen to show the horseman with his lance in the couched position, and the knight on foot with a conical nasal helm, a split hauberk, and a 'kite' shield with the top edge cut off straight. (David Nicolle)

probably reflected the Anglicization of the Norman elite rather than any direct military influence. The cultural impact of the Anglo-Saxons on the Anglo-Norman warrior aristocracy was seen as early as the reign of William II. New fashions – including long hair, moustaches and beards – appalled the older generation and the Church, who claimed that their youngsters looked like girls and were effete, if not worse. In fact such fashions probably stemmed from the Anglo-Saxon styles of the previously despised 'long-haired sons of the northern world'.

The old Anglo-Saxon term for a military levy, now spelt as *ferd*, remained in widespread use and was recorded in northern England as late as the end of the 13th century. The institution itself survived the Conquest as a militia to be called up in case of emergency. It may even temporarily have risen in importance as many minor raids from Wales or Scotland, full-scale invasions from Scandinavia and real or threatened attacks from Normandy kept the Anglo-Norman knights fully occupied. The *ferd* was not, however, a general levy, but involved only a select group drawn from the more prosperous peasantry. The Anglo-Norman army did not consist primarily of knights, and the *ferd* even served across the Channel in Normandy, but its lack of training was a serious weakness. This was perhaps the main reason why mercenaries largely replaced the Anglo-Norman *ferd* in the 12th century.

Urban militias drawn from a 'burgess' class were closely associated with the *ferd*, and similarly consisted largely of infantry, but neither force served separately from the knights. Yet the urban militias did remain more effective, that of London being particularly famed. They not only defended their city walls but were called upon to serve in the field. Such militias could be seen as a link between the standard infantry forces of the early medieval period and the increasingly effective foot soldiers of the 14th century.

The organization of Anglo-Norman armies reflected earlier Norman systems but was clearly more advanced. Among various senior ranks the constable had originally been in charge of the royal stables but now commanded the household knights. The master constable was in charge of court security, providing guards, door-keepers and marshals. The marshals under a master-marshal kept order, provided messengers, supervised the stables, organized hunts and had serjeants to help them. Among the full-time guards of Henry I's reign were a unit of royal archers. William II had earlier employed crossbowmen in his court, but it is not clear whether they formed a distinct unit. From such simple beginnings in an almost nomadic court a full military command structure was to evolve.

So-called household troops from the king's court were also sent to garrison important castles. Many of these were professional archers. Household knights

were clearly of higher status. Many were not strictly mercenaries, as their service was reinforced by oaths of loyalty and fealty even though they received no lands in return. Such household knights also served the powerful aristocracy. Some received only pay; others held small estates while living in the lord's hall. Those holding land would not be involved in agriculture nor even in its supervision, only being concerned with the rent on which they lived.

Wealth and status varied considerably within the warrior class, but a common code of conduct was emerging and is reflected in the many epic *Chansons de Geste* which survive from the 11th and 12th centuries. This form of literature also helped to spread and strengthen the new knightly ideals, which in turn reflected various influences. Above all they were a strange but powerful fusion of the previously antagonistic ideals of the Christian church and the ancient Germanic warrior code. Honor (reputation), truthfulness, reckless courage, military skill, pride in the face of superiors and humility in the face of inferiors, protection of the weak, the Church, women and children, and a love of display were all characteristic of the *mos militum* (customs of knights). To these the *mos majorum* (customs of barons) added nobility of blood (ancestry), learning, justice and generosity.

This was, however, a strictly masculine code. A less important 'romantic' culture was growing but as yet remained separate. Women were outside the system of knightly ideals until the 12th century, when influences from the Muslim world via Spain, Sicily and the Crusades led to a mingling of the romantic and knightly ideals. The result was the unique concept of Courtly Love, which was to be central to aristocratic behaviour in the 13th and 14th centuries. In its early forms the concept of Courtly Love was more down-to-earth and closer to the ideas of the Islamic *1001 Nights* (Arabian Nights) from which it partly sprang; only later were virgin-knights and ethereal, untouched ladies to dominate the literature of Courtly Love.

On a more practical level, the ideals of warrior behaviour restrained the unbridled violence seen in the 10th and early 11th centuries. Even the most powerful barons generally stuck to the rules, formally renouncing fealty in an act of *diffidatio* before rebelling against their sovereign. Besieged castles were normally given an agreed time in which to ask their lord for relief. If this was not forthcoming they could surrender honourably and with minimal violence. Rarely were prisoners executed, and then only as an act of exemplary terrorism.

The knight's life was naturally a dangerous way of living. In one recorded group of 15 *amis* (knights who trained together) three were slain in battle and one died in a fall from a horse. The lucky ones might subsequently inherit an estate, win back one lost by an ancestor, or earn a fief through their own merits. Only then would most men marry and consequently withdraw from the pool of immediately battle-ready knights. Naturally they remained warriors, but were now distracted by other responsibilities.

The declining ability of the landholding knights to fulfil their expected military duties was particularly noticeable in early 12th-century England. Such knights were, in fact, fast becoming the local gentry so characteristic of English rural life. When the king needed troops he often had to get them from either the household knights of his leading barons, from his own limited household or from mercenaries. Many such mercenaries were also landowners who held only small estates and therefore relied on an income as professional warriors. Some were knights, others simply soldiers. In the reigns of William the Conqueror and William II, however, the only mercenaries seem to have been poor knights serving as cavalry, but in Henry I's time mercenary serjeants are seen. During the civil war between Stephen and Matilda the country was reportedly flooded by mercenaries, mostly now infantry, from England, the Celtic states and the continent. Under Stephen and Henry II these mercenaries were numerous

OPPOSITE
Detail of a 12th-century Norman interlace carving on the south porch of Kilpeck church near Hereford showing a knight with sword. (Topfoto/Charles Walker)

The curtain wall at Brough, Cumbria, is of the 11th century, but the present donjon was built to replace the one destroyed in the siege of 1174. (Chris Gravett)

39

enough to form a professional army, some sections of which were grouped by ethnic origin: Bretons, Brabançons, Spaniards and men from the Welsh borders. Others were military specialists such as siege engineers, or spearmen trained to combat cavalry. As a standing army they were also available for less usual strategies such as winter campaigns.

Anglo-Norman warfare was characterized by some ambitious and large-scale strategy. New roads were cut through forests to enable an army to bypass castles and attack an enemy's heartland. A fleet could act in conjunction with an army, particularly during operations in northern Britain. The Anglo-Norman fleet seems, in fact, to have been quite an impressive force. Many ports had naval duties as 'guardians of the sea' well before the famous Cinque Ports of south-eastern England evolved. Their ships were often manned by *piratae*, a word that originally meant sailors trained to fight. Such fleets could even attempt a blockade of the English Channel against a threatened attack from Normandy. Prolonged guerrilla warfare was normally restricted to the Welsh Marches but was also seen in eastern England's marshy fen country.

The rise in courtly culture in Norman England was accompanied by an elaboration of male costume, though as yet by few changes in military equipment. This young squire has been serenading his lady on a psaltery. She is a noblewoman, and thus dressed in the simple yet flattering aristocratic fashion of the 12th century. (Angus McBride © Osprey Publishing)

The Celtic Nations

The role that Normans played in the other nations of Britain and in Ireland is less well known. It was, of course, also less important, yet the Norman contribution to the history of Celtic lands cannot be ignored. Wales, for example, retained its independence throughout the Anglo-Saxon period but largely lost it to the Normans. Norman colonization of the countryside was thin outside Pembroke in the far south-west, but most of the Welsh principalities soon became vassals of the Anglo-Norman king. In many ways the Welsh seemed to find integration into the Norman empire easier than did the Anglo-Saxons. Even as early as the reign of Henry I, Welshmen owed knight service, acted as castellans and even owned castles in Norman-held territory. Southern Welshmen helped the Normans invade north Wales in 1114, and may have accompanied Henry I to France in the same year.

A rising followed the death of Henry. By then Welshmen had learned the art of cavalry warfare, modifying it to their particular needs with smaller horses and lower saddles. They almost overwhelmed the newcomers, but after the rebellion failed Norman influence grew strong, particularly in south Wales. Even traditional Welsh epic poetry was affected in the late 11th and 12th centuries, adopting English military terminology as well as the new concepts of chivalry. Welshmen continued to fight alongside Norman troops as vassals of the king, and were still deeply involved in the tangled campaigns of John's reign.

Although the Welsh aristocracy adopted some Norman styles of combat and equipment, the fighting methods of the ordinary infantry changed less. Generally speaking a long spear was the characteristic weapon of the north, and bows of the south particularly of Gwent. Whether these latter were 'longbows' or short 'flatbows' is a matter of debate. So is the question of who was influencing whom in the gradual spread of archery in war rather than merely as a hunting method. Other Welsh equipment included javelins, small shields and relatively light mail and helmets.

The Norman impact on Scotland was different but in many ways more fundamental. Normans never tried to conquer this northern kingdom, though they almost achieved a peaceful take-over. A few Normans had served King Macbeth in 1052–54, but all appear to have been slain in battle. There was, in fact, very little use of armoured cavalry in Scotland before 1100, except perhaps in the Lothians. But even so the old Celtic forms of warfare had long been under Anglo-Saxon influence. A small number of Normans did help the Anglicized King Edgar defeat a Celtic rebellion in the north and west at the end of the 11th century, and in 1114 there may have been a few Normans in the Scottish army which marched south to help Henry I. King Edgar's policy of welcoming Normans was continued by his

younger brother David, who first governed southern Scotland and subsequently became king in 1124. It was he who gave large estates to his friend De Brus. This family originated from Brix in the Cotentin peninsula, and later took a leading role in Scottish history under the name of Bruce. The whole character of the Scottish nation had been changing since the northern kingdom of Alban conquered 'Welsh' Strathclyde and the Anglo-Saxon south-east of Scotland.

King David I, who also had large estates in central England, consciously remodelled Scotland's administration along Anglo-Norman lines. He encouraged Normans to come north by giving them senior office, thus strengthening his new feudal structure. Charters soon mention knight service, mounted serjeants, mounted and infantry archers. Along the island-studded west coast a peculiar variation of feudalism saw land being held in return for service with longships and oarsmen. There were many such compromises between Celtic and Norman systems. In the south and centre fortified royal towns, *burghs*, sprang up to be inhabited by Englishmen, Flemings, Normans, Anglo-Danes and of course Scots. Older forms of loyalty and kindred groupings, later seen as clans, survived in the western Highlands, while in the north-east the Celtic leadership survived but transformed itself into a feudal aristocracy. In fact it was the Norman newcomers who had to earn their way into the existing power structure. Nevertheless it is worth noting that 12th-century Scottish rulers, addressing their subjects in order of importance, referred to their 'French, English, Scots, Welsh and Galwegians'. Although the Normanization of Scotland was basically peaceful there was plenty of native resistance, both cultural and physical. Many risings were directed against the ruler and his 'foreign friends', particularly from the north and west. All were defeated as the building of castles spread across the land. These were of the simplest wooden motte and bailey type but, by the late 13th century, stone castles appeared. Most were built by members of a new French-speaking Scots-Norman aristocracy, such as the De Vaux family which erected Dirleton castle in East Lothian.

Dirleton overlooks the Great North Road. This was a major feature in Border warfare, but in the 11th and 12th centuries the Anglo-Scots border was not as fixed in the minds of the two nations as it was later to become. Many Scots, not least their king, thought that the old Roman frontier of Hadrian's Wall should be their southern limit. During the troubled years following the Norman Conquest of England King Malcolm of Scotland not only increased Scotland's degree of independence from English suzerainty but even pushed south, occupying the mixed Gaelic Scandinavian-speaking areas of northern Cumbria around Carlisle. This had earlier formed part of the kingdom of Strathclyde, the rest of which had been incorporated into Scotland only a generation earlier. Even the Anglo-Saxon regions of the south-east had only been taken in 1018. In 1093 the Anglo-Normans struck back, putting their client Duncan on the Scottish throne. In return the new king swore fealty to William II of England.

OPPOSITE
Dirleton castle was built by the Scots-Norman De Vaux family in the 13th century. The upper buildings date from the 14th and 15th centuries. (Topfoto/Doug Houghton)

The Normans in Ireland and Scotland. This Anglo-Irish knight of the De Clare family, c. 1225, is bearing down on a Hebridean warrior. In the background is a Gaelic Irish warrior. (Angus McBride © Osprey Publishing)

At the height of England's difficulties during the civil war between Stephen and Matilda the Scots took control of the rest of Cumbria and even parts of Northumberland. But within three years of coming to the throne King Henry II retook Northumbria as well as Cumbria and Carlisle. Thereafter the border was relatively static, but raiding, official or otherwise, was endemic for centuries. It was unlike warfare in southern England or Normandy. Here speed and the winning of booty were what mattered. War had, in fact, to be self-financing, with cattle, prisoners for enslavement or ransom, equipment of all kinds and – for the Scots at least – anything made of iron being a primary objective. On the Anglo-Norman side equipment and tactics were similar to those in the south, but probably lighter and with greater reliance on archery. On the Scots side inferior equipment and a shortage of both archers and modern-style cavalry led to a reliance on large numbers of infantry spearmen supported by an elite of axe-bearers. The old Viking war axe was to see a new lease of life in Scotland, where it evolved into the Borderers' famous long-shafted Jeddart axe in the 13th and 14th centuries. In the western Highlands the axe developed slightly differently into the so-called Galloglach axe of the Hebrides and Ireland.

Ireland

The Norman impact on Ireland was different yet again. Like Scotland, Ireland was changing under English influence even before the Normans invaded the island. It was not yet feudalized but was no longer the tribal society of earlier centuries. Many small Irish courts imitated the fashions of the Anglo-Norman court. Ireland was by no means culturally isolated. Trade was largely in the hands of Celto-Scandinavian *ostmen* of the Irish ports. Viking tradition was also very strong in the armament and military organization of 11th- and 12th- century Ireland.

As usual, the first Normans arrived as mercenaries, probably as armoured infantry, to reinforce the light cavalry who, despite their lack of stirrups, were already the main striking power of Irish armies. Most native Irish warriors fought without armour, using short spears, javelins or broad-bladed axes of Scandinavian form. Bronze maces would also appear in the 12th century. There are many descriptions of the Normans in Irish annals as 'grey foreigners' in iron mail, though the archers seem to have been more feared than the cavalry.

The invasion itself began with the recruiting of Norman and Flemish troops from South Wales by Dermot, King of Leinster. These men then called upon their own king, Henry II, for aid, and held on until he arrived in 1171. Henry's willingness to involve himself in the affair and to disguise it as a crusade was probably designed to divert Papal attention from the murder of Thomas à Becket, Archbishop of Canterbury. The Normans then went on to conquer part of eastern Ireland, but they never succeeded in subduing the whole island.

One of their main problems was a huge difference between Irish and Norman forms of warfare. This resulted in a kind of stalemate, for while the Normans fought to dominate people and land, the native Irish fought only to dominate people. The country was very under-populated and, at least in the north, the inhabitants were semi-nomadic and pastoral, their main wealth being in cattle. It was thus counterproductive to slay too many of the foe. Instead, harrying, plundering and limited but highly visible destruction were designed to extort tribute and obedience. Most warfare consisted, however, of cattle raiding with minimal casualties. When the Normans tried to hold a piece of territory the inhabitants often destroyed their own homes, burned their crops and migrated to another area. The Normans retaliated by trying to force Gaelic chieftains to return such refugees and by encouraging foreigners to settle the vacated land. In response the Irish concentrated on guerrilla warfare in marsh and forest where the Normans' technological advantages were reduced to a minimum. In the 13th century Irish resistance was stiffened by the recruitment of axemen from western Scotland and the Hebrides. First recorded as *gall óglach*, foreign warriors, in 1290, these mercenaries had probably been serving in Ireland at least 50 years already.

Gaelic Irish warriors on the 11th–12th century gilded container of the Stowe Missal. (National Museum, Dublin)

Within the area conquered by the Anglo-Normans the whole structure of society was changing. Feudalism was imposed by force along with its associated military systems. This was at first based on military service, but a form of commutation called royal service soon became widespread as it enabled the ruler to hire and pay mercenaries. In some areas more knights' fees were created than the king had originally intended. Leinster, for example, was able to field 180 although only 100 were owed. This meant a clear profit, and increased military potential for the feudal lord. Most knights and tenants were newcomers from England or Wales. Many disbanded mercenaries from England were also encouraged to settle in new towns which were, in reality, little more than villages. Wooden fortifications were also erected in almost every new Norman manor but, except along the border between Anglo-Norman and Gaelic Ireland, these were rapidly abandoned.

Within the Anglo-Norman zone there was considerable intermarriage between the old and new military aristocracies. The Scandinavian *ostmen* also continued as a warlike burgess class in the coastal towns. Divisions between the feudalized Anglo-Norman area and the Gaelic areas beyond became sharper as the pace of Norman Conquest slowed to a stop. It was along this border that most warfare naturally took place.

The areas under Anglo-Norman rule also enjoyed an economic and population boom, a huge spread of agriculture and a real social revolution

'Centaur' bowman wearing a conical nasal helmet: late 12th century *tympanum* showing Norman influence, *in situ* Cormac's Chapel, Cashel, Ireland. (Irish National Parks and Monuments Branch)

which pulled Ireland into the mainstream of European history for the first time. The towns expanded, particularly the ports, as did trade. Ireland was soon exporting its light and fast horses, not only to England but to the Continent. Within two generations of the arrival of the Normans, feudal Ireland was sending its troops to fight for the Anglo-Norman king in England, Wales and France. Ulster and Kildare even saw the growth of small iron industries, though these were largely confined to the castles. The impact of such developments was also felt beyond the area of Anglo-Norman control in the Gaelic regions.

In all the Celtic nations the Norman conquests, warlike or peaceful, were incomplete. In Wales the northern principality of Gwynedd remained free until Angevin times. In Scotland the process of Normanization did not lead to political control by England. In Ireland the area conquered by the Anglo-Normans covered less than half the country. The reason was, of course, partly local resistance, but it also resulted from political decisions by the Norman kings themselves. Many of their potentially most troublesome and certainly most powerful barons were based in the borderlands. What better way of ensuring that they did not become 'over-mighty' than by keeping Celtic realms in being just beyond their frontiers. These small but warlike states needed little money and less prompting to descend upon their Norman neighbours should these neighbours in turn make trouble for the king.

The Normans in Italy and Sicily

The first Norman mercenaries seem to have arrived in southern Italy in 1017 to fight in a revolt against Byzantine rule. At this time the area was divided between Byzantine provinces, autonomous coastal city-states and independent Lombard principalities. Meanwhile the island of Sicily was ruled by Arab emirs owing occasional allegiance to Tunisia or Egypt. Some 12 years later the Normans began to settle around Aversa, but not until 1041 did one band of adventurers under Robert Guiscard set about conquering territory in their own right. By 1059 Norman rule over much of Apulia and Calabria was recognized by the Pope. In 1071 Bari fell, and Byzantine authority collapsed.

The invasion of Sicily had begun 11 years earlier but was not completed until 1091. The various conquered regions were at first governed separately, but were united as a single Norman state in 1127, this being recognized as a kingdom in 1130. Almost inevitably the Normans were drawn into rivalry with the Zirid rulers of Tunisia. Early expeditions failed, but around 1134, a more determined invasion took advantage of internal Zirid squabbles, and by 1148 the Normans ruled a North African province from northern Tunisia to the Gulf

Roseto castle, one of the defences of the Calabrian coast of Italy. Its lower part might date from the Norman period. (David Nicolle)

Christian slaying 'pagans': early-12th-century carving, *in situ* west front, San Nicola, Bari. (David Nicolle)

of Sirte, even including the ancient Islamic city of Kairwan. This 'empire' had collapsed by 1160, partly because of the rising power of fundamentalist Almohades from Morocco, and partly because the heartland of the Norman state faced Byzantine invasions plus threats from the German emperor who ruled northern Italy.

At one time it looked as if Norman ambitions against Byzantium would be more successful. These also partly grew out of commercial rivalry in the Mediterranean. Invasion and counter-invasion culminated, in 1185, in a Siculo-Norman army capturing Thessaloniki and marching to within a few days of Istanbul (Constantinople), the Byzantine capital. But they were turned back; and within a few years the Norman kingdom was itself torn apart by a disputed succession. In 1194, after years of civil war and invasion, Norman rule ended when the German Emperor Henry VI of Hohenstaufen occupied the kingdom. This, then, was the chequered history of the most cultured of the Norman states, one built firmly upon traditions which the Normans had found when they came to the area in the 11th century.

These traditions were very mixed. While Arab troops had played a secondary role to that of the Berbers in the previous Muslim conquest of Sicily, they took a leading role politically, culturally and in the command of most military forces. Hence their importance in the development of Siculo-Muslim

Early Norman Italy and Sicily. The armour of the Siculo-Norman knight shows southern influences, which generally meant that slightly less armour was worn, and would have made them almost indistinguishable from their Italian, Byzantine and Egyptian neighbours. On the right is a Neapolitan infantryman whose arms and armour also reflect Byzantine and Islamic influences. On the left is a Sicilian infantry archer, lightly armoured, with a powerful composite bow. (Angus McBride © Osprey Publishing)

forces, whose traditions were subsequently inherited by the Normans. Troops of servile or slave origin, plus mercenaries, were important but the introduction of the *iqta* (fief) and the regional *jund* (militia) systems did produce some aspects of feudalism. Both these forms of military organization survived under the Normans. The *iqta* were transformed with little difficulty or alteration into fiefs for the new Norman Christian elite. Meanwhile the *jund* system of western Sicily, with its territorial militias based upon the *iqlim* or district, continued to provide the Normans with reliable Muslim warriors.

The many and close contacts between Muslim Sicily and southern Italy before the coming of the Normans also led to similarities in the military styles of the two regions. But whereas the population of southern Italy had been largely demilitarized under Byzantine rule, the Norman conquerors of Sicily were faced by a population of soldiers – Arabs, Berbers, local converts and others – who were prepared to defend their existing political supremacy. Later, after their defeat, the old military class of Sicily continued to fight for a new Christian king.

Italians, Byzantines and Lombards

Before looking at the Normans themselves, however, the Italians and Byzantines should be fitted into this complex military context. Both communities had an influence on the development of the Norman army, certainly on the Italian mainland and even in Sicily. The demilitarization of the local population under Byzantine rule applied to the rural rather than urban areas. As the Byzantine *themes* of Langobardia (Apulia), Lucania and Calabria developed economically they also became administratively more self-sufficient. Around 1040 the professional *theme* armies were disbanded and responsibility for defence largely fell upon local urban militias. Such predominantly infantry forces subsequently came to terms with the Norman invaders and helped eject the Byzantine authorities. Local militias were not, of course, necessarily Greek. The population of Calabria might have been mostly so, but that of Lucania was mixed, while Langobardia, with the exception of a Greek-speaking area at the very tip of the heel of Italy, was largely Italian.

One of the panels from the late-12th-century bronze doors of Trani Cathedral, showing Siculo-Norman warriors. (David Nicolle)

Late-12th-century capital in the cloisters of Monreale Cathedral, Sicily, showing sleeping guards at the Holy Sepulchre, in Italo-Norman dress. (David Nicolle)

A very similar system operated in those areas under Lombard authority, where armies reflected a strong Byzantine influence. The turbulent pre-Norman duchies of Capua, Benevento and Salerno were not feudally organized and their rulers again relied primarily on urban militias. In the countryside, castles were garrisoned by non-noble troops recruited by the castle's owner. In contrast there already existed in cities like Naples and Bari a class of citizens whose status and military obligations were sufficiently impressive for the Normans to enfief their cavalry elite as knights within a few years of taking control. Other cities put up such a spirited defence against the Normans – for example Capua in 1062 – that the conquerors subsequently left the protection of vital gates or citadels in the hands of local citizens.

Mounted troops were also fielded by the major ecclesiastical authorities and landowners. Nevertheless the military obligations placed upon church estates were lighter than those in Norman England. Many such church troops seem to have been mounted and armoured in the normal western European fashion. Expensive heavy cavalry equipment could probably be afforded because these church estates were generally more feudalized than were those of secular landowners. Secular militias did, however, include some armoured horsemen as well as light cavalry and numerous infantry.

These, then, were the military circumstances into which the Normans erupted so successfully in the 11th century and which they were soon to inherit. The Normans themselves were, of course, mostly armoured horsemen as they or their ancestors had been in Normandy itself. Not that Normans were the only northern Europeans to be attracted by the lure of southern Italy: Bretons, Flemings, Poitevans and men from Anjou are also recorded. But of course Normans dominated both numerically and in the leadership of the many war-bands.

In the early days their military organization seems to have been more communal than feudal with warriors following a leader of their choice rather than a hereditary prince. The feudal military obligations that later provided the foundation of the expanding Norman state were similar to those of Normandy and England, consisting of 40 days' duty with 'hauberk and destrier' and a suitable feudal following. The number of such 'one-hauberk' knight's fees was to grow quite large – 3,453 on the mainland alone, according to the *Catalogus Baronum*. This referred to the years between 1154 and 1166 but excluded Calabria and Sicily. New knight's fees that were created in Sicily tended to be small, which could indicate that they followed the pattern of the previous Muslim *iqta* land holdings. Perhaps they were also, as a consequence of their small size, large in number. Elsewhere there is mention of non-noble freeholders, probably new settlers, whose land tenure was on condition of military service. Such a structure was nevertheless firmly rooted in the pre-Norman administration. Variations between provinces also betrayed the pre-Norman foundations. In Apulia and Capua, Lombard elements are visible; in Calabria, Byzantine; and in Sicily, most noticeable of all, Islamic.

The Norman rulers could not rely solely on feudal resources despite a theoretical widening of military obligations, so that the entire adult male population could be called upon to fight. The serfs or *servientes defensati* were expected to provide their own equipment, while in Sicily the villein class, whether of Lombard (Italian), Greek or Muslim origin, had to undertake specific local garrison duties. In reality, however, the growing centralization and wealth of the Norman government seems to have led to a steady decline in reliance on local levies, particularly in traditionally well-administered areas like Calabria and Sicily. In turn there was a rapidly increasing reliance on mercenaries.

The employment of such professional soldiers introduced yet more elements into an already complex military situation. As early as 1054 Robert Guiscard recruited non-Norman Calabrians, Greeks or Slavs, for the invasion of

Late-12th-century capital in the cloisters of Monreale Cathedral, Sicily, showing a Norman knight with flower-shaped shield charge. (David Nicolle)

Sicily. Troops as well as sailors were drawn from Italian states like Pisa and Genoa, these being used to garrison coastal cities as well as to man the fleet. In fact it has been suggested that the Norman rulers of Sicily relied on strictly Italian troops far more than has previously been realized. Non-Muslim as well as Siculo-Muslim troops were, of course, needed to support the feudal core of the Norman army. The Normans made war on almost all their neighbours at various times, including the rulers of North Africa. It was here that non-Muslims were required, since it seems to have been agreed that Muslim troops would not be sent against their co-religionists. Altogether the Norman field army could consist of heavy and light cavalry, some of the latter were armed with bows though probably not fighting in Turkish horse-archery fashion, plus heavily armoured and more lightly equipped infantry. Other contingents of volunteers fought without pay but for booty alone. These *rizico* seem to recall the *muttawiya* volunteers who figured so prominently in previous Muslim forces.

A Muslim landed aristocracy also survived in western Sicily. Although probably depleted and in decline, it seems to have held a number of small castles and to have fielded its own forces of both infantry and cavalry throughout the Norman period and into the early 13th century. Most of the Muslim troops serving Norman rulers were clearly mercenaries paid by the treasury rather than being a part-time militia. Though paid, their service was in a way quasi-feudal, for it was performed in return for religious toleration extended

'The Betrayal' – marble candlestick made by Nicola d'Angelo and Pietro Vassalletto, c. 1170. (San Paolo fuori la Mura, Rome, David Nicolle)

'Triumph of Tancred', showing (top row) a miniature royal parasol; (middle row) Muslim musicians and spearmen; (bottom row) archers and crossbowmen of various origins. Late-12th–early-13th-century Sicilian manuscript. (*Chronicle of Peter of Eboli*, Ms.Cod. 120/II, Burgerbib., Berne)

towards Islam by the Norman government. These troops formed a standing army of light cavalry, skilled siege engineers and numerous infantry, of whom the archers were renowned for their speed of movement and rate of shooting. They were organized along lines that reflected the pre-Norman territorial *jund* and were sometimes led by men of their own faith. An elite, significantly drawn from the infantry archers, also formed a guard for the Royal Treasury or *Camera*.

The impact of these archers on military developments in medieval Italy might have been as strong as that of later English longbowmen on English and French tactics. Armed with powerful composite bows and short swords, they proved to be highly effective against heavy cavalry as the latter were often no more manoeuvrable than the light infantry archers. They could, in fact, sometimes move swiftly enough to act in conjunction with their own cavalry in a frontal attack. In earlier centuries the militia infantry of Italian cities had fought only with spear and shield, but in the 13th century the tactical role of the Normans' Siculo-Muslim light infantry archers seems to have been inherited by the famous crossbowmen of northern Italy.

The Normans of Sicily and southern Italy also inherited a flourishing, though probably small-scale, arms industry. As yet it is impossible to say how the products of this industry differed from or were similar to the arms and armour of neighbouring manufacturing regions in western Europe, Byzantium, North Africa and the Middle East. Sicily was rich in iron from around Messina and Palermo, as well as in the timber needed for fuel in metal-working. Armourers had reportedly been active in late 9th-century Palermo; and Muslim Sicily had certainly shared a general economic expansion, agricultural and industrial, seen in the western provinces of Islam from the 8th to 11th centuries. A comparable, though perhaps less dramatic, process of development was taking place in southern Italy from the 7th to 11th centuries. There was a growth of wealth and productivity in both the Byzantine provinces and the Lombard duchies involving agriculture, mining, metal-working and shipbuilding.

The lively Mediterranean trade of coastal cities like Amalfi during the pre-Norman period is well known, though the importance of Amalfi itself declined in the face of Pisan and Genoese competition from the 10th century. It is, however, worth noting that trade between the southern Italian ports of Amalfi or Salerno and the Middle East, particularly in traditional Italian cargoes like wood and iron, revived immediately after their occupation by the Normans. Thereafter it continued until relations with Egypt were ruined by Siculo-Norman attacks on the Nile Delta in 1153. In this context it should be pointed out that the Norman rulers continued their predecessors' strict state monopoly over the exploitation of forests and mines, and hence over arms production, as well as over the export of primary products.

Military Equipment in the Norman South

Students of the arms and armour of the Norman south are fortunate because three major and almost unique sources of information survive from the early, middle and late periods. The earliest are carvings over the north door of the church of San Nicola at Bari. Dating from the very early 12th century, they are believed to illustrate an episode in the First Crusade, either the capture of Jerusalem or more probably the fall of Antioch. The Italo-Norman baron Bohemond of course took most of the credit for this latter victory. The five defenders of the city in this scene mostly wear a form of lamellar armour and seem to have turbans. A conical helmet, a mail hauberk and possibly two mail coifs are also shown on the defenders. One may assume that the artist modelled these figures on the closest available Muslim warriors, namely those of early Norman Sicily. The only archer in the scene is also one of these men, all of whom are on foot. Other defenders are armed with spears, swords and kite-shaped shields.

The eight horsemen who attack the city look at first sight like typical Norman knights, but closer inspection shows considerable differences. Those attacking from the left are dressed in short-sleeved mail hauberks, carry only spears and seem almost to have stepped out of the Bayeux Tapestry. Of those attacking from the right one clearly wears a mail hauberk. The other three wear lamellar or, much less likely, scale armours, one of which is put on over a mail hauberk. This group of four men are armed with spears or swords. Bearing in mind the already fierce antagonism between the Normans and Byzantium, these lamellar-armoured horsemen are unlikely to represent Byzantine troops who, of course, played only a minor role in the First Crusade. Their appearance is therefore likely to indicate a high degree of lingering Byzantine influence on the arms and armour of the early, and as yet still disunited, Norman states in southern Italy.

The second major source of information is the unique Cappella Palatina ceiling in Palermo. Made of painted wooden panels in an almost purely western Islamic style in around 1140–43, it illustrates military equipment as varied as the cultures and population of Norman Sicily. It was probably made by Siculo-Muslim artists and it is natural that Islamic military styles predominate. Most, though clearly not all the warriors shown on this mid-12th century Cappella Palatina ceiling are likely to mirror the appearance of those Siculo-Muslim warriors who served in Norman armies. Four are shown as guardsmen wearing typical Islamic ceremonial costume, and they almost certainly look like the elite units which protected the Norman ruler and his treasury. Where apparently European mail hauberks, helmets, shields and weapons are shown, it should be borne in mind that such equipment was also used in western Islamic regions from Egypt to Spain.

Late-12th-century capital in the cloisters of Monreale Cathedral, Sicily, showing Italo-Norman infantrymen, perhaps from North Africa, one with a curved sword. (David Nicolle)

The third vital source for the military equipment of Norman Sicily and, to a lesser extent, southern Italy are the carved capitals in the cloister of Monreale Cathedral. This was built in the hills overlooking Palermo between 1174 and 1189. Although essentially late Romanesque in style, the capitals illustrate a great variety of warriors and their even more mixed equipment. They, again, probably reflect the mixed armies of later Norman Sicily, for the weaponry includes western European, Byzantine, Islamic and specifically North African styles. Four basic fashions are present. These are full mail hauberk and helmet for both cavalry and infantry; lamellar or scale armour, which is generally worn without a helmet by both cavalry and infantry; infantry wearing variously shaped helmets but no apparent body armour; and completely unarmoured cavalry and infantry. Shields are varied while weaponry is even more so, including long lance, short spear or javelin, mace, axe, short 'self-bow' of simple construction, and composite recurved bow. Swords appear as broad-bladed or pointed and almost triangular. There is even what appears to be a curved sword or sabre.

Such evidence, when added to the written sources, shows the armies of Sicily and southern Italy to have remained very varied, cosmopolitan forces up to and even beyond the fall of the Norman kingdom.

NORMAN SHIPS

Mediterranean transport ships, like this 13th century example (1), made the expansion and survival of the Crusader states and the Siculo-Norman empire possible. Note the *corridoria*, which, replacing an upper deck, were a feature of many Mediterranean 'round ships.' The Norman-French warship (2) was a development of Viking longships, the warlike dragonship and the more peaceful *knorr*. With castles added fore and aft, it dominated warfare in northern waters for many years. The Siculo-Norman war-galley (3) was a development of the famous Byzantine *dromon*. The main difference between medieval warships and their classical predecessors was that a ram had been raised above the waterline. Thus it became an oar-smashing, ship-disabling, rather than ship-sinking, weapon. This probably reflected the increasing cost of warships as the Mediterranean coasts became deforested. William the Conqueror's flagship *Mora* (4) had a lantern at the masthead, a monstrous figurehead comparable to those of earlier Viking ships and a new form of carved sternpost. (5) shows the profiles of archetypal 13th-century Mediterranean ships, a three-decker Venetian, the largest form of 13th-century ship (a), a four decker (b), a two-decker (c) and a *salandrium*, a specialized horse-transport (d). (Angus McBride © Osprey Publishing)

The Normans in
the East

Normans are recorded in Byzantine service within a few years of their appearance in Italy. In the 11th century most of the so-called 'Franks' in Byzantium seem to have been Italo-Normans or to have arrived via southern Italy. Some came as individuals, others in groups of as many as a hundred men. Their first operations were as part of Byzantine forces fighting the Muslims of Sicily, or against Pecheneg Turkish invaders in the Balkans.

Normans rapidly rose to military prominence, a certain Hervé acting not only as leader of the Norman mercenaries in around 1050 but also as one of general Nicephorus' two chief lieutenants. Almost inevitably, these turbulent Norman leaders soon quarrelled with their paymasters; but in Byzantium, unlike Italy and so many other areas, Norman efforts to carve out their own principalities all failed. Hervé broke with Emperor Michael VI and took a force of some 300 Norman troops to eastern Anatolia. Here, however, he came up against not only the Byzantine authorities, but Armenians, Seljuk Turks and finally the Arab emir Abu Nasr of Ahlat, who clapped Hervé in irons and sent him back to Byzantium. Yet Norman resilience was such that Hervé rose again to become *stratilate* of Byzantium's eastern army under Isaac Comnenus in around 1058.

There were already many Normans in Byzantine Armenia, Georgia and the Trabzon area. In 1057 two of the five eastern frontier corps consisted of 'Franks'. Their main base was Malatya. Others were based further south at Urfa (Edessa) under the command of the Duke of Antioch. The next leader of these Normans was Robert Crispin, known as Crépin the Frankopoulos. He died, supposedly of Byzantine poison, shortly after the disastrous Byzantine defeat by the Seljuk Turks at Manzikert in 1071. The Normans then found a third leader in Roussel de Bailleul who had, until 1069, been one of Robert Guiscard's lieutenants in southern Italy. He then took service with Byzantium, first against pagan Turkish raiders in the Balkans and subsequently in the Emperor Romanus' catastrophic campaign of 1071.

Manzikert brought the Byzantine Empire to its knees. Seljuks, other Turks, Armenians, Kurds and Arabs now struggled to take control of various parts of Anatolia. Roussel saw the potential of such a situation, and set out to create a Norman principality in the east. He came closer to success than had his predecessors, yet he too failed. From the fief that the Byzantines had given him in Armenia he fought against all comers but, like Hervé before him, Roussel was captured by the Muslims and sent back to his one-time foe, the future

An Italo-Norman
crusader, a serjeant,
delivers a message from
Tancred to the Armenian
lord, Oshin of Lampron,
wearing an essentially
Byzantine costume.
Beside the lord is a
Norman ex-Byzantine
mercenary. (Angus
McBride © Osprey
Publishing)

Emperor Alexius I Comnenus. Four years later Roussel also re-emerged into
imperial favour as the leader of the 'Frankish' mercenaries of Alexius I.

The fate of many other Normans in eastern Anatolia is more obscure and
perhaps even stranger. This strategic area had been strongly garrisoned by the
Byzantines, who generally sent their best western mercenaries there. After the
disaster of Manzikert many of these Normans or 'Franks' helped the Turks
destroy the Byzantines' Armenian vassal states of Taron and Sassoun. But a
revival of Armenian independence then occurred further south in the Taurus
mountains, Cilicia and northern Syria. Some 8,000 'Franks' under a certain
Oursel also moved down to the upper Euphrates valley and the northern edge

of the Syrian plain. Here many cities continued to recognize nominal Byzantine authority while paying tribute to the victorious Muslims. They survived, in fact, as pawns in the greater struggle between Seljuk Turks and the Arab emirs of Syria, but their autonomy was real enough. An Armenian general called Philaretus seized control of one such city, Antioch, in 1079. Originally Philaretus had commanded Byzantine forces along the south-eastern frontier, and as such he was well known to the Normans. Philaretus then went on to take control of a broad territory which included Urfa (Edessa). He is also said to have commanded an army of up to 20,000 warriors, the most effective element of which were the supposedly 8,000 Normans or 'Franks' who, under their new leader Raimbaud, had joined Philaretus as early as 1073.

Their first base was a fortress called Afranji, the 'Franks'' castle, near Harput on the left bank of the Euphrates. Others joined the garrison of Urfa and perhaps Antioch. Raimbaud himself died while defending Philaretus' tent against Thornig, the Armenian prince of Sassoun in 1074. It may also be no coincidence that merchants from Amalfi in Norman-ruled southern Italy continued to trade with Antioch during these troubled years, or that men from Bari, one of the main cities of Norman Italy, were trading at Tarsus in Cilician Armenia as late as 1097.

The career of Philaretus and perhaps of his Norman supporters came to an abrupt end around 1085, when the Seljuk Turks first captured Antioch then went on to crush both the Arab dynasties ruling Mosul and Aleppo and their Armenian ally Philaretus. Urfa itself fell in 1087 by treachery from within the walls. The city did, however, retain its autonomy under Armenian governors. Urfa also kept its own forces to defend the city and garrison outlying castles. These were primarily an urban militia, though mercenaries were hired when

The walled city of Mdina in Malta was already a fortified stronghold when Count Roger arrived before it in 1090. (Chris Gravett)

money was available. The fate of the Normans after this Seljuk takeover is unrecorded, but according to Crusader sources the warriors of Urfa at the time the First Crusade arrived were armed and armoured in what sounds like European style. Elsewhere, particularly in Antioch, the old military class of Armenians and Greeks were 'Turcified' – *turcaverant* – through intermarriage with the conquering Seljuks. A substantial section of the previous elite clearly came to terms with the newcomers, and it was they, or their descendants, who reportedly fled at the approach of the Crusaders. 'Franks' or Normans are not specifically mentioned. Nevertheless only 12 years separated the Seljuk seizure of Antioch and the arrival of the First Crusade. Might the offspring of Norman mercenaries, legitimate or otherwise, have been defending the city when Norman knights from southern Italy drew up beneath Antioch's walls?

Following the disaster at Manzikert Byzantium lost its main Anatolian recruiting grounds and so, under the Comnenid dynasty, Byzantine forces were increasingly dominated by mercenaries, amongst whom Normans continued to form an important element. A polyglot army was recruited from these Normans plus Germans, Frenchmen and troops from the Crusader states, particularly from the Norman principality of Antioch, which was at various times a theoretical vassal of the Byzantine Empire. The main Byzantine armies were, in fact, remodelled along essentially Norman-French feudal lines by the Emperor Manuel Comnenus, great emphasis being placed on heavy cavalry using the couched lance. This process led to further disaster at Myriokephalon in 1176, where the Byzantine Empire suffered a catastrophic defeat at the hands of the Seljuks second only to that suffered at Manzikert a century earlier. Crusaders from Antioch formed Manuel's right wing at Myriokephalon. After the defeat the emperor also sent a letter to Henry II of England, praising the courage of Manuel's Englishmen – almost certainly referring to Anglo-Saxon troops in his service. Many Normans also fought for Byzantium against their fellow countrymen under Robert Guiscard of southern Italy. Others were recruited to fight Pechenegs and Seljuks in the 1080s and 1090s. 'Franks' were found in the garrison defending Iznik (Nicea) in 1113, Corfu in 1149 and Varna in 1193. Others were involved in the civil war of 1180, while 'Franks' served Theodore Lascaris, ruler of Iznik, in 1259.

Many such mercenaries settled in Byzantium and founded long-lasting military families. These would often have held *pronoia*, the Byzantine equivalent of the western fief. The feudalization of Byzantium may, in fact, have been a legacy of the days when the Comnenid emperors recruited as many Normans and other westerners as they could find. Among those families founded by 'Franks' were the Raoulii, who were descended from a certain Italo-Norman named Raoul, and the Petraliphae, descended from Pierre d'Aulps. A group of warrior families called the Maniakates, descended from Normans serving the great Byzantine general Maniakes, settled in Albania. Here they were led by a certain Constantine

Humbertopoulos, whose name indicated descent from a westerner called Humbert. In 1201 a Constantine Frangopoulos ('son of the Frank') was given command of six war-galleys; and in 1285 another Humbertopoulos defended Mesembria in present-day Bulgaria against the Mongols.

From around 1190 to 1216 the first medieval Albanian state won a brief independence under native *archons*. It would be interesting to know if any of these claimed 'Frankish' or Norman descent. Certainly when the Angevins of southern Italy created a puppet Albanian state in 1272 many local lords readily adopted feudal titles and associated forms of behaviour.

In the First Crusade Normans played a disproportionately large role. They were also doubly represented, with Normans from Normandy forming one contingent and Normans from southern Italy forming a second, perhaps even more important force. This was led by Bohemond of Taranto, a disinherited son of Robert Guiscard. The Italo-Normans might have been few in number but they were well equipped, well led, and disciplined – and above all, they had experience of dealing with Byzantines and Muslims.

Emile Signol's 18th-century painting of the Crusaders taking Jerusalem, during the First Crusade, 1099. (Topfoto/Roger-Viollet)

The Principality of Antioch

The conquest of Antioch during the First Crusade and the subsequent establishment of the principality of Antioch did create yet another Norman state. Whereas Duke Robert of Normandy and the bulk of his troops left the Holy Land in 1099, a large part of the Italo-Norman contingent remained. Bohemond was already in effective control of Antioch, but the Normans' right to rule this city did not go unchallenged. Byzantium claimed at least suzerainty over the ancient 'duchy of Antioch', while many non-Norman Crusaders felt that Bohemond had been more interested in winning a fief than in conquering Jerusalem for the Cross. Then, in 1100, Bohemond was captured by the Danishmandid Turks, and his nephew Tancred was summoned north from Galilee to take command. While in Palestine Tancred had learned to win the active help of local Christian communities. In Antioch he used this experience to enlarge and consolidate the new principality. Tancred also encouraged Normans from Italy, Sicily and France to settle in northern Syria. He structured the new state along strictly Norman and strongly feudal lines, making it different from the kingdom of Jerusalem which was emerging to the south. At the same time Tancred recruited assorted mercenaries and found allies even among local Turkish chieftains.

Despite these efforts and those of his successors, the essentially western principality of Antioch was never able fully to establish itself in the mosaic of Middle Eastern states. Nor were its Norman military elite able to integrate themselves into Syrian society. They remained a thinly spread aristocracy which stayed alien despite sometimes adopting local, and particularly Armenian customs. The Normans and other westerners were isolated from the Muslims of the countryside by their religion and by the obligation to combat Islam with the sword. They were also separated from the local, largely urban Christians. These, though divided amongst themselves, far outnumbered the Normans, and were in turn regarded as heretics or schismatics. The only local community with whom the Normans built up a close working relationship were the Armenians, who were also a warrior people with their own neighbouring independent and to some extent feudally-organized states. Efforts to go beyond mere collaboration to political and religious union came to nothing: the cultural gulf was too wide. On an everyday military level Norman-Armenian co-operation, which had begun even before the conquest of Antioch, seems to have been commonplace. It was probably a man of Armenian origin, an armourer or his descendant, who betrayed Antioch to the Crusaders in the first place. An Armenian engineer from Antioch designed siege machines which the Crusaders used against Tyre in 1124. Armenian troops served in the garrisons of Antioch and Margat in 1118. At other times as many as 4,000 to 5,000 Armenian horsemen and 10,000 infantry were said to be employed by the Crusader states.

The principality of Antioch and the associated county of Edessa were in some respects separate from the other Crusader states of Tripoli and Jerusalem. Their political, economic and even defence considerations were often different. Antioch's position on the ancient trade route from Iraq and Iran to the Mediterranean also made it the richest of the Crusader states. Antioch itself was a flourishing centre of commerce and industry, famous for its textiles and glass. Many westerners came to settle in the cities, and such immigrants may eventually have formed half the urban population. Though neither knights nor professional warriors, they were probably the basis of the state's infantry levy. But despite this flourishing commerce and wealth, the importance of Antioch actually declined under Crusader rule, Muslim Aleppo gradually taking over as the commercial centre of northern Syria.

Iron was mined in the mountains and the associated iron-working tradition included a small arms industry. Most of the iron-working was done around Marash, but the area as a whole had, as recently as the 10th century, produced horse-harness, spurs, maces, some form of armour, sword scabbards and wood-framed saddles.

The direct line of Norman princes of Antioch ended as early as 1130 with the death of Bohemond II. Subsequent rulers were descended from his daughter Constance and a French nobleman, Raymond of Poitiers, who had been

Bagras castle overlooks the Orontes River and the Syrian plains beyond. Much of the walls date from the Armenian period, but it was a key position in the defence of Antioch. (David Nicolle)

summoned secretly from the Norman court of Henry I of England. Feelings of *Normannitas* nevertheless remained strong in Antioch, and no fewer than five more princes were named Bohemond, including the last.

The feudal structures that the first Norman princes built along Siculo-Norman lines also remained relatively unchanged to the end. Feudal ties were simpler than in Europe, because the military elite was tiny and fewer people were involved. Compared with the situation in Tripoli and Jerusalem the ruler of Antioch kept most of the land and castles in his own hands during the 12th century. Almost all the big fiefs were held by his relatives, the others generally being held by men of Norman origin. The great offices of state were typically Norman, with *constables*, *marshals*, *seneschals*, *chamberlains*, *vicomtes*, *bailiffs* and *chatelains*. The only Byzantine or Islamic offices tended to be legal or administrative, and even these are likely to reflect Norman experience in Sicily and southern Italy. In the cities, however, administration reflected a mixture of Byzantine, Islamic and newer Italo-French ideas, while in the countryside Arab-Islamic systems continued to operate.

The organization of Antioch's armies was overwhelmingly western. Cavalry were, of course, the most important element. All the Crusader states suffered

The knight of Antioch, c. 1268, left, wears the latest European armour, with some differences favoured in the Crusader states. Behind him rides a Norman-French Crusader of the same period. By this time there were no differences between Norman military equipment and that of the rest of France. His shield bears a red cross on green, a device favoured by French Crusaders. In the background is a Turcopole. (Angus McBride © Osprey Publishing)

from a severe shortage of horses during the early years, but the principality's problems were less acute, as the plains of northern Syria had long been famous as a horse-rearing region.

The small size of Crusader armies has often been exaggerated, as has the larger numbers of their Muslim foes; yet the total of Antiochene knights never rose much above 500. In the Middle East, however, the military obligations of such knights appear to have been open-ended and were not limited to the theoretical 40 days seen in Europe. Such numbers could be considerably increased by pilgrims and landless mercenaries from Europe. Antioch's wealth enabled it to pay for many mercenaries who remained vital to the expansion and survival of all Crusader states. There were also many serjeants of inferior status but similar military effectiveness, plus Turcopoles, and large numbers of allies including Armenians. One large castle could have a garrison of almost 1,700 in time of peace, though only 50 of these would have been knights. In time of war the garrison could rise to 2,200.

Tactics remained basically the same as those used by the Normans in Europe, but modifications based upon local experience did soon develop. In open country the cavalry were normally preceded or even boxed in by infantry armed with spears, bows or crossbows. Such infantry defended themselves with tall shields, spearmen being in front and their ranks opening to let horsemen make their charges. In the early 12th century all the cavalry operated together, knights and non-noble warriors, fully and more lightly equipped men. Faster and more mobile forces in which infantry were mounted were also used to intercept convoys and to raid deep inside enemy territory. Light cavalry, with spears of bamboo and perhaps javelins, appeared at the end of the 12th century, modelled on Arab rather than on the more specialized and alien Turkish horse-archer traditions. By this time the Crusader states had stopped expanding and had already been forced onto the defensive, thus perhaps becoming more ready to learn. In the 13th century tactics became more flexible, varied and sophisticated.

Infantry had grown in importance, as archers and crossbowmen proved to be the best defence against horse-archers. Earlier tactics were still used, but at other times the cavalry formed up in groups outside an infantry formation into which they could retreat if necessary. They now often made more limited tactical charges by one or two smaller groups of horsemen. Mounted serjeants still fought alongside the knights but were generally less heavily armoured.

Most Turcopoles appear to have been cavalry although they also included infantrymen. Their exact origins and even their function are still a matter of debate. A number of local Christians seem to have been enrolled as serjeants but they remained few. Many more Muslim prisoners of war had been converted to Christianity in the early 12th century, and may then have fought for their new masters. Such men are unlikely to have risked returning to the Muslim fold, as apostasy from Islam was a capital offence. Turcopoles were, in fact, almost invariably executed if captured. The few recorded names of Turcopoles also suggest Muslim family origins. The evidence indicates that although many fought as horse-archers this was not in Turcoman nomadic style. Instead Turcopoles seem to have been equipped more like the *ghulams* of the neighbouring Muslim states. These fought both as light cavalry and as disciplined horse-archers who shot in ranks, often at rest rather than on the move as did the tribal Turcomans. Some Turcopoles even held fiefs, which were normally listed as *serjeantries*.

The most enduring monuments of the principality of Antioch are its castles. Some were immense, and they still crown many of the hills of north-western Syria and southern Turkey. Most, however, were built during the principality's period of decline. The only big castle to be built in the 12th century was that at Sahyun; no less than 170,000 tons of virgin rock were cut away to make its eastern ditch. Smaller fortifications were also erected at this time, many overlooking mountain passes between the coast and the Muslim regions of inland Syria. Such castles were often updated structures from the 9th or 10th centuries, having originally defended the Byzantine duchy of Antioch or the Arab province of Aleppo. Most of the other cities and towns had been fortified by Byzantines, Armenians or Arabs before the Normans arrived.

During the 13th century important castles were sold to the Templars, Hospitallers or other military orders because the rulers of Antioch were increasingly short of cash and men to garrison these defences. Massive and sophisticated as they were, the castles ultimately failed, the main reason again being shortage of manpower. Antioch itself fell after a five-day siege in 1268 because the garrison could not man all its towers. Many castles were betrayed from the inside, and this tendency might have been a particularly serious example of the defensive, almost defeatist 'castle mentality' which gripped the Crusader states in the 13th century.

The military elite can hardly be blamed for such an attitude. From the time of Saladin their position became ever more obviously untenable. The county of Edessa had long gone and Antioch, like Tripoli and Jerusalem, controlled a shrinking area of countryside. Fiefs became fewer, until almost the whole knightly class was town-based. They still claimed feudal rights over villages and fields long retaken by Islam, but their status was maintained as a legal fiction unsupported even by wealth. The European settlers fled to the towns or back to Europe while a substantial number, including serjeants and maybe even knights, adopted Islam and became renegades. In 1223 the Patriarch of Alexandria claimed, perhaps with exaggeration, that about 10,000 such renegades were in Ayyubid service in Egypt and Syria. After the Fourth Crusade captured Istanbul (Constantinople) in 1204 large numbers of knights, serjeants and Turcopoles left Syria to seek their fortunes in Greece.

Nevertheless, the principality of Antioch clung on for another 83 years. It survived in name after Antioch itself fell to the Mamluk Sultan Baybars in an orgy of slaughter and destruction. Thereafter the principality consisted of little more than the port of Lattakieh, which itself fell in 1287 after an earthquake seriously damaged its walls. Ironically, the Mamluk Sultan Qalaun justified its seizure during a time of truce by using a legal nicety that the Normans themselves might have appreciated. As the current ruler of Antioch, Qalaun claimed that he had a right to all the old principality including Lattakieh, the remaining unconquered portion. Its last prince, Bohemond VII, died childless and perhaps broken-hearted six months later.

Revanda (Ravendel) castle was a typical outlying fortress of the Principality of Antioch. It was built on a mountain near the eastern frontier. (David Nicolle)

The Norman Knight

The knightly class was a true elite within Norman society. While the humble infantry embodied the power of mass, the knight exemplified the highest standards of military prowess. His instruction would begin as a mere boy. Future training included everything for a martial life: horsemanship, sword-fighting, using the lance, rules of war, dress and etiquette. When, as a young man, he finally became a knight, he would embark on a career of leadership and war which often had little glamour except in the eyes of others. This part explores the life of the knight, from the clothes he wore and weapons he carried, to some of the actions he fought. It shows the reality of the knight in battle – how he often fought dismounted, the battle of wits between archers and cavalry, and the use of the feigned retreat. This part also shows how the knight's economic fortunes were precarious, with a frequent dependence on crude battlefield looting.

Appearance and Equipment

Many, if not most, items of dress and armour worn and the weapons used by the Norman knight could be seen in much of north-western Europe during the 10th to early 13th centuries and were not specific to him alone. When good sword blades might be imported and fresh armour could be had from the battlefield, such intermixing of pieces is hardly surprising. As equipment became more expensive so the military elite became more distinct. According to the late 11th-century *Sayings of St. Anselm*, a true knight had to own a warhorse with bridle, saddle, spurs, hauberk, helmet, shield, sword and lance, the latter normally being of ash.

The 10th and 11th Centuries

Next to his skin the Norman knight wore a linen shirt which was pulled on over the head. Underwear consisted of a baggy pair of long breeches or braies which often reached the ankles and were tied under the shirt with a waist girdle. They tended to be close-fitting from knee to ankle. Woollen or linen knee-length stockings or chausses might be worn over them, often having an embroidered band at the top which may have served as a garter. Very occasionally the chausses reached above the knee; a few were fitted with a stirrup instead of a foot. Leg bandages were sometimes worn over the braies or chausses, bound spirally from the foot to below the knee. The criss-cross method of fastening was a style reserved for the nobility. Shoes were of leather and closed with thongs which passed through slits cut in the shoe.

Over the shirt came the tunic, again put on over the head. It was knee or calf-length with long sleeves that sometimes were puckered at the wrist, and was hitched up over a waist girdle or belt. Instead of a wide neck opening some tunics had a smaller one provided with a vertical slit at the neck which facilitated putting it on and which might be closed by a pin or a brooch. The tunic might be decorated with embroidered bands at the cuff, neck or hem and occasionally the upper arm, where the band probably also served to hide the join between the sleeve and the main tunic. Simple all-over designs were also used. Some tunics were slit at the sides. A super-tunic might be worn over the tunic when the knight was not in armour. This was similar to the main tunic but sometimes a little shorter, and might have looser sleeves. On ceremonial occasions those of high rank might wear long tunics.

PREVIOUS PAGE
The so-called 'Temple Pyx' of c. 1140–50 probably formed part of a reliquary. Made from gilt copper alloy, the three figures carry typical long shields with simple decoration. The lattice of the central shield is dotted, suggesting riveted reinforcing strips. Two of the helmets also have diagonal bands. (Glasgow Museums and Art Galleries, Burrell Collection)

This early Norman knight, c.1000, is wearing a *spangenhelm*, an early style of helmet still used in the 11th century and which may have survived into the 13th century: the exploded diagram shows the construction of the helmet. His mailcoat is split at the sides, a fashion far more suited to use on foot, but which appeared infrequently throughout the 11th century and into the 12th. His shield is of traditional circular form, and not of the kite-shaped variety only now beginning to appear. He wears a handed-down sword, pattern-welded with a contemporary 'tea-cosy' pommel, and a wood and leather scabbard. His iron prick spurs are of the cylindrical type used by knights in north-western Europe. (Christa Hook © Osprey Publishing)

A rectangular or semicircular cloak of varying length provided extra warmth. It was fastened by ties or a brooch at the front or on the right shoulder to keep the arm free but cloaks were not usually worn when in armour. A purse (a pouch tied at the neck) might be carried under the tunic, suspended from the girdle which appeared at intervals from the braies. Gold or silver rings were worn and were also a sign of wealth, echoed in the quality of brooches or pins worn. The hair in the 10th century initially may have been long in Scandinavian style, perhaps worn in a heavy fringe. Some may latterly have copied the continental bowl crop round the tops of the ears. In the 11th century the back and sides were shaved in a distinctive fashion which can be seen on the Bayeux Tapestry but which did not last. Faces were usually clean shaven. In England during the reign of Rufus (1087–1100) very long hair and beards came into vogue, possibly helped by the longer hairstyle worn by the Anglo-Scandinavians.

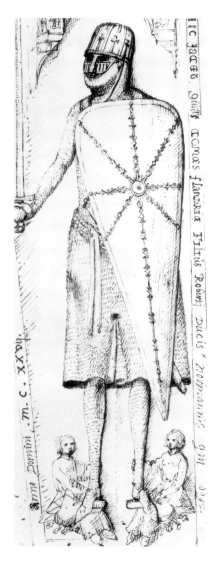

A sketch made of the now lost 12th-century effigy of William Clito (died 1127), Count of Flanders and son of Duke Robert of Normandy. His face is protected by a steel mask formed by expanding the nasal and which appears to be pierced with vertical slots for ventilation. The decorative crosses on the helmet may be a mark of rank, a sort of modified coronet. A ventail is drawn diagonally across the face and secured at the left temple. The shield bands are decorative and also act as reinforcement. (Courtesy of the Board of the Armouries)

The basic body defence of the Norman knight was the mailcoat. Mail consisted of numerous small iron rings each interlinked with four others to form a flexible defence. The coat so formed was pulled on over the head. Many of the first Normans would not have possessed any mail at all. Those who did would have had a coat which reached perhaps to the hip only and would be provided with short or elbow-length sleeves. During the first half of the 11th century there was a tendency for the coat to lengthen to knee length or even just below the knees. In order to facilitate movement, and to allow a rider to sit his horse more easily, the skirts were usually slit up to the fork at the front and rear. When mounted, this allowed the skirt to hang naturally over the thigh at each side. Some of the earlier coats may still have been made with side vents, a fashion better suited to footsoldiers. Short forms of the mailcoat continued to be worn, rather by infantry than cavalry, throughout the century but the longer style had become usual by the time of the Norman Conquest.

Occasionally the neck of the mailcoat was extended to provide a protective hood or coif. This was the origin of the word associated with such a coat – hauberk – which came from the Old German word for a neck-guard – hals berg. Indeed a few hoods may have been made separately from the mailcoat, but if this is so it was a fashion which did not last. Several shown on the Bayeux Tapestry, worked within 20 years of the battle of Hastings, lack any indication of rings which suggests they were of leather.

On the front of a number of hauberks seen on the Tapestry several straps may be seen. Some are arranged as squares and some as horizontal lines at the neck, the latter also seen on mailcoats worn by the English. The exact function of such features are unknown. They are rarely seen outside the Bayeux Tapestry, only appearing on a few other contemporary illustrations. One theory is that they represent a loose flap of mail hanging down prior to being tied up over the throat and chin. This, the ventail, is certainly mentioned in the Song of Roland of about 1100. Moreover, just such a square is shown in the open and closed position on a mid-12th century sculpted capital at Clermont-Ferrand, France. A few figures on the Bayeux Tapestry do appear to have a flap drawn up in a similar manner to that on the capital. However, we are left to wonder whether those with only a single horizontal strap at the throat are supposed to have such a flap closed or whether they simply echo the edging straps which appear on many mailcoats on the Tapestry. Again, the scene of hauberks being carried, together with some of the other sources, illustrate no mail hood to which such a flap would be tied, unless it is implied that it is hanging down loose at the rear. An alternative idea is that the square represents a loose mail flap tied over a vertical slit at the neck opening, which can be seen on other illustrations of such coats and was common on civilian tunics. A third alternative, and perhaps the least likely, is that it represents a reinforcement of mail over the chest or even a plate beneath held by ties.

By the time of the Norman Conquest a few senior knights wore mail hose or chausses. These may have been simple strips of mail applied to the front of the leg and laced up the rear. Alternatively they may have been full hose, both styles braced up to the waist girdle of the braies. Since shoes are worn by such figures on the Bayeux Tapestry we cannot be sure whether the foot was protected, though it seems unlikely. Interestingly, a few knights wear mail on the forearms. Though one or two figures may have sleeves extended to the wrist, and while at least one French manuscript shows that such sleeves were known by this time, those shown largely appear to be separate from the elbow-length sleeves of the hauberk. They may have been made like the hose and slid up the arm. If so, it did not last as a fashion. Many knights on the Bayeux Tapestry have coloured bands up the forearm; this could be conceived as a conventional way of rendering the puckered sleeve often seen at this time if it was also seen on civilian costume, which it is not. It may represent some sort of leather strapping wound round the forearm for extra protection, or even perhaps some padded under-garment. Such banded sleeves are also shown on illustrations of English warriors.

The helmet of the time was conical and almost invariably made with a nasal or nose-guard. Some were almost certainly made like the old-fashioned *spangenhelm*, in which vertical iron bands, usually four in number, spring from a brow-band and meet at the apex, the spaces between the bands being filled with iron segments riveted in place. Many helmets, however, seem to have been made from segments riveted directly to each other, whilst still others were beaten out of a single piece of metal. Though the nasal could be forged in one with the helmet, illustrations suggest that most

William confers arms on Earl Harold during his visit to Normandy, probably in 1064. The thick bands on the helmets suggest *spangenhelms*. The 'tails' on William's helmet are like the infulae on a bishop's mitre and may be a badge of rank, making him easy to spot from behind. The coifs do not appear to be of mail and are probably of leather. Notice the sword worn beneath the mail. (Bayeux Tapestry, Ancient Art and Architecture)

I VENERVNT ... AD DOL: ET:CONAN:

Unarmoured riders attack the castle of Dol. As this picture follows a scene of marching it may represent knights galloping straight into action, one man having donned his helmet. However, it may also represent retainers or even perhaps squires. (Bayeux Tapestry, Ancient Art and Architecture)

were made with an applied brow-band. Additional reinforcing bands might be added to these latter types. If the helmet was segmented the bands could cover the joints. Helmets might be painted, usually in the spaces between applied bands or else the segments themselves.

It is highly probable that all helmets were lined. As no lining and few helmets survive such ideas can only be hypotheses based on the presence of rivets and the examples of later helmets. It may be that a band of leather was riveted inside the brim, to which a coarse cloth lining was stitched, probably stuffed and quilted and possibly cut into segments which could be drawn together by a thong at the apex to adjust for height and comfort. The helmet would have been supplied with a tie at each side which fastened under the chin to secure it on the head. Contemporary references to lacing helmets is common. It also helped prevent them from being knocked over the eyes.

The final item of armour for the knight was his shield. The first Normans would have carried a circular wooden shield, probably faced and perhaps lined with leather. A bar riveted vertically inside the shield allowed it to be carried and to accommodate the knuckles a hole was cut from the centre of the shield. In order to protect the exposed hand a conical metal boss was then riveted over the front. A longer strap allowed the shield to be hung in the hall or slung on the back; it also prevented loss in battle if dropped. A strap for the hand rather than a bar seems to have been used occasionally by c. 1100, also being provided with an additional strap for the forearm. A pad to lessen the shock of blows may also have been provided. Although such additional strapping does not greatly assist in using such shields, some may have been added when carried by mounted men who might need to use the reins. Many shields are illustrated with an edging but surviving examples are very rare. Though such borders may

PORTANT:ARMAS: ADNAVES: ET hIC TRAhVNT:CARRVM CVM VINO:ETARMIS:

simply have been painted, it seems likely that leather, iron or bronze strips may have been used to reinforce the edges. A number of illustrations suggest that some shields were additionally strengthened by bands springing from the central boss to the outer edge. Some are also shown as rather ovoid in shape but whether this reflects a true shape is open to question.

In about the year 1000 such shields were supplemented by the introduction of a new type, the so-called kite-shaped shield. In this form the lower edge of the circular shield was drawn down to a point, the resulting shape being similar to the old-fashioned kite. It has been said that this form was ideal for horsemen, since the longer shape guarded the rider's left side and his vulnerable leg. However, such shields were initially seen in use equally by both cavalry and infantry. Moreover, many knights seem to carry their shields almost horizontally, as though attempting to protect their horse's left flank. The kite shield superseded the circular shield as the best type for cavalrymen, although the latter remained in use by some footsoldiers throughout the Middle Ages.

The carrying device on the new shield was no longer a metal bar. Instead there was an arrangement of straps, often a square or diamond (for hand and forearm) or the hand grasped a saltire, or else one or two straps together, supplemented by others for the forearm. Now redundant, the boss remained as an ornamental feature on many shields right through into the 12th and occasionally the 13th century. Many of these shields were decorated, especially with wavy crosses and beasts such as two-legged dragons. These were not true heraldic symbols, since the same person is sometimes shown with two or three different devices. True heraldry was not to emerge until the 12th century.

The foregoing formed the basic equipment of the Norman knight until the 12th century. The mailcoat appears from illustrations to have been the most

A supply wagon is dragged down to the waiting ships ready to sail for England. It is unlikely that spears were barbed or had lugs in reality. The helmets are hooked over the uprights of the cart and appear to have solid neck guards, though it may be meant to show the nasals of two helmets together. Each hauberk is carried on a pole by two men, since when not worn it represents dead weight. The coifs would hang down at the back. One sword is carried by a wrist strap. (Bayeux Tapestry, Ancient Art and Architecture)

popular form of defence. However, other forms of protection may have been used on occasion. Coats of scale, in which small scales of horn, metal or even leather are attached to a canvas backing, had been known in western Europe since the Roman Empire. At least one seems to be shown on the Bayeux Tapestry. The less wealthy may have simply worn a coat of hide. Unfortunately, this is a poorly documented area. The 13th century St Olaf's saga mentions coats of reindeer hide which could turn a blow as well as mail. One rider in a group of Norman horsemen on the Bayeux Tapestry appears to wear a coat of brown material which is of identical cut to the mail hauberks around him. Lamellar, consisting of small metal plates laced together, may have been adapted by some Italo-Norman knights.

It is possible that some form of padded garment was worn under the mail. The drawback with mail was its very flexibility, which allowed a heavy blow to break bones or cause severe bruising without actually tearing the links. Also, if links were broken they could be driven into a wound and cause blood poisoning. The form such garments took in the 10th and 11th centuries is likely to have been similar to that of the mailcoat. One or two garments seen on the Bayeux Tapestry may represent padded tunics but we cannot be sure. Even in the 13th century, illustrations of mail being removed do not reveal the padding below. It is just possible that the bands shown at the edges of the hauberks in the Bayeux Tapestry represent some padded lining, but this can only be supposition.

The weapon par excellence of the mounted knight was his sword. No other weapon was more esteemed or more celebrated, and the girding on of a sword was the mark of knighthood. The type in use in the 10th century and into the 11th century was a double-edged cutting or slashing sword. It had a blade about 79cm (31in) in length, tapering slightly towards the point. Down the centre ran the fuller, not a blood channel but a method of lightening the blade without weakening it. Some men may have preferred an alternative but less common form which was longer with more parallel sides, the fuller being quite narrow. Sword hilts were fairly short, since the sword was meant to be used in one hand. The crossguard was often straight but might curve towards the blade slightly. The pommel, which helped to counterbalance the blade and also prevented the hand from sliding off the grip, was usually either shaped like a tea-cosy or like a brazil nut. More rarely a simple disc pommel might be seen.

The sword was sharp as a razor but both hard and flexible, being capable of a thrust if necessary. It was carried in a wooden scabbard lined with wool or fur whose natural oils helped protect the blade from rust. The wood was often covered in leather and slung from the waist by a belt fastened with a buckle. In the 10th and early 11th century some may have been hung from a baldric over the right shoulder. The tip of the scabbard might have a chape to prevent scuffing, the mouth a locket. The scabbard might have occasionally been angled

Shortly after Christmas 1078, King William I marched on the castle of Gerberoi, near Beauvais and the eastern borders of Normandy, to besiege his rebellious son, Robert. Three weeks later Robert sallied out and attacked the besiegers. During the fighting William, now corpulent and about 50 years old, had his horse killed beneath him, possibly by Robert himself. Wounded in the arm, the king was saved ironically by an Englishman in his army named Toki, who gave William his own horse. Toki was then himself killed by a crossbow bolt. The king's other son, William Rufus, fighting on his father's side, was also wounded and Robert retired with his troops. Such a downfall was a great humiliation, William had been unhorsed and then lost the fight, which was especially unsettling as they were fighting other Normans. (Christa Hook © Osprey Publishing)

slightly back by joining it with a suspension strap to the side of the sword belt, in the manner seen on one or two Anglo-Saxon depictions of warriors. Occasionally the sword belt appears to have been worn under the mail, since many figures on the Bayeux Tapestry are shown wearing swords which have no visible means of support. This may be accidental, but several figures are seen in which the scabbard itself is worn under the mail, the lower end protruding from the skirt or through a slit, the sword hilt similarly emerging from another slit at the hip.

The other main weapon of the knight was his lance. In the 10th and, to a lesser extent, the 11th century the lance was essentially a spear, a plain ash shaft fitted with an iron head of leaf or lozenge shape and with a fairly long socket. The Bayeux Tapestry shows mounted knights using their lances either to stab or to throw. Although the overarm illustration has been questioned as simply a stabbing action, at least one lance is shown in mid-air on the Bayeux Tapestry. In the 11th century the lance was also being 'couched' under the arm so that the full force of the rider and galloping horse was imparted to the tip. The lances of senior commanders might be fitted with a small pennon with tails which was nailed behind the head. One semicircular flag shown on the Bayeux Tapestry seems to have a raven depicted on it, a throwback to the pagan raven symbols of the Vikings.

Maces were far less commonly used than the sword, and appear to have consisted of a wooden haft fitted with an iron or bronze head moulded with pointed projections. One depicted on the Bayeux Tapestry suggests a flanged

At the disaster at the
hillock, one knight strikes
overarm. The scene
shows how panic and
boggy ground can affect
even drilled horsemen.
(Bayeux Tapestry,
Ancient Art and
Architecture)

metal head, though this would be a very early date for this type. Senior
commanders such as Duke William might carry a rough baton or 'baculum',
presumably to signify their rank. This seems to be a descendant of the Roman
centurion's vine rod. Of crude construction, it also stood out in battle from
other maces. Axes were not popular with horsemen at this date, despite the
Normans' Scandinavian descent.

The knight rode a warhorse or destrier, so-called perhaps because it was led
on the right hand or itself led with the right leg. Destriers were specially
selected and carefully bred. Consequently they were extremely expensive
animals, costing at least eight times the price of a riding horse and often much
more. Such mounts, as the Bayeux Tapestry makes graphically clear, were
stallions whose natural aggression would be useful in a battle. Later medieval
sources show that warhorses were trained to lash out and kick and it is possible
that a similar desire lay behind the use of aggressive horses by the Normans.
These horses were perhaps similar in size to, or even smaller than, a heavy
hunter and were most like the modern Andalusian. Indeed, William himself
was sent gifts of horses by the King of Spain. The horse was deep-chested and
muscular so that it had the required staying power yet was nimble enough to
perform the necessary turns in battle.

Stallions required domination and their riders used curb bits and prick spurs
fitted with simple spikes. The saddle had developed by the mid-11th century
into a proper war saddle, provided with a raised pommel and cantle and long
stirrups so that the knight was almost standing in the stirrups and rode
straight-legged. This combination gave a sure seat in battle, braced his back in
the charge with a levelled lance and helped him to keep his seat as he cut with
his sword. To further brace his saddle it was provided with a breast band and in

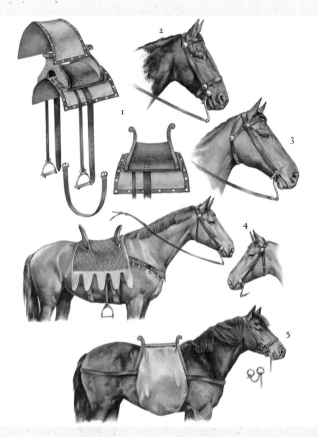

SADDLES AND BRIDLES

The saddles on the Bayeux Tapestry and on other representations do not give a great deal of detail. The pommel and cantle on most appear to curl outwards at the upper end and the saddles are usually reconstructed with a scrolled top edge. The 11th-century saddle (1) is basic, a tree of two pieces set either side of the horse's spine, the arçons (front and rear boards) carved to shape and with a central cut-out at the lower edge. Some form of padding would be nailed over the gap between the trees and a leather seat attached. The stirrups are long, the leathers passing under the saddle flap, probably looping through a slot cut in the tree and buckling under the saddle flap. Less likely, a metal hoop might be nailed to the tree through which the leathers are looped. The girths are nailed to the saddle and buckle on both sides to allow for adjustment. A saddle blanket is worn below the saddle to stop chafing. An overblanket may have been used. The 11th-century bridle (2) is of simple form, provided with a curb bit, most of these having their arms apparently joined by a transverse bar. The curb chain is positioned under the jaw. Illustrations rarely show any buckles on the cheek pieces. The reins were knotted together and most probably had a running ring for adjustment, a feature very occasionally seen in representations. Twelfth-century saddles (4) at first appear similar to the foregoing but as the century progresses the cantle develops a slightly more upright form and becomes more curved to the rider, while the front of the saddle bow often curves away from him. This form is less like a pommel but more like the wider form seen in southern European illustrations. Some arçons may have been painted. Cropper straps appear in art more frequently. Sometimes, as here, large decorative overblankets are worn, the arçons passing through slits cut in the fabric. Twelfth-century bridles often have no nose-band (3, 4), but some have a neck strap which sometimes joins to an extension of the browband. A sumpter horse (5) is shown with a saddle fitted with panniers. A leading rope is passed through the ring of the headstall. Others would be entirely of rope construction. (Christa Hook © Osprey Publishing)

some cases a crupper band as well. By 1100 a knight might own an additional warhorse. He also needed a palfrey or riding horse and ideally a sumpter horse or mule for his baggage. The squire might ride the packhorse or else a poorer-quality riding horse called a rouncy. All this equipment and horseflesh meant that knighthood was a very costly business.

The knights riding to Hastings are supported by archers clad in tunics except for one mailed and helmeted man who may be an officer. (Bayeux Tapestry, Ancient Art and Architecture)

The 12th Century

As well as the tunic seen previously a new, close-fitting long version came into fashion, slit up at the front and sometimes worn with a girdle which might carry the sword. This version might have bell-shaped or pendulous cuffs, which could be rolled back for action (1130s–1170s). Others had tight, turn-back ornamented cuffs. At the end of the century *magyar* sleeves, which gave a deep armhole, heralded the style of tunic of the next century. The braies shortened to the knees in mid-century, becoming drawers. Long hose became popular, pulled up over the drawers and made with a tongue at the upper front edge by which it was fastened with a tie to an exposed portion of the braies girdle. Hair remained long, parted in the middle and accompanied by beard and moustache. Younger men were often clean shaven with hair to the nape only. According to Orderic Vitalis, one method of distinguishing knights from squires in the time of Henry I was by the shorter hairstyle worn by the latter who were not allowed to grow their locks. Following the battle of Bourgthéroulde, William Lovel escaped disguised as a squire after cutting his hair.

The mailcoat of the 11th century could be seen throughout the 12th century and indeed into the next century. However, many representations show certain developments. The length remained at or just below the knee although some longer versions are seen occasionally. The sleeves now tended to extend to the wrists and towards the end of the century these had further developed into mail mittens. A half-way style can be seen on an illumination of Joshua in the Winchester Bible of 1160–70, where several figures have the hand covered in mail but the fingers left exposed. Once the whole hand was covered in mail a leather or cloth palm was necessary to allow for grip; since the sleeve and mitten were made in one, a slit in the palm enabled the hand to be freed as necessary. Often a lace was threaded through the links at the wrist and tied to prevent the mail sleeve dragging down onto the hand.

By the end of the century a quilted cap, similar to the civilian coif in shape, can be seen worn beneath the mail hood. Very occasionally a separate mail hood is shown but most were made in one with the mailcoat. Now the ventail flap is seen more often. Rectangular versions have been mentioned in connection with the capital at Clermont-Ferrand, one such covering the face up to the eyes. Other ventails took the form of a pendulous flap which was drawn up across the throat and chin to be secured to the mail coif at the temple by a lace. Some appear to have consisted of a simple lace used to close a vertical slit in the mail protecting the throat. Mail chausses became increasingly popular, though still occasionally worn with shoes. Some chausses had a lace threaded through the links below the knee to help keep them in place.

Many 12th-century illustrations show knights with a long undergarment flowing from below the mail skirt. It has been suggested that this is a padded *gambeson* but the form seems too loose for such a garment. Moreover, although in mid-century Wace mentions *gambesons* as an alternative to mail and though padded coats appear in the 1181 Assize of Arms and in conjunction with mailcoats in a description of the Third Crusade, these are references to infantrymen. The first descriptions of padding worn below the mail appear in the early 13th century. Although this does not negate the suggestion that such garments were worn earlier, it cannot as yet be proven. It may well be that these skirts are in fact the long gowns which have already been referred to as becoming popular in the 12th century.

By mid-century a new garment had appeared: the surcoat. This was worn over the mailcoat. A few illustrations show long sleeves and pendulous cuffs (again reminiscent of civilian fashion) but the majority were sleeveless and split up the fork at front and rear. For this reason it is rather hard to believe the idea put forward in one 14th-century chronicle that the surcoat kept the armour clean and dry. It may well have proved of some use during the Crusades to fend off the heat of the sun from the metal links. It is just as likely, however, that its origins lay in a desire to emulate the long flowing garments worn by the Saracens. Most surcoats were tied at the waist with a girdle or belt which was separate from that securing the sword. Early surcoats were often white or self-coloured and perhaps had a contrasting lining. Some were soon used for decorative display, although this was not necessarily heraldic. Heraldry was a very new science with rules of

The Norman kings of England changed the style of seal used by their Anglo-Saxon predecessors in order to show themselves as warrior knights riding their warhorses. This is the great seal of Henry I (1100–1135). Equipment shows little change to that of 1066 except for long sleeves to the mailcoat. (Public Records Office, London)

usage. One man ought to have one coat of arms only, which passed to his eldest son on his death. Rules also governed the use of colour on colour. Surcoats were not greatly used for heraldic display until the 14th century.

Scale hauberks continued in use. Wace refers to another garment, the curie, which, as its name implies, was probably of leather. Unfortunately no 12th-century representation seems to exist but 13th-century sources suggest it was a waist-length garment put on over the head and tied or buckled at the sides. It may even have been reinforced with iron. Some are worn by knights over mail but under surcoats, others without other armour by infantrymen.

This knight is Robert FitzWalter, c. 1190, wearing the latest equipment. Although some knights still looked similar to those at Hastings, changes had occurred. His mail skirt is shorter, and the sleeves are elongated into mail mufflers with a cloth palm. A lace threaded through the links helps keep the mail in place. Mail hose enclose the legs, and a lace below the knee helps to stop the mail from sagging. A surcoat is worn over the mail, and belted at the waist. The helmet is cylindrical and flat-topped and is fitted with a rigid face-guard pieced for ventilation. The spurs are still of the prick variety, but the arms now have a curve to accommodate the ankle bone. The shield is a little smaller and flat-topped, with FitzWalter's arms on it. The sword has a slight taper, and is fitted with a circular disc pommel, the commonest form of the next century. (Christa Hook © Osprey Publishing)

The conical helmet with nasal remained throughout the 12th century but variations appeared early. Many now had the apex tilted forward whilst some were drawn down at the rear to form a neck-guard. During the second half of the century hemispherical forms and, from about 1180, cylindrical types appeared, with or without nasals. Also at this time a few German illustrations show a bar appearing on the end of the nasal to protect the mouth. By the end of the century this had developed into a full face-guard, provided with two slits for the eyes and pierced with ventilation holes or slots to assist breathing. The cylindrical form was a popular type for this new development. Used in conjunction with a neck-guard, this new helmet foreshadows the great helm of the 13th century. That of Richard I has a tall fan crest, presumably of metal, on which a lion *passant guardant* is painted, echoing those on his shield. Other helmets might also be painted, though not all such decoration carried heraldic significance.

In addition, a new form of helmet, the kettle hat, made its appearance mid-century. The Scandinavian chesspieces from the Isle of Lewis in Scotland suggest that two forms were in use: one had a cylindrical top with a deep angled brim; the other was very like the 20th-century tin hat. Primarily a footsoldier's helmet, we know from 13th-century sources that occasionally knights wore the kettle hat in preference to the stuffy helm, a situation which may have been met with in the late 12th century also.

The kite-shaped shield continued throughout the 12th century. However, by the 1150s many shields began to have the top edge cut straight, allowing the

St Benedict frees a prisoner, a manuscript of c. 1070 from Monte Cassino in Italy. This is one of the rare chances to see a saddle from the front and shows a rounded bow similar in shape to a southern French picture which shows a cantle. (Photo12.com, Oronoz)

knight to peer over without the sides curving down away from him as they did on the 11th-century form. Many shields were curved to the wearer's body. By the end of the century the length of some shields had slightly reduced. Shield bosses continued in a decorative function, for example the newly discovered conical boss from the castle at Repton.

The double-edged cutting sword described earlier remained the main knightly weapon. Towards the end of the century a new type with a slightly tapered blade and shorter fuller emerged and became the most popular style of the next century. Alternative pommels also appeared. One was shaped like a lozenge and was fashionable after about 1175. Swords were still often worn beneath the mailcoat. Others show the popular method of fastening: the longer end of the belt was slit into two tails which were passed through two slits cut in the other end and knotted together.

As well as pennons similar to those seen on the Bayeux Tapestry, some triangular types were also used. Wace distinguishes between the gonfalon of the baron and the pennon of the knight. A number of bronze polygonal mace heads have survived which may date to the 12th century. Though light in comparison to later versions, they would be capable of disabling an unarmoured man or causing damage through flexible mail.

By the later 12th century the arçons on the knightly saddle had developed so that the rear arçon curved round the knight's thighs and that at the front also curved. A long saddle cloth, sometimes with a dagged lower edge, was sometimes laid over the saddle, the arçons passing through slits in the cloth.

Construction and Repair

Little contemporary mail has survived, although the so-called mailcoat of St Wenceslas at Prague may be of 10th-century date and a rolled mailcoat, probably from the battlefield of Lena in 1208, is preserved in Stockholm. Later medieval shirts show that mail weighed approximately 14kg (30lb). Most of the weight was taken on the shoulders but the drag could be reduced by hitching the mail over a waist or sword belt.

A mailcoat was the end product of a process which took many hours of labour. The exact method of making mail in the medieval period is unknown but scraps of information plus intelligent guesswork have arrived at a not improbable method of construction. The links began as drawn iron wire which was wound round a rod. The links so formed were then separated by being cut down one side of the rod. This left a number of open-ended rings. The ends of each ring were then hammered flat, overlapped and pierced in readiness to receive a tiny iron rivet. Every ring was interlinked with four others, two above and two below and then riveted shut. Since only every other row of rings needed to be riveted

OPPOSITE
'David and Goliath' and 'The Death of Absalom' from the Winchester Bible depict mailed men whose hands are completely covered to form mufflers. The horse at lower left has a cloth laid over the saddle, provided with slits to pass over the arçons. (© Photo Scala, Pierpont Morgan Library 2004, M.619 f.1v)

in order to join the rows above and below, the other rows could be welded shut. However, surviving medieval mail usually consists of wholly riveted rings. An 'idle' ring was only linked with three others and so could be used to decrease the number of rings in a row or the number of rows, so allowing a garment to be shaped. Thus a small hole under the armpit prevented the links from bunching up. The mail garment was designed with the rivet heads on the outside so that they did not rub against the clothing underneath and so wear it and themselves away. It is possible that certain tools were in use which overlapped, flattened and pierced each link in one movement but this can only be hypothesis. It is likely that the mailmaker actually made up the garments, leaving the more repetitive work of producing the links to his apprentices.

Scale armour would be made by riveting the upper edge of each scale to a leather or canvas backing garment and overlapping downwards so the top of the next scale was thus covered. Padded garments would have consisted of two layers of cloth or canvas stuffed with wool, hay, hair, old cloth or tow and quilted, usually vertically but perhaps also in a diamond pattern, to keep the stuffing in place. Some may have been made from many layers of linen.

Helmets were made in several ways. In order to make a segmented helmet each segment, usually four in number, had to be shaped, overlapped and riveted together. Those made from one piece were drawn up from a flat piece of iron or steel hammered out over a shaped iron stake secured in a hole in the anvil. The metal was annealed, that is heated and cooled, to make it workable. Once formed, applied bands, neck-guards or face-guards were riveted on. In the case of *spangenhelm* the iron framework was forged and fitted together before the segments were fixed inside with rivets. Internal linings would be secured with rivets along the brim.

Many shields were made from several planks of wood glued side by side. It may be that some – circular rather than kite-shaped – were of laminated form, that is of perhaps two layers, each of which was placed with the grain running at right-angles to its neighbours for added strength. Some kite-shaped shields may have been formed from a single piece of wood. The earliest surviving shield is not Norman but belonged to the von Brienze family. It may date to the late 12th or early 13th century, although its rounded top was cut flat at some time between 1230 and 1250. It is 15mm ($^5/_8$in) thick and may originally have been 100cm (3ft 3in) long, being covered in parchment on both sides. Most shields were probably made from lime wood or possibly poplar. The dished appearance of some circular shields and the curved surface of many long shields was probably achieved through steam heating. Leather, when used, would be tacked at the edges on the rim or at the rear. Enarmes and guige were riveted through the wood, the heads visible on the outer face. Bosses were similarly riveted through to the rear.

The sword had undergone a change of manufacture. Until about 900, sword blades were produced by pattern-welding. Since a good blade was handed down and since the knife known as the *seax*, together with spear heads, continued to

A Norman armourer's workshop was often of detached stone construction because of the dangers of fire. Some may even have been used to smelt the iron. This forge has a stone-built hearth with a canopy of earthenware tiles to draw the smoke away. A pair of hand-pumped bellows supplies the draught and charcoal keeps the fire hot. In front, set into a tree trunk, is a rectangular iron anvil. Windows would be kept to a minimum or omitted entirely. A torch is a controllable source of light which means the armourer can see when the metal in the fire has reached the right temperature by the colour it becomes or the sparks that adhere to its surface. The other tree trunk has holes to take iron formers or stakes shaped like mushrooms, and a slight depression used to shape shallow depressions in metal from the inside. Here a conical helmet has been heated and is being beaten out. The armourer is surrounded by the tools he might need, and water for quenching hot metal after shaping. The inset shows suggested tools for making mail. (Christa Hook © Osprey Publishing)

be pattern-welded until after the Norman Conquest, a description of the technique is called for. Rods of iron and carburized iron (a soft, impure form of steel) were beaten and twisted together to form a sandwich which was then twisted with similar sandwiches to form the blade, hammered out and flattened and shaped. The twisting of the metals meant that when the blade was finished and polished, a wavy line was seen running down its length, the pattern.

By about 900, however, improvements in the forging of steel meant that new types of sword could now be made. In order to harden the steel it was first quenched to temper the metal. The very hardness, however, gave this steel a brittleness which the older iron and carburized iron had not possessed. It was therefore necessary to employ the steel in such a way that the sword did not shatter easily. In order to achieve this the smiths used the steel in various combinations with the more malleable iron to produce harder but flexible blades. Some swords had tough steel edges welded on to improve their sharpness. It is impossible to know which methods were favoured the most, since different smiths favoured different combinations. Some felt that honey was a better medium for quenching because it created fewer bubbles. Similarly, the reaction of quenching could differ from sword to sword within the same smithy. Moreover, many surviving swords have not been analyzed at all.

Sword blades might be decorated. Grooves were cut into the blade and the decoration was hammered into the heated surface. On the other side another design might spell a name such as 'ULFBERHT' in Roman letters. Other names were also used, especially at this time: 'INGELRIF'. These were probably originally the names of swordsmiths, but by the time of the Conquest they had come to denote the factory. Many seem to have been based in the Rhineland, from whence swords were sent to their customers.

The most common smith's name when set into the narrow fullers of the longer swords and their derivatives was: 'GICELIN ME FECIT' ('Gicelin made me'). On the reverse, especially of the latter, might be found a religious inscription, usually 'INNOMINIDOMINI' or a garbled version of it. Other metals were also used for decoration: latten (which was a type of brass), silver, pewter or tin. Well-written religious phrases in latten or white metal were especially seen, some misspelt or obscure, usually on the long swords or their derivatives. Crosses might flank an inscription. Rarer decoration came in the form of symbolic pictographs and mystical designs.

The metal crossguard was slotted on to the tang and secured by the grip. This was formed from two pieces of wood or horn channelled out to take the metal tang, then glued over it and probably covered in leather and perhaps bound with thongs. The pommel was slotted over the end of the tang which was then hammered over to secure it.

The repair of a knight's equipment in the field depended on what was damaged and whether a smith or armourer was on hand. In the invasion of England there would have been a number of armourers travelling with the host. For small-scale skirmishing it is doubtful whether a skilled technician would be available until the knight returned to his home base or reached another castle.

Mail might tear but still render the garment usable until such time as it could be repaired. It is doubtful if a village smithy would have the type of tools required for the tiny holes and rivets needed to close up links. He could probably beat out a dented helmet, however, until a more skilled repair could be effected by an armourer. Rents in cloth were probably stitched up by squires or, when an army was on the march, by some of the women that accompanied it.

This portrayal of the murder of Thomas à Becket dates to the late 12th or early 13th century and illustrates a form of helmet which seems to be provided with a solid chin-guard, a feature rarely seen elsewhere. The bear on the shield alludes to Reginald FitzUrse, one of the murderers. (Topfoto/ Charles Walker)

Shields, although tough, were not designed for long usage. Viking sagas note the effects of sharp weapons against shields during formal duels, when the wood was hacked to pieces leaving only the metal bosses intact. Damaged shields would be discarded rather than repaired, only the boss and perhaps any metal fittings or straps being salvaged. Swords were prized items and only an armourer could deal with damage, though again a blacksmith could straighten out a bent weapon temporarily if no swordsmith was to hand.

The fallen warrior, in this scene of David and Goliath, wears chausses which show how they were laced under the shoe. Notice the rendition of the chausses, a feature of this period which has led some to argue that different types of armour are being worn. (British Library, Add. Ms. 14789 f.10)

Whilst speaking of repair it is perhaps worth noting the kind of services available to the knight himself should he be wounded. Good care was probably given by monks, who used numerous herbs in their healing. However, a knight was likely to receive the attention of surgeons if in an army or of great rank, or of lesser men if himself of humbler rank. Knights in southern Italy might be lucky enough to be tended by men trained at the great school of Salerno. Head wounds were less common in knights because they usually wore helmets but they were more likely to suffer dislocated shoulders from falling off their horses. Such wounds were frequently treated by placing a ball covered in wool under the arm and forcing the joint back. Throat wounds, often from a lance, were usually considered untreatable. Wounds were often left partially open for a day or two until pus formed, before stitching up. The more enlightened used egg white and other remedies as opposed to boiling oil or hot cautery irons found elsewhere. Amputation might be done with an axe but suturing of blood vessels was known. Barbed arrows were removed either by covering the barb with a tube or quill, or by pushing them through to the other side and breaking off the head before withdrawing the shaft.

Training

The training of the Anglo-Norman knight was the same as that of his fellows in Normandy. It began when a *puer* (boy) of around 12 years joined a band of *amis* (comrades) to train 'like brothers' in a *compagnie* or *maisnie*. Schooling involved horsemanship, the training of horses, use of weapons, archery, self defence, wrestling, hunting, what would now be called 'fieldcraft', riding, operating as a group, and the rules of spoils and plunder. The extravagant dress of young men was part of their group solidarity, which was itself a vital element in military training. Once trained they became *armigers* (squires) but might have to wait years before being 'dubbed' as knights, often all at one time.

References to squires tend to suggest that while some boys of good birth were so-called, a much higher proportion were in fact non-noble attendants who would never attain knighthood and who were paid – often erratically – for the job they performed. From 11th- and 12th-century accounts and from the more detailed rule of the Knights Templar of the 13th century a picture of these duties may be formed.

The squire was often heavily laden, carrying his own and his master's pack and weapons. According to the Rule, he rode either the pack-horse or a rouncy and led his master's saddled warhorse. In the battle line he took the riding-horse to the rear after giving the knight his shield and lance. If a spare warhorse was owned, a second squire followed his master at a safe distance, ready to assist if the first horse was killed or blown.

When on campaign the squire set up the knight's tent before riding out to forage for firewood and water, especially for the horses. Squires often seem to have set out in groups, sometimes with an armed escort. They were also prominent in sieges and when a place was sacked. Young men of good birth were more likely to be the ones who helped a knight dress and put on his armour, or who carved at the table. They also may have worn armour and fought, as suggested by a reference on the Bayeux Tapestry.

It is obvious that a professional cavalryman must work hard to acquaint himself not only with the niceties of riding with minimal hand control but also with the use of the lance and sword from horseback. According to Abbot Suger in the early 12th century, a *puer* destined for knighthood was placed in the household of another lord when about 12 or 13 years old. Thus William Marshal was placed in the household of his uncle, William of Tancarville, in 1155. Such a move might be easier for some than for others since some lords, such as Henry I, were actively on the lookout for new young blood to join their ranks and had the money to support their training. Lords who could not place their sons in the household of the king or a great magnate did the best they could.

This Norman knight from around the time of the Norman Conquest wears a mail hauberk split front and back to facilitate movement, particularly when mounted. His mail has a coif and ventail. He wears a segmented helmet, perhaps the most common form in use in 1066. It was constructed from four shaped iron segments riveted together, to which a browband and nasal were attached, as seen on the exploded diagram. The shield is now kite-shaped, defending the left side, but capable of covering much of the horse when held out horizontally. The sword is carried under the mail, a slit at the hip providing access to the scabbard mouth. The weapon was usually buckled on by a waist belt. His tinned spurs have a pyramidal spike to goad his horse. (Christa Hook © Osprey Publishing)

Boys were taught to ride at an early age. The Carolingian comment, 'You can make a horseman of a lad at puberty, after that, never', was echoed by the remark, 'He who has stayed at school till the age of twelve, and never ridden a horse, is fit only to be a priest.' The boisterous stallions were not easy to control, which explains somewhat the use of a harsh bit and prick spurs. Boys therefore had to learn to master these wilful animals as well as to ride with their legs, allowing their hands to concentrate on using the shield in the left hand and the weapon in the right. The left hand is sometimes shown holding the rein as well but close combat would mean either laying the rein on the horse's neck or else keeping the shield fairly still.

Hunting was a tough sport and knights were killed in accidents. In this early 12th-century hunt, a boar has been brought to bay by greyhounds and is grappled by heavier alaunts, powerful dogs that were often hard to handle. The knight, distinguished from the squires by his long hair, has elected to attack from horse-back, which involves skill in controlling his horse, and a steady aim. The boar spear has lugs to stop an enraged boar from running too far on it. The use of the bow and crossbow in the hunting field was probably the only time a knight or squire would carry one. (Christa Hook © Osprey Publishing)

It took much practice to be a good fighter. References occasionally occur, such as that of the knight accidentally killed while practising the javelin with his squire. Illustrations of the 13th- and 14th-century show how warriors trained at the pell, a tall wooden post driven into the ground at which they could practise their sword cuts. Later medieval texts, following Roman manuals, describe training weapons as being of double weight to develop the muscles. Once the lance began to be couched under the arm it became necessary to learn how to stay in the saddle under the shock of impact and how to grip the lance firmly so that it did not slide back under the armpit when contact was made. The lance of the Norman knight had no ring behind the hand to ram against the armpit and prevent friction burns.

There is no reason to think that trainee knights did not practise in the same way as is shown in 14th-century manuscripts. This involved early training by use of a wheeled wooden horse pulled by companions. The pupil aimed at a shield nailed to a post and, once the shield was struck, the wooden horse continued to be pulled to teach the youth to grip firmly with his legs and to hold on to the lance, so preventing either loss of the weapon or an ignominious unseating. The same target could be challenged when riding a warhorse. As well as inanimate opponents, apprentice knights could fight each other or another knight, to learn not only the basic cuts but also feints and the offensive use of the shield.

The trainee was dubbed a knight when about 21 years old, a translation initially made by a stout buffet about the ears, the only blow the young man would have to receive without retaliating. Banquets, victories or the starts of campaigns were often marked by the making of knights. The ceremony was performed by another knight, usually the lord of the household but sometimes the king himself. The new knight's sword was belted round him and his spurs buckled to his feet. He then showed off his prowess, sometimes in a celebratory tournament.

Given money and weapons, the new knights would then be sent to serve a lord as a group, or graduate into the household knights of the lord in whose *familia* (military household) they had trained. As a new member of an elite equestrian society the young man was now known as a *juvenis* (youth) and remained so until he settled down, married and had children, after which he was referred to in written texts as a *vir* (man). Since some knights, such as William Marshal, did not marry until they were into middle age, their years as a youth could last for some time. They maintained their training by riding at dummy targets and practising skill at arms with other knights or boys.

It was youths, as knights errant, who rode out to seek fame, money, wives or positions. They took service with lords, sometimes in far-flung lands, either as mercenaries or as household knights and flocked to theatres of war. Those younger sons with little prospect of a part of the patrimony were on the lookout for a rich heiress who could provide them with land. They took part in tournaments that were emerging in the 12th century. Here was an excellent training ground. The tournament of the day consisted of a battle between two teams of knights wearing full armour and using unblunted weapons. The field might stretch over a large area of the countryside and contestants had every incentive to fight hard since defeated knights forfeited their horse and armour. Thus good fighters such as William Marshal stood to make a fortune and toured events looking for gain and glory.

As men of action, Norman knights were perfectly attuned to the hunt. It supplied additional food for the table but also provided the chance to improve horsemanship by galloping after game over rough country. Certainly it could be dangerous; Richard, son of William the Conqueror, is said to have been gored to death by a stag in the New Forest, which his father had created. Accidents were common and not all caused by the enraged quarry. The same forest witnessed the death of another of the Conqueror's sons, William Rufus, killed by an arrow which some have tried to suggest was the result of an assassination plot by his brother, Henry. Against wild boar or rarely the brown bear, the hunt provided the chance to demonstrate courage in tackling such animals with sword or spear. Moreover, the hunting field was the one place where the knight might show his skill with the bow or crossbow.

Tactics

The Norman knight was the shock element in the armies of the day. Initially cavalry battles are poorly documented but probably consisted of groups of horsemen, each under its lord's *gonfanon*, galloping against the enemy. Such *conrois* may have used their lances in various ways; certainly the Bayeux Tapestry shows little co-ordination of movements and couching the lance is not a priority. It was probably not until the late 11th century that couching the lance became usual, so that Anna Comnena speaks of the knight of the First Crusade being able to punch a hole in the walls of Babylon. This method enabled *conrois* to charge in a solid line, knee to knee and so close that it was said of one group of feudal knights in the Third Crusade that an apple thrown into their midst would not have touched the ground.

The initial charge with the couched lance was begun at a trot, only breaking into a gallop at the last moment so as not to tire the horses or lose formation. Similarly the lance was held upright at the start and only levelled on nearing the enemy. The idea was to drive the iron into an opponent or else to unseat him or overthrow both horse and rider. For this the man or his shield must be hit squarely and the lance gripped firmly and kept clamped under the arm. Late medieval tournament books advise not looking at the oncoming lance point as this will make you flinch or close your eyes; instead you should concentrate on the oncoming target. The charge was followed up by drawing the secondary weapons and raining blows. The tournament books suggest that in the mêlée in the lists the knight should strike and press on to the next, not turning round as this wastes time and becomes tiring – advice likely to apply equally to earlier centuries.

The initial charge was important for, if it could be held, the attack might peter out. To this end the Byzantines, uncomfortable when facing Norman

Warhorses poke their heads above the gunnels of the ships during the crossing to England in 1066. They are probably wearing halters as no bits are shown. (Bayeux Tapestry, Ancient Art and Architecture)

cavalry, would sometimes try to break them up by throwing down caltrops to maim the horses or else by using light wagons as an obstacle. Against solid infantry the mounted knight was more at a disadvantage. Here the use of volleys of javelins, delivered by groups of horsemen who then wheeled away, are possibly suggested by the Bayeux Tapestry. Such tactics were probably copied from the Bretons and against a phalanx of infantry may have proved more useful than a charge with couched lances. Any weak spots so caused could then be exploited by groups of knights bursting in with drawn swords. In either case the knight was soon reduced to a long contest of hard knocks with secondary weapons where his stamina and strength would be tested to the limit.

Although he could fight on foot, Anna Comnena noted that the long shield and spurs seemed to be a disadvantage for the dismounted knight. However, against both foot and horse he could employ the trick of the feigned flight to lure them out. As already noted in the first part, this manoeuvre has been the subject of much controversy. The usual argument has been that it would panic the rest of the army, or that the enemy would guess what was afoot. It is simply the chronicler's way of covering up a real retreat, say the critics. It was especially suited to the *conrois*, since one or more such units could be employed. Many fought with the companions they knew and trained with, and thus a feeling of camaraderie and fellow-thinking could be utilized to reduce possible confusion. Moreover, feigned flights had been a part of cavalry tactics for centuries. Certainly the Bretons had been using them since the 9th century and it is possible that the Normans were influenced by the latter. Norman knights are recorded as using feigned flights to great effect at Arques in 1053 and Cassel in 1071. They also used this tactic in Sicily, at Messina, in 1060.

Enemy arrows were a problem since the warhorse was unarmoured and his rider's limbs and face were partly exposed. Here it was necessary to avoid a head-on confrontation and to try to take the enemy in the flank. When faced with eastern horse-archers the heavier horses and the solid charge of the mailed knights could do little against enemies who refused to stand and, mounted on swift horses, harassed the westerners with arrows, particularly on the flanks. It meant that such enemies had to be forced into a position from which the charge could be launched, or ambushed to allow the knights to close quickly. Bohemond formed a reserve of mounted knights in an attempt to counter flank attacks on his charging knights. He also made good use of his infantry to form a screen behind which the cavalry could wait for an opportune moment to deliver their charge. The armoured spearmen could in their turn cover the archers and crossbowmen who could keep their enemies at a distance. In this way each arm of the army complemented the others and provided an effective countermeasure.

It might be thought that Normans who broke through and pursued a defeated enemy would be difficult to rally. The fact that they could be halted, even when individuals used their lances in different ways rather than in a concerted charge, testifies to the discipline and order seen on the field.

OPPOSITE
Normans in Italy charge Byzantines, who hated the solid lines of horsemen, with levelled lances. This solid tactic was now becoming the usual method for a cohesive charge, as the 11th century ended and the 12th began. Though many knights wore the same armour as seen in the West, others were influenced by more eastern styles encountered in Byzantine Italy and Sicily with its overlays of Muslim culture. (Christa Hook © Osprey Publishing)

Detail from an Anglo-Norman manuscript c. 1150. On the left are infantrymen, with an archer poised to shoot his bow. In the foreground and bottom left men are sharpening swords. (Eadwine Psalter, Ms.R. 17.1, Trinity College Lib., Cambridge)

Typical Engagements

The effectiveness of the Norman cavalry charge, with or without the couched lance, is demonstrated in a number of battles. Val-ès-Dunes in 1047 was a struggle between Duke William of Normandy and a force of Norman rebels. There is little reference to the presence of infantry and it appears to have largely involved clashes of bodies of horsemen in which the stronger or more skilful, under William and King Henry, won the day. Even against mixed forces the power of a Norman assault could be decisive. In 1081 at Durazzo an Italo-Norman charge broke the Byzantine line which included horse-archers. At Monte Maggiore in 1041, about 2,000 Normans in revolt against their Byzantine masters faced a larger army drawn up in two lines. The Norman horse and foot attacked in spearhead formation – presumably a kind of wedge – and drove the first line in on the second, causing confusion and ultimate defeat. In 1053 the battle of Civitate again saw Norman knights, this time from Apulia, quickly routing a larger Papal force of Italo-Lombard cavalry and infantry in the first charge. However, the Norman knights under Humphrey de Hauteville and their reserve under Robert Guiscard were held up by a group of about 700 Swabian mercenaries until Richard of Aversa's horsemen returned from the pursuit and forced them into squares which were gradually dissipated.

Hard pounding was used far more at Hastings in 1066. According to William of Poitiers, the lines of the Normans and their allies consisted of archers in front, infantry behind and knights in rear. This strongly suggests an initial softening up with missiles, followed with an assault by the foot. The cavalry were to be used to break open the gaps so formed and to pursue the routed enemy. Such tactics made sense. For one thing, the Normans probably had fewer horsemen than they would have liked and were confronted by a solid dismounted phalanx. Secondly, warhorses were expensive and were more likely to be killed by footsoldiers than by other mounted knights. Moreover, as we shall see, this combination of elements in Norman armies was usual. In reality, the Norman foot at Hastings were unable to effect breaches and the cavalry were committed in a desperate attempt to break the English line, made more secure by being positioned on a ridge which denied flank attack. Victory was only achieved towards evening when a combination of mixed cavalry and infantry assaults and arrow showers finally saw King Harold killed. The English position had shrunk so much that the ends of the ridge were seized by cavalry who then rolled up the line.

The ferocity of English resistance was not lost on the Normans. It must have reinforced their belief, shared by other feudal commanders in Europe, that dismounted knights were often tactically desirable. Indeed, Norman forces often appear to have dismounted a part of their cavalry while keeping others as a mounted reserve. Moreover, archers were usually placed in front so that the resulting army consisted of similar elements to those at Hastings, although the shortage of cavalry here meant that the infantry consisted of footsoldiers, knights only joining them when their horses had been killed.

A shield of the von Brienze family. This example was probably made in the late 12th century, being modified between 1230 and 1250 by having the top arch cut off. The wood, 15mm (3/5 in) thick, is covered on both sides with parchment and the lion is painted silver on a blue field. The rear straps have been cut away, leaving fragments held by rectangular washers; there are traces of the pad for the fist. Originally the shield may have been about 100cm (40 in) long. (Swiss National Museum, Zürich, LM3405.178)

A mailcoat, split at the sides in the old fashion, is worn by this warrior in a depiction of the Massacre of the Innocents. His sword is carried under the mail but on the right side rather than the left, possibly a mistake of the artist. (British Library, Ms Cotton Nero C 4f.14)

During the later 11th and 12th centuries, there were few fundamental changes in Norman warfare; when knights fought in their most characteristic manner as cavalry they still operated in small, closely packed *conroi* units. The habit of wrapping a horse's breast-strap around the rear of its saddle showed that so-called 'shock tactics' with the couched lance were even more important than before. Similarly, the participation of unarmoured cavalry decreased dramatically. The classic tourney or tournament of the 12th century was still very much like real cavalry warfare, with *conrois* of knights fighting in a mêlée. This was certainly not a free-for-all, as it involved manoeuvring by cavalry units and sometimes even the involvement of infantry, who assaulted any broken *conrois* in the flanks.

When open battle took place it was common for much of an army, including the knights, to fight on foot. The tactic of dismounting some of his knights to form a solid defence supported by horsemen won the day for Henry I on several occasions. In 1106 he was besieging Tinchebrai when his brother arrived with a relief force. Instead of backing off, Henry chose to fight. He placed his infantry in the front line and dismounted knights in the second, with a contingent of 700 cavalry with each. Robert apparently also dismounted some of his forces. He then launched a cavalry charge against Henry's right wing. Henry of Huntingdon noted that they had been well trained in the wars of Jerusalem, probably a reference to the solid charge with couched lances. It broke through

Henry's first line but was held by the second, a similar charge on the left wing making little progress. However, Henry then sent a hidden reserve of perhaps 1,000 cavalry under Helias of Maine against the entangled Normans on his right and won the day. At Brémule in 1119 Henry I dismounted all but about 100 of his 500 knights when he encountered the invading forces of Louis VI of France. It was a small-scale affair since Louis himself had only about 400 knights. The French came on in two or three divisions and the first, though apparently lacking discipline, actually broke the Norman cavalry screen. However, on confronting the dismounted knights it was surrounded and cut to pieces, as was the next division. Louis, himself wounded in the head, fled. At the battle of the Standard near Northallerton in 1138, knights fought on foot to stiffen the English levies against the opposing Scots. Again archers completely disrupted the undisciplined Galwegian charge and, though the Norman cavalry of David of Scotland had some success, they were withstood probably by the Norman mounted contingent fighting for Stephen. At Lincoln in 1141 both King Stephen and the rebel forces placed wings of horsemen on either side of a centre of infantry and dismounted knights.

The danger in attacking archers is well illustrated by the battle of Bourgthéroulde in 1124. This battle is important, not so much for the historical outcome – no king was present – as for the concise tactical description given by Orderic Vitalis. Henry I's household knights confronted the rebel Waleran of Meulan who was returning from an attempt to relieve Vatteville. After discussion the royal troops decided to dismount one section and support it with the other which remained mounted. A screen of archers was placed in front to shoot down the enemy horses. Mounted archers, who almost certainly only used their horses for movement, were sent against Waleran's right wing. His knights had their mounts shot from under them and Waleran was captured. Henry was on the receiving end when attempting to relieve Alençon in 1118, however. An Angevin force of knights, followed by archers and other infantrymen, charged a Norman force of mixed cavalry and infantry. The Angevin knights were dismounted, and behind them Angevin archers in a second force advanced and took their toll of the royal troops; a charge by Count Fulk from the siege lines then broke Henry's forces.

Flank attacks have already been noted in the sudden onslaught of cavalry used by Henry I at Tinchebrai. At Nocera in 1132 the rebel, Rainulf of Avelino, secured victory over Roger II of Sicily by wheeling his force of 2,500 Apulian Norman horsemen against the flank of the Sicilian forces who had pushed back the rebel left wing. Several references occur of knights ambushing enemies. In 1119 the Norman garrison of Tillières, by keeping the paths patrolled, surprised French raiders who were on their way to besiege it. A large-scale ambush was that of Duke William's attack on the French/Angevin rear, trapped by the tide while crossing the ford at Varaville in 1057.

Motivation

The sons of the Norman nobility, like those in other parts of western Europe, had limited opportunities. The eldest, especially in England, would usually inherit the patrimony but for the rest the main outlet was either the church or a military career. The eldest was expected to become a knight, other younger sons who chose war as a profession also found knighthood expedient. Some became vassals of great lords, receiving land or living as household knights. Some would marry a rich heiress and so obtain land; some would become rich through tournaments. Others became soldiers of fortune, seeking wealth abroad and eventually carving out kingdoms in Italy, Sicily and the Holy Land. Still others hired themselves out as mercenaries. Thus Norman knights sold their services to the Byzantine Emperor soon after arriving in Italy. All were endeavouring to promote their career in a harsh world which, to men of their birth, offered only the Church as an alternative.

We know from Orderic that not all such men were uncultured, for the knights of Maule used to enjoy holding academic conversations with the monks in the cloisters of the priory there. Others, such as the Earl of Chester, had a noisy household crowded with men and dogs. He was a man who uncaringly rode roughshod over the crops of his peasant tenants when out hunting yet was

Huntsman dressed in mail and helmet, and carrying bow – a 12th-century carving *in situ*, north door, La Martorana, Palermo. (David Nicolle)

careful to keep a poet at his court. In the 11th century knights were brought up on epic tales of heroes, stories short on love interest and long on blood and fighting. In the 12th century Courtly Love themes crept slowly in from southern France and romances, often with Arthurian themes, began to arise. Moreover there was a certain *esprit de corps* among knights, even if often for the fact that a captured knight meant ransom money. Loyalty to your lord was, however, an important concept, as was honor. Peasants fared badly during unrest and footsoldiers were cut down with impunity after a defeat. A few men were exceptionally cruel and treacherous; Robert of Bellême had a liking for torturing prisoners rather than ransoming them. Yet men were not unaware of the evil they did. The Conqueror on his deathbed was, so it was reported, weighed down by guilt at the blood he had shed. Some knights, after a life of violence, took the cross and went on a pilgrimage or crusade. Others entered monasteries so they would die in monkish robes, for nearly all believed ultimately in God's power.

It is obvious from the many speeches made by commanders before battle that their soldiers needed encouragement and that they were often nervous of the outcome and feared death. This was used to advantage in the Crusades by the reassurance that those who died would go straight to heaven. Men also feared defeat, which prevented many battles from developing in the first place. Older and wiser minds often tried to persuade younger commanders against making a stand, because of the dangers inherent in losing a pitched battle, often with good reason. It was safer to destroy villages and crops, to show up an enemy's failure as a protective lord, and to threaten war, than to actually engage in it. Some men avoided becoming knights by paying *scutage* instead. Originally this was a money payment raised on those too young, sick or old to become knights and probably used in England during the reign of Rufus. However, already in Henry I's time the sheer cost of becoming a knight caused some to pay *scutage*. Finance outweighed ideas of chivalry.

The silver seal die of Robert FitzWalter, probably dating to the early 13th century. The enclosing helm is rather similar to that of Richard I. The knight wears a surcoat and his horse a long caparison or trapper which bears his arms. The testier or head covering may be of pourpoint to guard the animal's head. (Topfoto/British Museum/HIP)

Bohemond

Tall, broad-shouldered, muscular, slim-hipped but slightly stooping, white-skinned with a clean-shaven face where the white mingled with red, blue-grey eyes and blond hair cut to the ears; this portrait of Bohemond of Taranto comes down to us from the Byzantine princess, Anna Comnena, who saw him when a young girl. Despite a certain charm, she recalls how forbidding and savage he seemed, how untrustworthy he was and how quickly he changed his mood to suit the moment.

Bohemond was the son of Robert Guiscard, the tough Norman adventurer who had arrived in Italy in 1041 and carved himself a large slice of southern Italy. Bohemond was born to Aubrée and christened Mark but because of his size in his mother's womb received the nickname of Bohemond after a giant of that name.

The boy soon took after his father and joined him on his aggressive sojourns. In 1080 Guiscard, under a Papal banner and probably with an eye on the imperial throne, set sail from Otranto with Bohemond. Having captured Corfu they advanced on Durazzo. Although Guiscard had to return to Italy to help the Pope and quell a revolt, Bohemond was left to press the attack. So adroit was he that he almost reached Constantinople itself before being rebuffed at Larissa in 1083, when the Byzantines themselves are said to have used a feigned flight. The Normans were now steadily pushed back and the Balkans lost.

When Guiscard died in 1085 his son, Roger 'Borsa', was designated his successor. Angry at being disinherited by his lacklustre half-brother, Bohemond immediately seized Oria, Otranto and Taranto and in 1090 took Bari as well. He was only stopped by the formidable Roger, 'Great Count' and conqueror of Sicily, who now pushed north to consolidate and increase his possessions in southern Italy.

In 1096, contingents of knights who formed part of the First Crusade rode into the shifting political struggles of southern Italy. While Borsa and Roger were uninterested, Bohemond took the Crusader's oath and set off. Although he possibly had some genuine desire to free the Holy Places, he may also have seen an opportunity to revive his expansionist designs, either in the empire or in the east. Having passed through an uneasy Constantinople with his followers, he took a prominent part in the battle of Dorylaeum against the Turks; by the time they reached Antioch late in 1097, Bohemond was an acknowledged leader.

Antioch would be a suitable prize, and Bohemond went all out to acquire it for himself. He defeated relief forces by keeping his own men in reserve until the Muslims thought victory was theirs. A second relief force from Aleppo was also broken when the crusading cavalry lay in wait. Although the first mounted charge by the Crusaders failed to break the large force, it was then lured on to ground with a lake on the left and river on the right where the Christians were protected against flank attack. A final full charge then broke it. Bohemond led the assault which took the city on 3 June 1098, assisted by treachery within. He also led the whole army out to defeat Kerbogha who had arrived to take back the city, in the most complete victory of the First Crusade. In this he emerged from the city with the footsoldiers in a screen to protect the horsemen until the critical moment. The mounted charge which followed crashed into the enemy ranks and secured the ultimate victory. In the face of this his request to take possession of Antioch was unopposed except by Raymond of Toulouse, whose own men finally forced him to leave Bohemond in Antioch. Careful to legitimize his position after the fashion of Norman conquerors in Italy, Bohemond was invested as Prince of Antioch in 1100 by Daimbert, Archbishop of Pisa and Papal legate, thus cutting himself from the Byzantine emperor and from any interference from Jerusalem.

In 1100 Bohemond was captured by the Turks and only released three years later. Returning to the west he was treated as a super-hero and began stirring enmity against the Emperor Alexis, accusing him of treachery in having turned back from Antioch when the Crusaders needed him. In 1106 Bohemond, newly married to the daughter of the king of France, preached a crusade in Chartres Cathedral against Alexis. The following year, with Papal backing, this restless warrior moved once again against the Byzantine Empire. Knowing Antioch was safe under his warlike nephew, Tancred, he set about besieging Durazzo, the fortress guarding the gateway to the Balkans. When assault proved useless, Bohemond sat down to starve it into submission. Unfortunately, Byzantine ships thwarted his plans, blockading the coast and cutting him off from Italy. Soon the Byzantine army, with Turkish mercenaries, hemmed him in and waited. Trapped, his own men dropping with disease and famine, the prince had no option but to surrender to Alexis in September, 1108. Forced to agree a treaty with the emperor, he returned humiliated to Apulia and died three years later.

Logistics

An apprentice to arms would be supplied by his lord with the items necessary for his training. He might possess a sword or even some armour as a gift from his father. Alternatively arms, armour and horse might be received from the lord who knighted him or even the lord who took him into his service, an echo of the old Germanic idea of the lord as gift-giver. Less romantically, such possessions might come from battlefield looting, the ransoming of captured knights or as spoils from the tournament. Any weapons or armour received in this way might be given to one's own followers, since their appearance reflected the generosity and wealth of their master. Alternatively such booty could be sold and the money used for other purposes.

Mail, helmet and sword were tough and might take a fair amount of punishment before they needed replacement rather than repair. Mail in particular was long-lasting since any damage could be mended with new rings. This was just as well considering the cost of such equipment. Shields and lances, on the other hand, might need regular replacement depending on the frequency of action. For knights living in a lord's household the cost was borne by the lord; for those on estates the bill was laid at their own door. Warhorses cost a fortune, which is one reason a knight was set above other men, and the loss of such an animal through wounds or disease was a real setback to any knight with little financial backing.

Landed knights supplied their own food from the produce of their estates, whereas household knights and mercenaries were fed by the lord. On castle rota, landed knights would be fed at the lord's expense. On campaign the whole force expected the king, duke or lord to make provision for supplying their needs. In some cases this meant carrying supplies on pack animals or in carts; on the Third Crusade Richard I took so much that many of the footsoldiers were forced to carry some of the baggage. However, this was never the whole answer. It was vital that a sizeable force was ensured provisions to keep it in the field. This might be done by fortifying castles to allow a supply line to be kept open through hostile territory, often a slow process. Alternatively a force would simply ravage the surrounding areas, which brought in supplies unless the foragers were careless; when one half of a French/Angevin invasion force scattered to plunder round Mortemer in 1054 it was set upon by the Normans and destroyed. That is why those foraging for food were often accompanied by incendiaries who burned villages and destroyed what they could not take, including peasants and their crops. Squires were often grouped into foraging parties, sometimes accompanied by a knightly escort. This was a far less

risky way of waging war than by direct confrontation which might end in disaster. Of course, two could play at that game; keeping an armed force in the vicinity of a hostile invader often rendered him impotent, since he dare not throw out foraging parties. Thus thwarted, supplies would dry up and he would be forced to withdraw.

These knights from a 12th-century French chess set wear segmented helmets with nasal guards, and carry kite shields. (Photo12.com, ARJ)

Norman Stone Castles

Castles are the most visible legacy of the Norman period in Europe. They were centres of aristocratic power, projecting political might and military muscle over the surrounding region. Castle construction grew in sophistication throughout the Norman centuries, from the early adaptations of existing timber fortifications through to massive and complex stone fortresses such as Château-Gaillard and Dover. Yet while they gave the impression of being almost impregnable fortifications, Norman castles were in fact highly vulnerable. Defensive options were limited, and mining brought down even the thickest of curtain walls, while sieges could subjugate the occupants through thirst and starvation. This part fully explores the design and development of the Norman castle, explaining key features from the ditch to the donjon, and detailing the methods, materials and organization involved in construction. It also looks at the social life of these great buildings – how castles were communities within themselves, with each inhabitant contributing to the castle's function and, in times of war, its defence.

In Normandy, castles seem to have arisen in response to the situation in north-western Frankia after the death of Charlemagne (Charles the Great), whose vast empire had also encompassed Germany and parts of northern Italy. As his sons and grandsons squabbled over territories, there was an inevitable breakdown of central government, probably already in evidence owing to the problems of ruling such a vast area. Into this came the Vikings, rowing their shallow-draught vessels up the rivers to plunder where opportunity arose. With little central authority, people in threatened areas, notably in north and west France, were thrown back on their own defence. Nobles set themselves up to protect their lands, recruited knights and other soldiers to serve them, and protected their homes with fortifications. The castle, known in written texts as *castrum*, *castellum*, *munitio*, *municipium* or *oppidum*, was also a symbol of authority. The mounted men within could control an area at least 16km (10 miles) around, the distance a horseman could comfortably ride out and back in a day.

At first, these castles were predominantly built of earth and timber, but a number included stone defences. Their expense meant that initially such examples were rare. The new stone towers were not known as 'keeps', since the word was not used in the medieval period (it first appeared in the English language in 1586 in Sidney's *Arcadia*). The more usual word in France was *donjon*, a term derived from the Latin word 'dominium' (an allusion to lordship), which is still used in the French language today. The term was not only used to signify these towers but might also denote a motte or the area of a castle that was the lord's preserve. They were also known as 'great towers'.

Written evidence, relating to the great tower at the ducal castle in Rouen built in the mid-10th century by Duke Richard I (942–96), indicates that stone castles soon appeared in Normandy. The same duke is said to have erected a fortified palace at Bayeux, and his successors carried on this trend. In Normandy, castle building other than by the duke always presented a potential threat to central authority, since feudalism was never as controlled in Normandy as it would initially be in England after the Conquest of 1066: the dukes tried to control construction where possible. Duke Richard I, for example, enfeoffed his brother, Raoul, with Ivry. In the first half of the 11th century castles were already being built not only by magnates but also by lesser vassals, though for the latter the cost involved would mean many were of earth and timber. During the century (mainly the first half), some 26 castles were founded between Caen and Falaise, in the area of Le Cinglais. Large numbers of castles were raised during the unsettled times following the death of Robert the Magnificent in 1035, while young Duke William was a minor. Le Plessis-Grimoult had stone defences, and was held not from the duke but from the Bishop of Bayeux until Grimoult de Plessis lost it in 1047 following the battle of Val-ès-Dunes, when William broke rebel power. His youngest son, Henry I, was responsible for much building in the duchy during his time as

both duke and king. The vast Angevin Empire that the latter's grandson, Henry II, acquired by inheritance and marriage gradually brought many French castles into his orbit whose walls had not been built by Normans. The death in 1199 of Henry's son, Richard I the Lionheart, finally gave the wily Philip Augustus the opportunity to seize Normandy from King John, which he did in 1204.

The Normans also exported their castle designs. The first Normans had arrived in southern Italy and Sicily as mercenaries in about 1017, employed by the Pope as a counter to pressure from the German emperor in the north and the Byzantines to the east. The Normans gradually spread over southern Italy and founded the territories of Apulia and Calabria. In 1053 a Norman army from Apulia defeated papal forces at the battle of Civitate. Others crossed to Sicily in 1061 and by 1091 had conquered the whole island, which became a kingdom. As in Normandy, the newcomers were keen to assimilate ideas and culture they saw around them. Sicily, a rich mixture of Greek, Arabic and now Norman styles and customs, situated on the Mediterranean trade routes, was a cultivated and fertile kingdom.

Instability lay behind much of the castle building during the early period in the new territories. The castles were often built on pre-existing Lombard examples and gradually the autonomous nature of the latter was altered as feudal ideas took hold. In the more mountainous regions of Molise in southern-central Italy, however, and in inland regions, the feudal administrative traditions that

The late 11th-century donjon at Valmont, with its flat pilaster buttresses, is seen on the right, with the smaller tower butted against its left side and the later château to its left. The machicolated parapet and enlarged windows were added in the 15th century. (Chris Gravett)

The walls of Caen have been altered over the centuries but still retain the essential line of Duke William's castle of 1047. Some of the rectangular towers may be of late-12th-century date. (Chris Gravett)

went with the castle came up against earlier, Roman, forms of organization that were not to be overlaid. Such areas were new to the Normans. In Molise, the Norman strongholds were more administrative centres for managing the surrounding country. Sometimes villages or markets flourished near new castles, in areas where it was thought commerce would benefit. The rest of the land was poorly inhabited except for small urban enclaves. In more lowland areas such as Apulia and Calabria, feudal notions on similar lines to those in Normandy prevailed. In Apulia small warrior bands, often commanded by Greeks or Lombards, made the initial conquests, and central authority was slow to become established. In Sicily the island was conquered by a single effort, resulting in many small fiefs and a few large autonomous lordships that took a long time to be modified, including comital families who were a source of instability. The large monastic foundations also resisted feudal services, though the latter gradually came to prominence.

Other Normans would sustain the restless tradition these people made famous, a tradition that would carry them on the First Crusade under Bohemond of Taranto to set up the first Crusader principality, with Bohemond proclaimed Prince of Antioch in 1100.

It has been argued that the English castle began with the Anglo-Saxons, it being pointed out that they sometimes occupied defensive structures, or with the Normans. Since a castle is a home as well as a stronghold, the communal burhs seen in England before the Norman Conquest, and designed to protect a number of people, do not qualify. Only a thegn's private dwelling, with ditch and palisades, suggests possible continuities with the castles of the Normans. Contemporaries of the Normans, such as Orderic Vitalis, certainly thought of castles as a novelty and the lack of them in pre-conquest England as a contributing factor to defeat; yet it may be only their use as centres of seigneurial administration by the

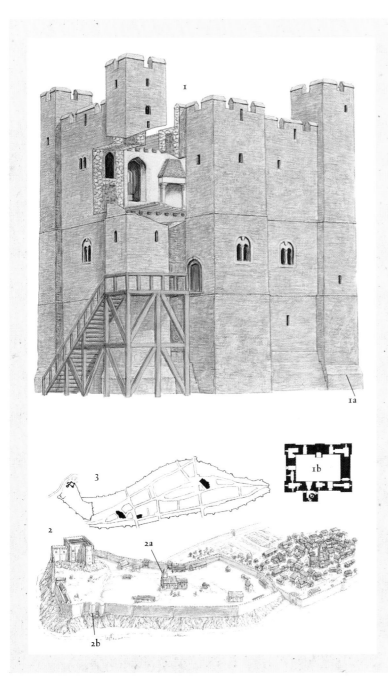

The great rectangular donjon at Chambois (1) was built around 1189 by William de Mandeville, a vassal of Henry II, in what was by then a rather archaic style. The tower is 25m × 15m (82ft x 49ft) in surface area, and 26m (85ft 4in) high, consisting of three floors. The entrance was at first-floor level via a door set in a slim tower butted against one side. In the 15th century a spiral stair was added inside the latter, but when originally built communication between floors appears to have been by ladders. The base has a battered plinth (1a). Also shown is a plan of the donjon (1b). The main floors have attractive two-light window openings and generous fireplaces. The castle of Falaise (2), birthplace of William the Conqueror, is set on a crag. The donjon was built traditionally in 1123 by Henry I, and now consists of a store cellar and a main floor containing the entrance. This was divided internally into a hall, chamber and antechamber, with a chapel in one corner. Several years later a second, smaller, donjon was added, presumably for additional residential space. The large bailey contained the chapel of Saint-Nicolas (2a). The southern gate flanked by two semi-circular towers (2b) may date from the second half of the 12th century. Many towers also survive on the extensive town walls, but, like some of those on the castle walls, they have been rebuilt or added later. The plan (3) shows the castle and town walls as they survive today. (Adam Hook © Osprey Publishing)

Normans that truly sets them apart from the defended houses of the English thegns. The use of a tower to display the lord to his subjects, evident in some early Norman stone gateways, certainly seems to echo the Anglo-Saxon burhgeat with an opening in its upper storey.

The White Tower in the Tower of London, begun c. 1077, as it appears today. The large windows replaced the originals in about 1700. The apse of the Chapel of St John has resulted in the rounded south-east corner. (Chris Gravett)

Timber castles spread far and wide after the Conquest, and were quick to erect in a hostile land. All castles were a statement of a lord's power, however, and large stone towers built in England would have seemed like skyscrapers to an Anglo-Saxon population mainly used to wooden buildings. One of the first was a fortified palace (begun c. 1077) in the south-eastern corner of the City of London, being so impressive that it gave its name to the whole castle – the Tower of London. Others followed, at first few in number, for the time it took to construct a large stone structure (the White Tower did not reach its full height until after 1100) meant that the earth and timber castle was a far more urgent requirement. We have noted how Orderic viewed castles as a contributing factor to Norman success, and castles were certainly of great value. Troops from within could hold down an area, sortie to snipe at or harry the supply lines of an enemy force, or join up with similar garrisons to form effective opposition. Conversely the enemy would need to take hostile castles as they progressed, to prevent such

The tower at Chepstow, Gwent, built c. 1072, has a thin wall on the strongly defended river side, but still has a first-floor entrance, an import from first-floor halls in Normandy. (Chris Gravett)

action. However, recent research has suggested that for the most part there was little danger of serious revolt after 1069.

As William consolidated his new kingdom in England, castles were soon being erected in towns and cities – sometimes planted as the army passed through to crush revolt elsewhere – to control the populace and to command any road or river traffic flowing through the place. They were built along the south coast, to guard ports and river estuaries and to deter any future invasion. However, many seem to have appeared simply to replace the headquarters of English lords. As castles proliferated down the social ladder (there may have been about 600 by the turn of the 12th century), the Norman kings may have lost some control over the building activities of their vassals. Some castles spawned a new town around their base, one of the most successful being Ludlow in Shropshire, built by Roger de Lacy. At first this was a deliberate policy of the king, but magnates soon took up the idea, and by 1100 some 21 new towns had been created. Lords also desired to build castles as heads of their honors (their collective estates), and so we find fortresses springing up in smaller places such as Richmond, Yorkshire, where the earl had his main seat.

Royal control of castles may have been more a matter of public sponsorship, and evidence of 'licensing' during Stephen's civil wars seems to imply that some lords were merely asking for royal confirmation in uncertain times, while actual 'adulterine' castles are rarer than once thought. When Henry II took power in 1154 the unlicensed castles he wanted to destroy were those of political enemies, rather than exemplifying a general royal control policy. However, Angevin kings were interested in acquiring castles, not least because castles – especially those held by a sheriff – gave stability and political clout.

Castles also proliferated in areas of unrest, particularly the borders with Wales and, to a lesser extent, Scotland. Marcher lords guarded roads and rivers with castles, and soon the areas along the borders were thick with fortresses, often on Roman sites. A number of these were stone fortresses from the start, such as Chepstow in Gwent. As the Normans penetrated South and North Wales, they created castles there too. However, the number of castles successfully besieged raises the question of whether their military role was considered their most prominent function. In Scotland most of the new castles built by the incoming Normans in the 12th century were of earth and timber: as in England, they were ideal when speed of construction was necessary. The kings of Scotland seem to have actively supported the settlement of Anglo-Normans in Galloway, to help control the area. Stone castles were rare until the early 13th century, when they became more common in the Lowlands. Cobbie Row's castle in Orkney, which claims to be the oldest stone castle in Scotland, was not built by the Normans but by a Norse chief in about 1145. Probably the rectangular donjon at Castle Sween on Loch Sween is the earliest in Norman style, but it only dates to about 1220. Similarly in Ireland, when Henry II launched his invasion in 1169 the castles that appeared were usually of motte and bailey type. So useful were they that timber-towered castles were still being built in the late 12th and early 13th centuries, alongside still rare stone fortresses such as that at Carrickfergus. However, despite Gerald of Wales writing that the new castles in Ireland were to subdue the natives, groups of mottes were usually placed in frontier areas, probably to check raiding. The erection of most other castles, especially those built of stone, suggests a desire to demonstrate a Norman lord's presence. Only later were additional fortifications needed to resist external threats.

Gradually, more stone fortifications were used to strengthen defences, perhaps at first comprising a simple ring wall, but also occasionally a donjon. As well as these, other elements – gatehouses and mural towers of stone – that had been built from the outset gradually increased in number. Donjons multiplied during the 12th century until many castles could boast a great tower

of lesser or greater proportions. In the later 12th century the donjon would be the subject of experimentation, as polygonal and cylindrical versions appeared.

In recent years there has been much study of Norman castles and in particular of the donjon. A rather different picture is beginning to emerge of some of these great monuments, but it may never be known exactly how they were employed. The uses these buildings were put to have for many decades been rather stereotyped. The various floors have frequently been labelled – often without a shred of evidence – as basement, entrance and/or garrison floor, great hall and private solar. Recent review of the known facts has caused a major rethink of key aspects such as whether some towers were built for different reasons, and how they were actually employed. In a number of cases we have to say simply that we do not know for certain and probably never will. We can, however, make educated guesses.

The interior of the tower at Chepstow. The beam holes for the first floor are clearly visible; the far end may have been screened off to form a private chamber. The pointed arch at the end plus the walls above the round openings are early-13th-century insertions as are the pointed window openings. (Chris Gravett)

Design and Development

Normandy

In Normandy the duke was technically in charge of all castle building, but in practice some lords put up their own defences: allodial land (which the family alone owned) existed here too. Some castles were the direct responsibility of the ruler: Henry I of England in particular pursued a programme of adding strong stone fortifications to a number of sites as Duke of Normandy. When the Norman duchy expanded, notably under Henry II, many other castles came under the Norman/Angevin umbrella. Some, such as the huge donjon at Loches, were pre-existing stone fortresses in many ways similar to Norman examples but constructed previously by workmen from other duchies or counties.

Castle building in Normandy has an earlier history than it does in England. As mentioned previously, the first castles erected in Normandy were mainly of earth and timber, for economic reasons. The simplest form was what we now call a 'ringwork', consisting of a courtyard protected by a ditch, the earth from which formed a bank on the inner side, topped by a palisade (a row of stakes). However, some castles were already using stone for the walls or had replaced timber with stone. Longueville-sur-Scie was first built for the Giffard family in the 11th century at the bottom of the Scie valley near the town, and is in the form of a vast oval delimited by earthen walls, with no motte (a mound of earth). The castle was rebuilt in the late 11th to early 12th century on top of a hill on the site of Saint-Foy priory, as a large oval enceinte with walls but no mural towers. A wall of the gate-tower (mentioned in texts as a large tower at the entrance, facing the plateau) survives behind a facing wall, but there is no trace of a donjon. When the castle of Le Plessis-Grimoult was abandoned in 1047, it consisted of a 4m (13ft) high earthen rampart topped with a stone wall with one or more mural towers and a stone gatehouse.

William the Conqueror's move to make Caen his new centre saw the construction of an impressive castle on a rocky outcrop in about 1060, covering 30 hectares (74 acres). The long curtain wall initially lacked mural towers, but was provided with some rectangular mural towers probably in the late 12th century. Their irregular and wide spacing, with consequent loss of effective defence, belies the residential layout of the original castle.

The motte first appeared as an element in castle design during the 11th century. Sometimes natural but usually artificial, it was set at the side of the courtyard or sometimes within it, forming what is now termed a motte and bailey

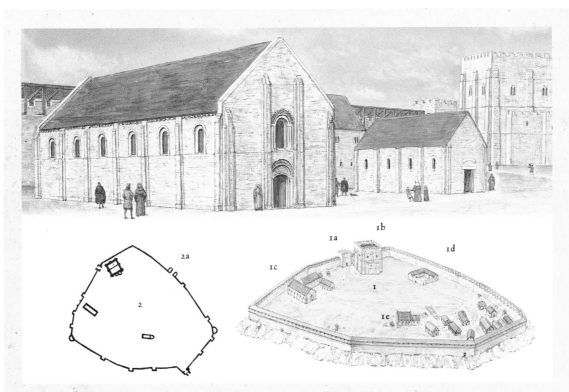

CAEN CASTLE, NORMANDY, c. 1170

The fortress built on the ridge by the town of Caen was gradually altered over the centuries. The initial layout was that of a wall surrounding a large enclosure (1), some 266m × 233m (872ft 8in x 764ft 5in) in area.

The entrance was via a rectangular gate-tower to the north (1a). To the west an early hall (aula) had a chamber (camera) added on the east side and a chapel (capella) of St George at right angles. In the 1130s the castle was strengthened as shown here. Henry I

added a large rectangular donjon near the gate (1b), also serving as additional protection (now only the base remains). This was augmented when he constructed a large rectangular hall, now known as the Exchequer Hall (1c), some 30m × 11m (98ft x 36ft) in internal area. It appears to have been a large ground-floor hall, though it has also been suggested that a kitchen on this floor served a main floor above. In the bailey stood a cistern (1d) and the church of St George (1e). In our reconstruction the curtain walls have been provided with wooden hoardings.

On the south and south-west sides especially are 11 open-backed rectangular mural towers, whose date is uncertain but which may date to the last quarter of the 12th century. The plan (2) shows the castle with these mural towers and gates in situ. The northern gate-tower was destroyed in about 1220 when Philip Augustus added a large chemise and ditch around the donjon. The existing eastern gate, Porte des Champs (2a), was added by Philip after the northern gate was pulled down. (Adam Hook © Osprey Publishing)

castle. At Maulévrier-Sainte-Gertrude there is additionally an arc-shaped outer bailey whose walls cross the ditch at each end to join those of the inner bailey. The puissant shape of the motte emphasized the nature of lordship, and the summit also allowed a better view, often being crowned by a palisade enclosing a wooden tower. The palisade might be replaced with stone, forming a shell keep, sometimes with buildings. For example, between 1120 and 1130 a polygonal wall was built

The so-called Exchequer Hall in Caen castle was damaged in 1944, but restored. It is one of the earliest and finest secular halls in Normandy. (Chris Gravett)

round the motte at Vatteville-la-Rue, with buttresses. Similarly at Gisors, the Conqueror's son, Henry I, built a wall around the top of the motte in the second quarter of the 12th century, a polygonal structure of 22 facets, each corner covered by a flat pilaster buttress, with three turrets on the north side. Hacqueville is one of the best-preserved examples in Normandy. The mound is some 53m (174ft) in diameter at the summit, with a 12th-century wall, the remains of which are included in the present farmhouse. On the summit, a square cellar with four rooms was reached by a right-angled stair lit by a basement window. Sometimes, as at Château-sur-Epte, the stone walls followed the side of the motte down to connect with those around the bailey. Occasionally a stone tower was raised on the motte, though this was a difficult procedure. Most artificial mounds, despite being made from layers of rammed earth, were not sufficiently settled to withstand the weight of a stone tower on top, unless it sat on the natural ground level and the motte covered the lower stages. The castle of La Haye-du-Puits is now ruined, but the huge motte on which the main stone castle stands is well preserved. The site originally featured an earth and timber castle, but probably in the 12th century (perhaps the first quarter) the palisade on the motte was replaced by a circular or polygonal stone wall; added to this was a slender, quadrangular stone donjon of three stages, which probably replaced a timber tower.

At this time, stone was already being used in north-west France to construct large square or rectangular buildings. The earliest survivors are not Norman, but located further south, in the area of the Loire. The famous castles of Doué-la-Fontaine and Langeais represent perhaps the first stone buildings still visible. Doué-la-Fontaine has been dated to about 950: it was built to serve as a ground-floor hall, but was altered to a tower with a first-floor entrance after a fire. Langeais was built perhaps in 994 or 1017; it too may have been a castle hall

The walls of Caen. (Chris Gravett)

rather than a tower. The stone hall at Brionne that was attacked by Duke William doubled as a donjon. Stone curtain walls would always hold the advantage over those of timber because they were fireproof, but initially some stone buildings may have been erected with defence as only a secondary consideration.

It is by no means clear exactly what function the earliest stone towers were designed to fulfil. Some of them were cramped and lacking in charm, while others would have provided comfortable accommodation. It would be dangerous to label all donjons as performing a similar role. Some of the larger examples may have been designed primarily as statements of power, to be employed for important functions rather than everyday use. The expense involved in erecting such a building would, of course, be enormous, but it would imply that its owner was a man of vision and substance. Used for official receptions, its impact on visitors perhaps familiar only with wooden secular buildings would be notable. Some others may have been designed both for receptions and as a withdrawing area for the lord and his family. Some smaller donjons perhaps served as a solar tower, an adjunct perhaps to a timber great hall that has now vanished. The smallest towers are difficult to relate to any domestic purpose because of their cramped interiors: it should be remembered that even a lord and his immediate family would have servants to hand, who might sleep in the same room. Perhaps such small towers served mainly as military watchtowers, while still displaying wealth and power in their construction materials.

While impressive remains and donjons survive in many places cited in documents, most of these donjons were erected in the 12th century and do not accurately represent a castle when first built. They may have replaced initial timber structures, or been a new addition to the castle. Unfortunately, very few stone towers survive from the early period in Normandy. The remains of the

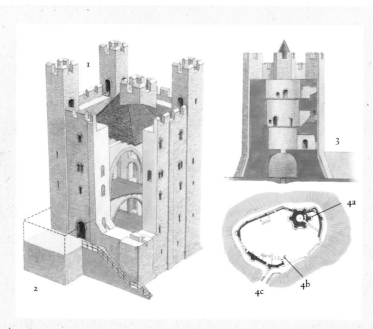

The two main levels below, graced with beautiful Romanesque arches, had no provision for sleeping accommodation (the mural barrel-vaulted chambers are too small). The builder was probably Aubrey de Vere, who is likely to have erected the great tower to celebrate his elevation to the rank of earl in 1142. The forebuilding (2) is now in a ruinous state; its precise form is uncertain.

The circular donjon at Conisbrough, Yorkshire (3), was one of the newer designs of tower in the late 12th century, but still possessed large buttresses. Internally it was provided with a single room on each floor and a vaulted basement; the main rooms had fireplaces and sinks. This was presumably a solar tower designed for the private use of the lord and his family. A hall and kitchen originally stood in the bailey, shown in the plan view. (4a) is the keep, (4b) is the gateway, and (4c) the barbican.
(Adam Hook © Osprey Publishing)

THE DONJON: HEDINGHAM AND CONISBROUGH

The exact purpose of the donjon or great tower has been the subject of much debate. A universal feature is that it demonstrated the power of the lord: though many could also provide a robust refuge, they were probably not designed primarily for this purpose. Some are likely to have served as private suites for the lord. The tower at Castle Hedingham, Essex (1), one of the best preserved, has recently been studied in detail. It has been demonstrated that the so-called top floor was simply roof space, the windows at that level being designed to enhance the building's

tower at Ivry-la-Bataille date to around 1000: the architect is said to have been beheaded by Aubrey, wife of the holder, Count Raoul d'Ivry, to prevent him building for anyone else. Others that were raised in the early period (though not necessarily in stone to begin with) include Tillières, Falaise, Le Homme (the present l'Isle Marie), Cherbourg and Brix, under Richard II (996–1026) and Richard III (1026–27); and Cherrueix (and perhaps others) under Robert I, the Magnificent (1027–35).

In his account of Duke William II's attack on the castle of Brionne in 1047, William of Poitiers describes it as having a stone hall 'serving the defenders as a donjon (arx)'. At Avranches, detailed study of what little remains has led both Impey and Nicolas-Méry to suggest a construction date of between 1000 and 1040: the tower must have been impressive, covering an area of 37m × 27m (121 × 89ft). The square tower at Valmont is another early example, probably from the 11th century, though it now forms part of a much later overbuild. The castle remains, however, a simple enclosure with the donjon at one side. The building itself is an unfussy square tower, with walls 2.4m (7ft 10in) thick and about 22m (72ft) high, with a single room on each floor: it may have been a solar tower for a vanished hall. It has three buttresses along three sides (those by the corners do not join to clasp them), which supported a primitive wooden gallery.

The tower at Ivry-la-Bataille has led some to speculate that it may have been the prototype for the earliest Norman donjons erected in England, namely those at the Tower of London and Colchester: both of these have an internal cross-wall and an apsidal corner marking the chapel. Moreover, although Ivry-la-Bataille was by then several decades old, it must have held some status, since Orderic Vitalis, writing in the first half of the 12th century, refers to it as the 'famous tower'. There must also have been some fortification at Rouen in the early period, since it was the first city of Normandy and would remain so even after Duke William shifted his power base westward to Caen. Some form of tower can be seen on the Bayeux Tapestry, but exactly what it looked like can only be speculation, as it was completely destroyed. Rufus's brother, Henry I (1106–35), undertook a programme of building leading to the appearance of extant donjons in a number of castles. Most of the donjons are square or rectangular, have internal cross-walls, pilaster buttresses and first-floor entrances. Some of these forms are similar to towers built by Henry in England. As Duke of Normandy, Henry had already been busy at Domfront: the Bellême family had built a fortress there in the first quarter of the 11th century, before Henry erected his donjon (after 1092 and before 1123). Henry made Domfront his main base in Normandy. The castle sits on the end of an outcrop, dominating the Varenne valley, and is cut off from the town by a deep ditch. In the 12th century the town was surrounded by a wall with 24 towers, remains of which are still visible. Only two walls of the donjon remain, about 28m (92ft) high and 3m (9ft 10in) thick, with four or perhaps five floors. It was one of the largest towers in Normandy, with a total external area of 26.3m × 22.4m (86ft 3in × 73ft 5in), and an internal one of 20.3m × 16.4m (66ft 7in × 53ft 9in). The corners were clasped by granite buttresses with a further buttress in the centre face of each wall. Internally, the space was divided by a cross-wall and further subdivided by another at right angles on one side. Neither the ground-floor nor third-floor walls have any loops at all. The entrance was on the first floor of the western wall via a gate in a vaulted arch some 6m (19ft 8in) above ground. There may have been a cistern in the north-west angle and also cellars separated by walls. Flooring was supported on beams running into holes. The donjon became a model for Henry's later work as duke and king, such as at Caen, Arques and Falaise.

Falaise features a rectangular buttressed donjon (the *Grand Donjon*) in the north-west corner of the site, overlooking a cliff and a stream running below. The south-east corner was expanded to form the St Pritz Chapel, with a small newel stair. The ground floor is blind (i.e. without loops for light) and the first

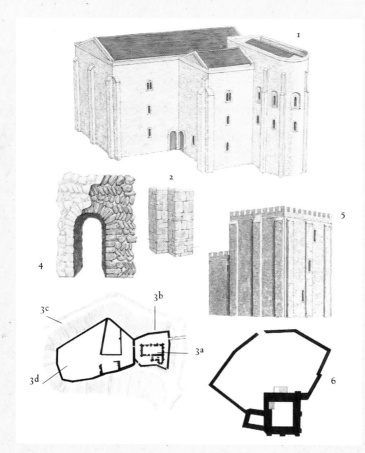

fact that Orderic Vitalis refers to it as the 'famous tower' even in the 12th century suggests it was of suitable stature. The absence of ashlar and the square buttresses (2) are symbolic of its early date. The apsidal end is that of the chapel within, and there was one main large room and a smaller at the side. Perhaps due to a change in plan or later demolition or collapse, the smaller room was extended to form a second wall, the original outer wall now becoming a spine wall dividing the larger and smaller rooms. A similar design, even to a similar apse, was to be seen again in the White Tower begun by William the Conqueror in London in about 1076. The tower (3a) is set within a chemise wall (3b) and ditch (3c) that seems to have been built at the same time or possibly earlier, and which is connected to a lower court (3d), as shown in the plan view. The later towers have been removed from the plan. Also shown is an external doorway seen from the inside of the great tower (4). The rather plain tower at Valmont (5), dating from about 1100, is seen here without the later machicolated battlements. It forms the nucleus of the castle, whose basic enclosure is shown in the accompanying plan (6). (Adam Hook © Osprey Publishing)

EARLY TOWERS IN EUROPE
The site at Ivry-la-Bataille provides some of the most extensive early remains of a donjon in Normandy. The donjon (1) was built in several phases. The earliest form, dating probably from the early 11th century, is tentatively reconstructed here. The tower, 32m × 25m (105ft x 82ft), may have been a storey lower, but the

floor is the only other level to survive. Access to the donjon was by a straight stair up to the first floor on the east side, with the main newel in the north-east corner. During the mid-12th century a second, smaller, rectangular tower (the *Petit Donjon*) was attached to the west side of the *Grand Donjon*, with access through the wall. It had a small room block jutting north along the west face.

Henry I largely rebuilt Arques-la-Bataille. The castle consisted of a generous bailey with deep ditches, opening on to the plateau on the south. The curtain walls have been rebuilt and ruined over the centuries, but there are two square mural towers along the south face, and a possible third, that may be of the period of Henry I. The rest are D-shaped 13th-century structures, and there are later gatehouses. The French *doyen* of reconstruction, Viollet-le-Duc, studied the ruined castle in conjunction with a plan of 1708, and reconstructed both the castle site and the donjon, making the latter conform to how he thought it once appeared. Henry's donjon is now in a ruinous state: it was some 20m (65ft 7in) square and about the same high, positioned at an angle close to the curtain in the north-west corner of the inner bailey, where it also guarded the postern gate. It had an internal cross-wall, main stairwell in the south corner, and the south-eastern face was provided with two large buttresses. The external straight stair was enclosed in a large forebuilding accessible by a doorway on the south-east face and opened onto the second floor. The lowest floor was vaulted throughout. Viollet-le-Duc interpreted the buttresses as connecting at second-floor level by semi-circular arches. A mural dead-end passageway on the fourth (top) floor ran from the stair newel along the south-east side, and contained two pairs of lights that opened into it, suggesting arrow loops, though there is no embrasure inside the passage. Another passage ran back via an extension to the north-west curtain wall.

In 1123 Henry I rebuilt the small donjon at Vire, which would become a key residence of King John. The first courtyard was backed up by a second behind it, in which there was a chapel to Saint Blaise: at the rear the donjon rose up. Only the west wall and half the south wall survive to any extent. The donjon measures externally 14m × 13.4m (45ft 11in × 43ft 11in) and 9.6m × 9.2m (31ft 5in × 30ft 2in) internally. The destroyed north wall was some 2.3m (7ft 6in) thick, while that on the south is 2.1m (6ft 10in) thick. The external angles are clasped by flat buttresses that project 0.3m (11in). The walls are of sandstone; internally the donjon was divided into two unequal rooms by a north-south partition wall. There are four floors (the ground floor without openings), with the first floor higher than the others. On the top floor the surviving west wall has a row of corbels to carry the floor beams that presumably ran to those of the vanished cross-wall. On the ground floor there is a simple narrow window embrasure. The two main floors seem to be the first and second floors, with the first floor served by a fireplace and a window converted later in the Middle Ages. On the second floor two windows open on the west wall (Chatelain noted there should be one in the middle of the south wall), and on the third floor the windows are very narrow, which has been attributed to the fact that the garrison who guarded the battlement were located here. The crenellations were replaced in the 14th century by machicolations.

Not all donjons were built by the Anglo-Norman kings of course. At Brionne the tower has been attributed to Robert I of Meulan in the early 12th century to replace an earlier castle on an islet in the River Risle in the town, which had been besieged in 1047 and 1090. The donjon has one and a half walls surviving to a height of about 17m (55ft) but originally was 20m (65ft 7in) square, its walls 4m (13ft) thick and supported by buttresses. It consisted of three floors, the lowest being blind; the first floor had windows. The donjon appears to have been partially

The locations of key Norman castles in Normandy. The boundaries shown indicate the Norman bishopric boundaries, as opposed to the modern-day regional and departmental zones.

rebuilt, perhaps in the second half of the 12th century, as a fireplace is blocked by 12th-century rubble. On the top floor traces of a single roof gable are visible on the interior wall face. A row of quadrangular holes along the upper part of the northern wall was probably for wooden hoardings. Tancarville was the seat of the Chamberlains of Normandy from about 1100. There is a 12th-century square residential tower (the Tour-carrée) at the north-west angle. The donjon built by William de Mandeville at Chambois – measuring 21.4m × 15.4m (70ft 2in × 50ft 6in) externally, with a height of 25.7m (84ft 3in) – dates from the second half of the 12th century and is the best preserved in Normandy. It was built using small blocks, with four turrets rising in limestone freestone. It has a windowless ground floor and two floors above, pierced by geminate (two-light) windows. The entrance on the first floor was reached via a small forebuilding on the south-eastern side. Each floor has a large chimney, and each corner houses a mural chamber.

During the 12th century cylindrical or polygonal donjons began to appear, which benefited from an absence of weak corners and blind spots. A multi-angular design has several advantages. The angles, being shallower than the traditional right-angled corner, bonded the stones in more tightly and made it less easy to pick them out. On the battlements there were no blind corners presented by the merlons that met at right angles, which forced a defender to poke his head out to see directly in front, thus presenting himself as a target. Gisors was provided with an irregular eight-sided polygonal donjon on the motte by Henry I, about 20m (65ft 7in) high and of four stages. Between 1170 and 1180 Henry II raised the donjon by two storeys and added five buttresses to reinforce it. At Bricquebec a polygonal donjon sits on the motte but whether it is partly 12th century or wholly 14th century is unclear. Mortemer has a buttressed cylindrical donjon built by a half-brother of Henry II in the late 1100s on similar lines to Orford in England. Richard I built a circular donjon at Bonneville-sur-Touques at the end of the 12th century. Conches-en-Ouche was built around the same time on an escarpment at the junction of ducal lands and those of the Tosny family.

The cylindrical donjon, closely surrounded by its enclosure, is set on a partly man-made motte and cut off from the plateau by ditches 10m (32ft 9in) deep and 20m (65ft 7in) wide. It has a main hall vaulted with ogival (pointed) arches. The walls are 2.6m (8ft 6in) thick and are pierced by six openings. There are stairs in the thickness of the wall as well as a rising shaft up to the main hall. At Neaufles-Saint-Martin the motte carries the remains of a cylindrical donjon built in the 1180s by Henry II, 20m (65ft 7in) high and 14m (45ft 11in) in diameter, with three floors on corbels, the top floor with bonded oculi (circular openings). La Roche-Guyon has a late 12th-century donjon *en bec* (literally, 'in beak'), with one side drawn out to a solid stone vertical edge, to deflect missiles and present a solid obstacle to siege engines. Château-sur-Epte, founded in 1087 by William Rufus, has a bailey of some 70m (229ft) and a motte of 50m (164ft) diameter at ground level: at the top is a very dilapidated circular tower probably added by Henry II in 1184, which is surrounded by a wall pierced (probably later) with loops.

A number of towns, especially those that grew next to castles or had a castle planted in proximity, were given curtain walls and mural towers, though often surviving examples date from the 13th century. The town that grew at the foot of Falaise castle had a dressed wooden palisade at the end of the 10th century, which was replaced by a stone wall under Richard II. This was repaired by both Duke Robert the Magnificent and William the Conqueror, but a new wall was built by Henry I in c. 1123. Repaired over the centuries, the wall eventually had about 50 towers and six gates, and ran for approximately 2km ($1^1/_4$ miles).

Southern Italy

In southern Italy (and Sicily) the Norman adventurers saw to their own defences, largely adding to existing Byzantine, Lombard or Arab structures as they saw fit. Local craftsmen must have been employed in these endeavours. In some instances the latter's influence on the final design is tangible.

The castle of Melfi was the first to be taken over by the Normans. The rectangular donjon was built in the late 11th century but is now enclosed. Part of it can just be seen above the 13th-century curtain walls. (Chris Gravett)

The earliest Norman strongholds in Italy were the hill fortresses of Aversa (given to Rannulf by Segius IV in 1030 for services; he subsequently became Count of Aversa and was perhaps the first to give up brigandage) and Melfi (already a hilltop stronghold that had been heavily fortified by the Greeks). In 1044 Gaimar the Iron Hand opened up the mountainous and rather desolate region of Calabria, and built the important fortress of Squillace. Between 1050 and 1060 Aversa expanded to become the Norman principality of Capua (1057) and Melfi the duchy of Apulia. In 1056, Robert Guiscard (later Duke of Apulia and Calabria, and the founder of the Norman state of the Two Sicilies) placed his recently arrived younger brother Roger (later Count of Sicily) in Mileto. Molise County, roughly present-day Isernia, came into being in 1055, and Loritello County in 1061 (the eastern part of the modern-day Molise region).

We know that prior to 1055 Robert Guiscard had begun building strongholds in Calabria, such as at the old Byzantine fortress of Rossano on the Ionian coast (which came under William of Grantmesnil and was the centre of his honor), and 'Scribla', a hot and potentially malarial fortress guarding a mountain pass in the Val di Crati, and San Marco Argentano in the area of Cosenza. Also in this area lay Scalea, which was built in 1058 and looked down on the sea from on high.

Of particular note among the castles built in Apulia are Mount Sant'Angelo, whose pentagonal Tower of Giants was erected by Guiscard; Castelpagano, run by the Norman count Henry; and the castles to the south of the River Fortore such as Dragonara and Fiorentino (built by the Catepano Bojannes), Bovino (built by the Norman Dragone or perhaps by the counts of Lorotello, on Roman remains), Deliceto (erected in 1073 by the Norman Tristainus) and Serracapriola (dating beyond the Normans to the 9th century). Additionally, fortified convents were to be found at San Marco la Catola, San Marco in Lamis, Ripalta, and Calena.

Many surviving castles were modified at a later date, such as the Langobard town fortress of Roccapipirozzi, and few original examples remain. Early castles were often (though not always) built of wood, increasingly supplemented by, or wholly in, stone. Typical features include an inner courtyard, and a first-floor entrance: often, later additions were made such as reinforcements to walls, or domestic buildings, which altered the walls of the enceinte. At Conversano, 18km (11 miles) from Monopoli, the castle is trapezoid and three of the 12th-century square towers survive, together with a cylindrical 14th-century example. Towers, such as Morrone, were usually built along river courses, often on mid-slope within sight of each other and of a town.

In the early Norman period existing city walls and defences were utilized by the incoming Normans. Where ecclesiastical and military powers enjoyed good relationships, church, castle and residential buildings stood together and town squares were formed. Vastogirardi was a fortified burgh of an irregular shape with thick walls surrounding an open courtyard, and buildings attached around the inner sides with vaulted ground floors: it provided a solid defensive structure with two entrances diametrically opposed.

In more mountainous regions the town would spread along the ridge, with the church still the focal point. Town walls would evolve and the castle might find itself in the role of citadel, the place of final defence. Later castles were often built on the edge of an existing town, such as Venafro on the hill of Sant'Angelo. At Fornelli the Normans appear to have improved existing structures by integrating curtain wall sections and reorganizing towers: it was later heavily rebuilt. Longano and the Oratino make use of rocky ridges with escarpments, with Oratino including Norman work in its four-sided tower. Such towers were sometimes used as mural or corner towers, with dressed corners, as at Cercepiccola and Gambatesa. The latter is set on a ridge overlooking the confluence of the River Fortore and the Tappino stream. First mentioned in the mid-12th century, it is a four-sided structure with inner courtyard and two square corner towers, but the walls have been much altered.

Naturally strong hill or mountain areas abound in Molise province, making for excellent strongholds such as Mount Ferrante and Mount Santa Croce. Such places might be of Samnitic origin, reused by the Romans, and the Normans named them *castellum vetus* ('old fortress'). Old walled burghs were reused, but additional fortresses were built in the Norman period and later. Polygonally cut local stone was used, or else large rough-cut stone set in irregular rows. Castle walls built on rocky outcrops or along hill crests might have their foundations

The key Norman castles and sites in southern Italy and Sicily. The regional names given refer to the modern Italian boundaries, as oppposed to historical demarcations.

set in carved terraces, such as at Pescolanciano, known in the time of William II and with a trapezoid floor plan. Castel Bagnoli del Trigno was a Langobard castle on a rocky spur overlooking the Trigno River valley. The Normans modified the existing fortifications, building escarped walls, slightly pronounced, and overhanging on three sides. The front entrance wall is more prominent. Castropignano castle (another Langobard fortress) sits on a rocky ridge cut off from the town by a ditch (now filled in): it too was rebuilt by the Normans. It consisted of a four-sided castle with donjon and towers, including an entrance tower and one overlooking the River Biferno. The curtain wall displays a variety of building techniques, using calcareous stone set in regular pattern, and overhangs the rock, which is sometimes cut into terraces or escarpments. The gatehouse has a guardroom with two long arrow loops.

In some cases (for example at Roccamandolfi, on a hilltop overlooking the Matese pass) platforms and ramps were created by shovelling earth and protecting them with straight walls. The tops of outcrops or long ridges were adapted and surrounded by curtain walls sometimes set with mural towers and bayonet entrances, by spurs, 'rompitratta' walls, or (rarely) 'caisson' structures. At Roccamandolfi, the enceinte follows the irregular hillside and incorporates a four-sided structure, possibly a donjon. Cylindrical and D-shaped towers were added, while on one side the walls are integrated almost with the rock: on the southern side holes for horizontal wooden beams added within the masonry show construction techniques. This work is known as *opus gallicum* ('Gallic work', based on an ancient technique), and Molisian examples reflect the swift construction necessary. In the Magliano tower in the town of Santa Croce timber beams form a double mesh of bars radial to the masonry. Another example is Riporse castle in Longano, where a four-sided enceinte rests on an earthen mound, possibly a motte. Inside are the ruins of a square tower and cistern, with two out of four D-shaped mural towers remaining. Regular rows of small stones with much mortar are evident. Another example is the ruins of Castellerci at Palata.

In the lowlands the standard form of castle was the *castrum*, usually on the outskirts of towns or villages: these were initially strongholds for troops. The earliest examples were first Scribla, built by Guiscard, and later San Marco in Calabria. The *quadriburgium* was a four-sided building with corner towers: many have been overbuilt so as to incorporate the Norman castle, for example the palace at Larino. The term *castellum* could mean a strongpoint outside a settlement, a *castrum* or a light structure placed against a besieged gate, or later a citadel built within a burgh. Donjons, square and later cylindrical, were built, but were also copied by later builders. The donjon at San Marco Argentano in Calabria was built by Guiscard in 1051. At Campobasso, the donjon was erected by the Normans on the site of a Lombard tower with remains of Samnite walls beneath: it was situated in a four-sided castle, with four circular corner towers added later. Riccia castle, on the eastern side of two hills and overlooking the valley formed between them, was built on an ancient site and has an enceinte with three circular towers and a cylindrical donjon comprising a basement and three stories. The master tower of the 'sea' castle at Palermo, documented in the 12th century, is a cylindrical tower with spur, as is the late-Norman donjon at Bovino. Donjons were placed either well within the defences or in the most prominent position. In Molise they are almost always on the edge of an old town, usually isolated from the walls.

Sicily

The brothers Roger and Robert Guiscard executed a similar plan of castle building in Sicily. In 1060 Roger launched an abortive attack on Messina but captured it after a second invasion. Robert spent a week reinforcing and extending the walls and towers, raising ramparts and throwing up earthworks; a cavalry garrison was installed. Following the wishes of the local Greek Christians, Robert built the first Norman castle in Sicily in 1060–61 at San Marco d'Alunzio in the Val Demone, near the classical Aluntium: the ruins still survive. Petralia Soprana near Cefalù soon followed. From about 1062 Roger made Troina, perched on its hilltop, his centre of operations for several years. Between 1071 and 1074, following the capture of Palermo, he endeavoured to consolidate his hold over northern Sicily. He built a castle at Mazara in 1073, whose ruins survive; and one at Paternò the same year (the ruins have been heavily restored). Further castles were located at Calascibetta, Trapani, Lentini, Termini and Milazzo. In 1087 Roger Borsa rebuilt the fortifications of Agrigento, and Enna finally passed to the Normans by agreement with its ruler, Ibn Hamud, who retired to Calabria. Much of this work involved restoring walls and adding new stonework or towers to existing ones. Some fortresses had proved to be quite effectively protected, as the Normans discovered.

A solitary Norman tower of the castle at Caltabellotta survives on its heights, overlooking the Chiesa Madre. Adrano (or Aderno) has a large rectangular

The castle of Caccamo in Sicily. (Chris Gravett)

Adrano in Sicily (1) is divided by a cross-wall and subordinate walls to form hall, chamber and chapel (shown in the plan view, 1a). By the late 12th century the Normans had become much more immersed in the surrounding Lombard, Byzantine and Muslim styles. The main illustration (2) shows the palace tower of La Ziza in Palermo, at the time of building (1162) set in gardens among fruit trees and pools. The grand entrance leads into a large central room rising through the floor above to a honeycombed ceiling, with a frieze running in and out of wall niches. In front of the palace stands a covered fountain with water channels running into the main tower. A plan view of La Ziza is also shown (2a). La Cuba (3), also in Palermo, likewise shows strong influence from Islamic art and architecture. Built about 1180, it was set within a lake in the royal park and had a first-floor entrance.

(Adam Hook © Osprey Publishing)

NORMAN SICILY
When the Normans arrived in Italy and spread across to Sicily, they tended at first to build defences similar to those in their homeland. Hence the rather plain tower of

tower that lacks buttresses of any kind. The first-floor entrance is reached by a straight stair along the outer wall. Provided with two barrel vaults, it is divided internally into two separate rooms, one of which is further subdivided. There is a chapel on the second floor. The stair vice is set in the centre of one wall rather than at the corner. The surrounding chemise with small round corner towers is probably late 13th-century work.

Two notable palace towers survive in Palermo. La Ziza (from the Arabic word *aziz*, meaning 'magnificent') is the best preserved, and was begun by William I 'The Bad' (King of Sicily 1154–66) in 1162: it was finished off by his son, William II 'The Good' (King of Sicily 1166–89). A tall, two-storey rectangular building heavily influenced by Arab decoration, it has rooms set round a principal, central room that rises through them. La Cuba, also in Palermo, was built by William II. Set in an ornamental lake within the royal park (alas, no longer), it has a first-floor entrance, though much of the fabric has now been destroyed. Nearby are the remains of a smaller, second building, the Cubula, and not far off the remnants of arcading (on the east front of the Villa Napoli) that mark the site of the small Cuba Soprana (a pre-Norman palace).

The remains of the 11th–12th-century Torre Pisano in the fortified palace of the Norman kings of Sicily at Palermo is austere, despite the decorated windows. (Chris Gravett)

Britain

In Britain as in mainland Europe, many Norman stone castles were adaptations of existing earth and timber castles, by the simple exigency of pulling down the timber palisade around the bailey and replacing it with a stone wall. Some ringworks were changed to an enclosure protected by a wall in this way. In a number of towns with existing Roman defences, some repaired by the Anglo-Saxons in their turn, the invading Normans made use of the sturdy Roman stone walls, with their famously hard cement. By siting a castle in the corner of such urban defences the Normans acquired two ready-made walls, and they only needed to provide the other two to create a square, rectangular or oval bailey. The great stronghold of the Tower of London started life in this way, as did Exeter castle. At the Tower of London the first Norman defences were of earth and timber on the other two sides, until a stone curtain wall replaced the palisades in the reign of William Rufus. There is no obvious sign of a motte, though it is possible that the area originally contained an Anglo-Saxon ditch, now entirely destroyed. At Portchester in Hampshire the Normans cut off a corner of the Roman fort in similar fashion.

Many ringwork castles have either lost their early stone defences or they now form only a part of the defences that survive. They were usually quite plain, comprising a wall thick enough to provide a fighting platform protected by crenellations. Occasionally a mural tower, square or rectangular in plan, might be set along the wall, but these were rare in the early period after the conquest of England, and usually confined to weak spots in the circuit, such as covering angled turns.

The only tower on the wall might be the gate-tower, approached across the ditch by a wooden causeway and often a drawbridge. It was soon realized that a gate in a wall needed additional protection, and in some cases this was afforded by placing a tower next to it as a guardian. From this the idea of placing the gate passage within the tower soon developed, running through it from front to rear, with access controlled by at least one door and possibly a portcullis. There might be one or more rooms over the passage, with wooden floors (at Newark there are two floors), within which would be housed any operating mechanism necessary for the portcullis, or perhaps for a drawbridge. Above that were the battlements. The side walls were sometimes drawn forward as deep buttresses to form a rudimentary barbican. Newark has a spiral stair enclosed in a turret at one corner. Compared to later gatehouses, with their huge flanking towers, machicolated battlements and multiple defences along the passage, these early examples are relatively simple. However, they might form the strongest part of an enclosure castle that was lacking a donjon.

Within the enclosure itself, the bailey was filled with all the buildings necessary for the inhabitants of the castle to subsist, especially if trapped inside the walls. The domestic buildings within Norman castles have not been studied to any great degree. On many sites later building has covered or destroyed the evidence, whilst on abandoned sites there has been relatively little exploration. Where this has been carried out, a picture emerges of a courtyard packed with all kinds of buildings, very different from the often half-empty castles depicted in artistic reconstructions until recently. Most were of timber, sometimes with stone footings to help protect the wood against rot, and many walls were constructed of wattle and daub. This process involved filling a timber frame, made from interlaced osier or willow twigs, with wattle. Each wattle panel was then daubed with a mixture of mud and dung, which set hard and formed a relatively insulated outside wall. A few buildings, such as two-storey halls, or sometimes the chapel, might be built of stone. Roofs were often of thatch, but some might be wooden shingle or slate. All castles would require a chapel, and if it were not in the donjon itself then a separate building would need to be built in the bailey. At Richmond the 11th-century chapel was located within the ground floor of a barrel-vaulted mural tower. Perhaps the most famous surviving chapel is the delightful, 12th-century circular example at Ludlow in Shropshire. It is decorated internally with arcading.

As with ringworks, some motte-and-bailey castles were adapted by replacing the timber palisades on the motte with stone, to form the so-called shell keep. Sometimes walls ran down the side of the motte to protect the stairway. Inside the walls on the summit, buildings of timber or stone could be butted against the walls. In a few instances a small tower was also added on top, the shell wall acting as a sort of chemise or skirt.

The castles that appeared in England immediately after 1066 usually lacked a stone donjon, the very building that many think of when a Norman castle is mentioned. The development of the donjon in England, and the use to which it was put, has been the subject of much recent debate. M. W. Thompson has promulgated a theory for the spread of such buildings in Britain.

One of the earliest stone towers in England is that of Chepstow in Gwent, which, it is generally agreed, was built before 1072 by the Conqueror's companion, William FitzOsbern. It stands on a cliff above the River Wye, a long rectangular building between two long baileys. One wall, on the cliff side, is little over 0.9m (3ft) thick, the others being 2.9m (9ft 6in). There is a decorated hall (with arched recesses) on the first floor. Thompson believes this building to be a *domicilium*, a first-floor hall of the type seen in France, with a thin wall one side but with a first-floor entrance, like a donjon.

The White Tower in the Tower of London is one of the earliest donjons in England, probably begun in 1077. It is of the type usually referred to as a 'hall keep', in which each main floor is divided internally by a cross-wall to produce two rooms of unequal size. The cross-wall also helps to reduce the span required for timber floor beams. The rooms are usually interpreted as forming a hall with an adjoining smaller chamber, though it is often difficult to prove whether they were actually used in this way. However, external access is always into the larger room. Sometimes further, smaller rooms are created by the addition of internal walls. The Tower took at least another 20 years to complete, at first apparently having the roofs visible above the parapet, and only being finished around 1102 by when the walls had been built up. There may

The location of key
Norman castles in the
British Isles.

well have been an intervening period of slow growth, since William Rufus, who
succeeded his father the Conqueror in 1087, was more interested in the
building of Westminster Hall, and it is more likely that the later spurt of
activity at the Tower was due to his brother, Henry I (acceded in 1100). Similar
to the Tower of London is the donjon at Colchester in Essex, which also
possesses an apsidal, rounded corner. Unusually, it was constructed on the
foundations of a Roman temple to the Emperor Claudius. It too is a very large
building but not overly high, and it is commonly thought that the top floor has
been destroyed, though this has been called into question.

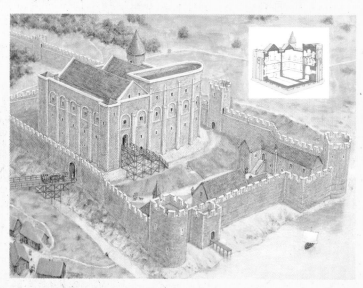

THE TOWER OF LONDON, c. 1100

The Normans utilized the old Roman city wall, repaired by the Anglo-Saxons and seen here running down to and then along the banks of the River Thames, to form two sides of their new castle. Ditches and palisades around the other two sides formed an enclosure. In 1097, William Rufus replaced the palisades with stone walls. Previous to this, in around 1077, Gundulph, Bishop of Rochester, began work on a new tower that would not reach its full height until about 1102. The eastern curved corner betrays the internal apse of the royal chapel of St John, a feature not initially planned, as the foundations reveal an original squared corner. The apsidal corner echoes that of the contemporary castle at Colchester. The first-floor entrance to the castle was reached by timber stairs. Internally, see inset, the 'White Tower' (a name deriving from the 13th-century whitewashing it received) had its two floors divided into two rooms of unequal size, usually defined as 'hall' and smaller 'chamber'. A third room, the smallest, led from the chamber; on the second floor this room was the chapel. There is no evidence for a kitchen. In addition to its role as a contemporary skyscraper aimed at impressing the populace of London, the palace of the Tower may have been intended primarily for important functions, with the luckier guests brought up through a series of increasingly impressive rooms to meet the king. (Adam Hook © Osprey Publishing)

It has been suggested that these two donjons at the Tower and Colchester are based on the ducal example in Rouen, now vanished: as Thompson has pointed out, though, they are unlike the majority in France. Thompson's theory is that these donjons were a new concept in a relatively hostile land: the hall and separate chamber were placed side by side in a large tower adapted from the type usual on the Continent, often now classed as a 'solar tower', in which single rooms were stacked vertically. This provided a defended group of facilities under one roof. However, the tower at Ivry-la-Bataille in Normandy, which dates to about 1000, also has an internal dividing wall and apsidal corner, and may have been the inspiration for the brand new towers in England. Moreover, the defensive qualities of a castle as opposed to its symbolic role are now being questioned, and by the time these first hall keeps were completed there was little threat from the English, though baronial unrest was always a possibility.

So what were these new, great towers designed for? As with the donjons in Normandy, the function of these towers is uncertain. There is no record that William I ever visited the Tower of London, nor were the other Norman kings regular incumbents. Perhaps the rooms in the White Tower were designed for

Colchester castle, Essex, has the largest plan area of any Norman castle in England. It is similar to the White Tower, though quite low. It is not known if it ever had additional upper floors. (Chris Gravett)

a kind of theatrical pageantry, whereby visitors were deliberately led through this hugely impressive stone building, their excitement increasing until they reached the king himself; perhaps only the most important guests were allowed to attain an audience in the upper chamber, the innermost sanctum of the monarch. This may have been the idea behind some of the larger donjons with their hall and adjoining chamber often duplicated on two floors, in which public and private rooms stood side by side, but since this rather neat division is a modern delineation it is more difficult to assess the role of these towers in contemporary eyes. Some public business might be conducted in the inner chamber, for example. Moreover, if a constable was in charge during the king's frequent absences, did he perhaps live within the lower chamber and hall? If little used by the monarch, a project into which a vast amount of work had gone then had slight value other than as a statement of great power, which may, of course, have been the main intention. If the king or lord of the place had his (perhaps temporary) residence there also, then so much the better.

Several early gate-towers possess a large opening high up, rather like a door that opens on to nothing. It seems that these are located for the lord to stand and be seen by the populace, another theatrical display, this time in affirmation of his control over the area by his physical presence in his tower. One such opening appears in a gate-tower at Sherborne, Dorset. The donjon built over the gate at Richmond, Yorkshire, has several openings that almost certainly led on to a wooden balcony looking towards the barbican and the town market place beyond. These deliberate and dramatic window displays did not last, though.

Castle Hedingham, probably built by Aubrey de Vere II in 1142. The forebuilding has been badly damaged. (Chris Gravett)

In some instances the lack of obvious accommodation within a donjon is so noticeable that the only conclusion to be drawn is that the tower in question was designed for little else but public function such as banquets or for a visitor to be received by the lord or king. A particular example is Castle Hedingham in Essex (c. 1140), which has barrel-vaulted mural chambers so small that they could have served little purpose other than as store cupboards. Here too guests may have been led along a prescribed route ultimately to meet the Earl of Oxford.

Some early towers are quite puzzling. While several buildings in undefended sites are indisputably palaces, such as Clarendon, several examples within fortifications have thin walls and ground-floor entrances, though otherwise have the unequal internal division of a donjon. An example is Castle Acre in Norfolk, begun in the late 11th century by William de Warenne, Earl of Surrey, as a rectangular stone dwelling within earthworks. The walls were then thickened internally and during the 12th century the south side was demolished and the north side raised to make a tall donjon.

The main floor at Castle Hedingham, showing the recessed window openings and the mural gallery. (Chris Gravett)

Many hall keeps survive in Britain and many suggest that, while not on the scale of palaces, they were residential, reinforcing the idea of the lord in his tower. Some 12th-century examples are quite refined when compared to the White Tower. Castle Rising has blind arcading carved along the external walls. As late as the 1180s, Henry II built the huge hall keep at Dover, by then a rather redundant building unless seen as an impressive statement of power and a royal residence. In the 12th century hall keeps were sometimes provided with a forebuilding, a rectangular stone building that butted against the main tower wall and masked the main entrance. Often stone stairs rose to the main entrance door and might be enclosed by the forebuilding. These stairs might be unroofed and open to the elements, to allow defenders to drop offensive material on any attacker using them: a few later examples were provided with arrow loops. However, the forebuilding also provided a stately entrance to the tower itself, as the visitor ascended to the main entrance doorway. The example at Dover was even provided with a stone bench that was centrally heated.

Hall keeps remained popular, though towers comprising a simple set of single rooms one above the other were also built. The floors vary in number from three to six. One of the earliest examples is St Leonard's Tower at West Malling in Kent, built in the later 11th century by Gundulph, Bishop of Rochester, who also built the White Tower. It is enlivened on its external walls by a blind arcade of round-headed arches, and has four floors reached by a single corner spiral staircase. Another early tower is that at Oxford, which is slightly stepped. It may be this type of tower without a dividing wall that was the usual form in Normandy and in other areas of northern France, and therefore the ones at West

Malling, and Oxford too, are early examples of the style built by the Normans in their newly conquered land. The modern term 'solar tower' suggests that these formed private apartments for the lord while a larger hall (often now vanished) would have formed the main living area somewhere nearby. Notable later examples include the polygonal Orford (Suffolk), circular Conisbrough (Yorkshire) and the almost cruciform tower of c. 1200 at Trim in County Meath, Ireland, where the visitor was guided through rooms to the lord. The number of mural rooms built into the designs often resulted in rather thin walls.

Compared to some hall keeps these solar towers are usually quite modest, with an internal area of between 36 and 100m² (387 and 1,076ft²). However, consideration must also be taken of how decorated such towers might be, regardless of size. Some have inadequate heating but are well-built and even decorated; perhaps such towers, provided with braziers, were used as sleeping quarters for family members or guests. Several towers, small and lacking refinements, give the impression they could have been little more than watch towers but even they would suggest to contemporaries that the holder had some wealth and status. There is evidence that solar towers may derive from wooden towers built on mottes or with mottes built up around them, as happened at several solar keeps. This, incidentally, may suggest the origin of the motte itself.

Donjons share many features, though not all display every characteristic. The main door is nearly always placed at first-floor level, reached by an external stair. In many instances the latter may well have been of wood, capable of being destroyed if the entrance had to be protected in time of danger. Internally access between floors was usually by spiral vices set in the corner wall thickness, or

Castle Acre, Norfolk; the remains of the chalk and flint house built by William de Warenne within the earthworks dates from the late 11th century, probably before 1085. The door and windows were blocked, floors removed, walls thickened, a curtain wall erected and the timber gatehouse replaced by a stone one. The addition to the north half of the building in 1140–60 turned the 'country house' into a donjon. (Chris Gravett)

occasionally by ladder and trapdoor. Few British donjons have straight stairs in the thickness of the wall. Some vices travel from basement to roof level, others occasionally miss alternate floors, forcing a detour across a room to reach a second stair to the next level, an obvious defensive advantage. Some corner buttresses are carried on up to form turrets. Additional buttresses are sometimes set against the wall face. Windows are usually small, sometimes being slightly larger on the upper floors, and occasionally of two-light construction. They are sometimes decorated with mouldings such as chevrons or billets. In many donjons the window opening splays into the room to maximize the light received. In some examples, however, a round-arched embrasure is set in the wall around the window. From these, or sometimes directly from the internal wall face, passages set in the thickness of the wall lead to small barrel-vaulted chambers or to privies. Some rooms are provided with round-arched fireplaces: those at the White Tower originally had hoods to help contain the smoke. From such fireplaces flues carried smoke out to openings usually set either side of a buttress. Where no fireplace exists, it must be assumed that heating was

Corfe castle, Dorset, c. 1105, was slighted during the English Civil Wars. The cavity cut by sappers trying to demolish the donjon in 1646 can be seen at the bottom of the annexe, below the two latrine chutes. (Chris Gravett)

147

provided by portable braziers. Windows must have been provided with wooden shutters with drawbars, or in a few cases thin sheets of horn might be set in place. Some chapels may even have had glass in the windows, so rare it was probably removable to allow it to be carried on progress with its owner. A well was, of course, vital. Tales of defenders sucking the moisture from saddle leather, or drinking one another's urine or the blood of horses, illustrates the lengths men would go to in order to stay alive when the water ran out.

As in mainland Europe, during the latter part of the 12th century British builders began experimenting with the shape of the donjon. Odiham in Hampshire has buttresses attached to each of its eight angles; Orford has huge buttresses attached to its multi-angular sides; Conisbrough is cylindrical but is still provided with massive buttresses that break up the design. These buttresses actually add projecting angles to the design, and it is debatable therefore to precisely what extent defence was a consideration, underlined by the fact that rooms and passages were contrived in the wall thickness, thereby weakening it. Gradually cylindrical towers were built without buttresses, as in the late 12th- and early 13th-century donjons at Pembroke, Skenfrith or Tretower, the areas in the West Country and Wales where such donjons found favour, or, for example, at Barnard castle in County Durham or Nenagh in Tipperary. The example at New Buckenham in Norfolk is apparently unique with a cross-wall, while Pembroke is actually provided with a stone dome rather than a timber roof, and has two concentric fighting galleries around it. A further advantage of such donjons is that they use less stone, though the circular interior feels less practical for domestic purposes. These polygonal and circular

The gate at Exeter, Devon, probably dates from the castle's foundation in 1068. It is now blocked up, but it is clear that the walls extended to form a primitive barbican. The arch is open behind. (Chris Gravett)

donjons may perhaps be seen as late forms of solar keep. Finally, the donjon was to be eclipsed by the strength of the outer defences, as the mural towers, hitherto relegated to a handful set at vulnerable points along the walls, or acting as gatehouses, were enlarged and multiplied in number. An early example of about 1180 is the splendid castle built by Roger Bigod, Earl of Norfolk, at Framlingham in Suffolk, which is distinguished by having no donjon: the defence relies solely on a strong line of towers set along the bailey walls.

Tour of a Castle: Château-Gaillard

BELOW
A view of Château-Gaillard
from the east, with the
River Seine behind. The
donjon can be seen on the
right. On the left the outer
bailey with its triangular
curtain is cut off from the
main castle by a deep
ditch. (Chris Gravett)

OPPOSITE
The deep ditches of
Château-Gaillard with the
middle bailey west wall
visible. The outer skin
of ashlar reveals a pattern
of white and grey stripes.
(Chris Gravett)

Château-Gaillard (or 'Roche d'Andeli', to use its official name) was built by Richard I of England on the banks of the River Seine in the Norman Vexin, the disputed territory claimed by both the Norman dukes and the French kings. In the valley of the Andelle, Richard decided to block further incursions by the French King Philip in 1194, and so he built Radepont as a new line of defence on the river. There may have been a castle here in the time of Henry I, but the existing fortress is the work of Richard I, along with Moulineaux and Orival. He then turned his attention to the two Andelys, Grand and Petit Andely. The River Gambon flows into the Seine from the north, and at the confluence is an island on which the little town of Petit Andely was set out: to the west of it lies a further, smaller island, the Ile d'Andely. To the north-east, on the far bank of the Gambon, lay Grand Andely. Both towns were fortified by Richard, with walls and towers; one of the latter remains on the west of Grand Andely. Two bridges crossed the Gambon to connect the towns with the Ile d'Andely, which was also walled. Close to Petit Andely, rising above the Seine, is a chalk spur that overlooks the little town, and it was here that the king chose to site his new castle. Its position on the Seine would command river traffic moving both north towards the Norman capital of

Rouen, and south towards Paris. Construction of the castle was swift: begun in 1196, it was completed in an amazing 13 months. Richard is said to have remarked, 'How beautiful is my one-year old daughter'. The size of the project makes it all the more impressive. Richard called his new castle 'Gaillard', usually interpreted as 'saucy', though it can also mean 'bold' or 'strong'. He swore that it was so good that he would hold it if it were made of butter. However, the king died in 1199, and it was left to his younger brother, John, to uphold the boast.

The site for the new castle was well chosen: the steep, sloping rock face meant that a hostile army's only practical approach was from the south-east. This was enhanced by the digging of a deep ditch around the landward side to the north and east.

Richard had envisaged a castle with several courtyards. At the south-eastern end he constructed the outer courtyard, the first obstacle for an attacker. The top of the ridge here was provided with a circuit of walls, roughly triangular in plan, with the apex facing south-east and covered by a large circular tower, with two further towers behind. It is assumed that another tower lay at the south-west angle, though the walls here have now been destroyed. The third angle to the north-east hosted the entrance itself: it comprised a rectangular gate-tower flanked on one side by a D-shaped tower (this does not survive). A gate passage flanked by two towers (as built at Dover by Richard's father,

The inner corrugated wall at Château-Gaillard, seen from the middle bailey. (Chris Gravett)

Henry II) was not employed, despite the use of modern cylindrical towers at Château-Gaillard. The outer courtyard was cut off from the rest of the castle by a ditch cut through the solid rock. Access to the second, middle courtyard was via a bridge over the ditch but only fragments of the entrance gate of the middle bailey have survived. The gate may have been through a central opening in the wall or possibly more to the north-east end, but either way does not appear to have been heavily defended. The bridge itself seems to have been a dog-leg shape in order to line up both gates. The middle courtyard was also protected by a curtain wall that ran in a rather angular oval around the rest of the promontory. The wall facing the outer court had a cylindrical mural tower at each end, of which only foundations of the landward example survive. The rather straight section of wall on this side survives only as foundation, and at the north-eastern end is fragmentary, but it had at least one further cylindrical tower approximately halfway along its length. On the south-western (or river) side, meanwhile, a straight section pierced by five loops runs about halfway along the length of the court to a square, open-backed tower with loops at the outer angles. A short missing section then becomes an irregular length of foundation to the north-west point, where the wall angle becomes acute, almost like a beak, and runs to join the inner wall before becoming fragmentary again as the circuit is completed. Within the middle courtyard the foundations of a rectangular building, possibly a hall, abut the south-west curtain, and foundations of other buildings abutting the opposite wall are visible. Traces remain here of a possible chapel with aisle pillars and apses, seemingly overbuilt. Here there was also a well.

Within the north-western section of the middle bailey stands the inner bailey, cut off by its own ditch that runs almost entirely around it, stopping short on the north corner. The shape of this court is an irregular oval, and it consists of a curtain wall whose outer surface, where it faces into the middle courtyard, is formed of close-set lobes pierced by arrow loops. This corrugated wall gives multiple fields of fire. The rear wall is plain, however, since immediately across the ditch lies the wall of the middle courtyard.

These elements provide a fine example of concentric defence, the inner wall supporting the outer. The inner courtyard is reached by a bridge across the ditch, leading to a square gate-tower with small side rooms. Within this courtyard lies the last line of defence, the donjon. To the north of it, domestic ranges were butted against the curtain wall, following the slight zigzag form of the latter.

Unlike many earlier examples set within an enceinte, Richard's donjon had already moved from lying within the enclosure to forming part of the curtain wall. It bulges out on the plain section of curtain wall, with its other side, which faces the inner courtyard, drawn out to form a massive solid stone prow, a donjon *en bec*. Internally the tower remains round: the stone prow is designed to deflect missiles aimed at it should the inner courtyard be captured, and to

CHÂTEAU-GAILLARD

Gaillard, the great castle built by Richard I in 1196–98, presented a formidable obstacle to an opponent. The only real line of approach was from the south, and here the attacker was met by a rock-hewn ditch and a triangular outer bailey that formed a large barbican to guard the main entrance. Richard used the latest circular towers, though the gate into this area is flanked only by a single tower. The gates connecting with the main or middle courtyard over another ditch have no supporting towers. In the middle courtyard are the domestic buildings that included a chapel, probably where the soldiers gained access via the latrine chute during the siege of 1204. Arrow loops have been added in the crenellations, though the wall-tops have not survived. The inner ward has a corrugated wall, whose missile coverage is shown in the top left inset. Its gate was set closely between two semi-circular towers. Within is the donjon *en bec*, with a solid stone 'beak' to deter mines and deflect missiles. The top part is now missing and it is not certain if the great buttresses acted as machicolated parapets, with slots for dropping material. To the left of the castle a towered wall drops to the River Seine, and a triple line of wooden piles bars the river. In the upper right can be seen the fortified town of Petit Andely connected to the fortified Ile d'Andely. A plan view of the castle is also provided, at bottom left.

(Adam Hook © Osprey Publishing)

The donjon *en bec* at Château-Gaillard presents its solid pointed edge towards the inner bailey. The deep battered plinth is also visible, together with the deep buttresses that may have carried an early machicolated parapet. Note the use of white and grey ashlar. The entrance was to the right of the 'beak'. (Chris Gravett)

thicken up this area of masonry. The base of the tower is provided with a deep battered plinth. Buttresses rise up the sides, expanding as they do so, but unfortunately the top of the donjon has been destroyed. When Viollet-le-Duc attempted to reconstruct this castle in the 19th century he added battlements to the inner corrugated curtain complete with wooden hoardings. He may have been right, since it seems such a powerful fortress would not be devoid of these

useful additions. However, when he similarly reconstructed the donjon, he interpreted the expanding buttresses as acting like corbels and carrying the battlements above, each buttress joined to its neighbour by an arch. Thus he surmised that slots left in the fighting platform above the arched section allowed materials to be dropped on those below. Unfortunately this theory can neither be proved nor disproved. The donjon was entered via a door on the first floor.

Some of the surviving stone retains evidence of horizontal banding. Some outer walls feature pink or grey stone, but others do not. The donjon also has similar ashlar blocks but it is difficult to conclude that this was regular banding as the sequence does not appear to follow a set pattern.

Below the main castle, down the side of the spur on the west side, a further buttressed wall was built, to cut off an inlet in the cliff. Next to it rises a cylindrical tower built into the chalk face itself, and from here a wall foundation runs down to the river bank. Here a timber stockade stretched across the Seine to bar access to river traffic.

Shown below from the south-western side of Château-Gaillard is the inner bailey with donjon. The foundations of the building next to the middle bailey wall on the left may be the lower room of the chapel. (Chris Gravett)

Tour of a Castle: Dover

Of the numerous surviving Norman castles in Britain, one of the most impressive must be Dover. It combines a massive yet old-fashioned donjon with the most up-to-date concentric defences, barbicans and D-shaped towers, and incorporates work from 1066 to 1216 and beyond.

The castle at Dover is one of the largest in Britain. Perched on the heights above the town and looking out on the Straits of Dover, it occupies a strategic position of considerable importance. The site was not new, having been an Iron-Age hill fort, and already contained a Roman *pharos* or lighthouse and Saxon church when the Normans arrived. Some work, namely a bank and ditch to the south of the church, may have been carried out under King Harold as part of his alleged agreement with Duke William while on his visit in about 1064, but could also be part of William's work in 1066. The earthworks around the site ran well beyond the *pharos* and church, down to the cliffs that formed a natural barrier. The Normans concentrated on the upper, northern end, beyond the church. The earlier defences erected by the Conqueror, which are largely lost, were greatly improved upon by Henry II in the 1180s. In an area cut off from the rest of the complex by a ditch, he created an inner bailey surrounded by a towered curtain wall. Inside this space he built a huge hall keep, already rather outdated in style. All this work cost almost £6,300, an impressive sum. Beyond this area he began to construct an outer circuit of defences around the northern end of the site, beginning on the eastern side by the southern end of the inner walls, and running north-west on a similar axis. However, work was halted when he died in 1189, and was not taken up again until the reign of his son, King John. He spent over £1,000 between 1207 and 1214 on improving the defences and adding domestic buildings.

The huge donjon is one of the largest in the country, 25m (83ft) high, and 30m × 29m (98ft × 96ft) in area, with a battered plinth. The walls, of Kentish ragstone rubble with Caen ashlar dressings, are 6.4m (21ft) at their thickest, with a pilaster buttress in the centre of each side: spiral stair vices are set in the south and north corners. Around the north-east and part of the south-east sides is a forebuilding providing stairs through three towers: the stairs (mostly modern, now with a right angle turn to the ground) were originally open to the sky to deny shelter to attackers (they were enclosed in the 15th century). The majority of rectangular windows are also reworkings of the 15th century. There seems to be an original doorway into the basement, an odd feature that would be a weak spot, though the door passage was defended by three doors with drawbars. The stairs rise to the lower chapel entrance in the first tower, with its porter's lodge (or perhaps a sacristy), then turn, and pass over a drawbridge pit to reach the second tower. Beyond is the third tower with guardroom, and to the left the decorated entrance doorway on to the second, or principal, floor. Leading from this passage is the vaulted well chamber with its shaft set in the thickness of the walls. It is lined with Caen stone for 52m (172ft) of its depth and additionally penetrates the chalk for 21m (70ft) or more. Only in the well chamber could water be drawn, to safeguard the supply if the basement was captured. From here two lead pipes, each 137mm (3 $^1/_2$ in) across, carried water via wall conduits to the lower floors. The second floor was almost certainly the royal suite, divided by a cross-wall into great hall and chamber. The larger hall, entered from the stairs, has a door leading into the great chamber, where more exclusive audiences would be held. In the wall there are two mural chambers, one with latrine, perhaps the king's private bedroom. On the south side a passage connects the two rooms and leads also to a sacristy and second chapel in the forebuilding tower. Above the hall a mural passage runs right around the building, but is broken in the middle of the north-west wall, where it forms two ranges of back-to-back latrines with loops. Below, the first floor could only be reached by the spiral stairs. It is laid out rather like that above but with less elaborate decoration, and the lower chapel can only be reached from the forebuilding. Below is the ground-level basement, with a narrow loop at each end of each room and a long mural storeroom in the south-west wall. The

The inner ward of Dover castle, built from about 1170 by Maurice the Mason, for Henry II. The tops of the towers were later cut down and the battlements are missing. In front of the twin-towered gate the barbican has now been destroyed. Behind the walls looms Henry's great donjon. (Chris Gravett)

Dover castle in Kent was a huge and powerful fortress. This is a reconstruction of the castle as it probably looked during the reign of King John in the early 13th century, before the siege of 1216. The first concentric castle in Europe, the outer gatehouse (1) was provided with an earth and timber outwork or barbican (out of view at the bottom left); both would be damaged in the siege of 1216 and the gate blocked and rebuilt. The outer ring of curtain walls has arrow loops and internal embrasures (2). Some towers built by John are in the latest D-shape design (3), being curved where they face the field, while the one in the lower right (4) is polygonal. To its left, the square tower (5) may well be a chamber tower serving a hall complex behind it. The older mural towers on the far left of the outer ring (6 and 7) are the rectangular towers of Henry II, though beyond them at the angle is Avranches Tower (8), shown also in closer detail (9), a tiered firing platform covering the re-entrant of the old earthworks. The inner circuit of walls (10) was built by Henry II, and consists of square mural towers, two of which form gate-towers to defend the northern entrance (11). This is itself defended by an offset stone barbican (12). Another similar gate and barbican lay on the south side (hidden). Within this circuit rises the great donjon (13), probably built to serve mainly as a royal residence and for receiving important guests. To the rear stands the old Anglo-Saxon church of St Mary (14) and the Roman pharos (15), in a low enclosure that Henry III would raise within great earthworks.

(Adam Hook © Osprey Publishing)

RIGHT
The curtain at Eynesford,
Kent, built c. 1100,
protected a timber tower
with a mound built up
around it. The flint-walled
stone hall replaced the
latter in the 12th century.
(Chris Gravett)

OPPOSITE
The donjon at Portchester
was possibly built by
Henry I. The date when
the upper two floors were
added is uncertain.
(Chris Gravett)

battlements are modern, and the flat roof was built in 1799; the original would
have been much steeper in design. The vaults on the second floor were added
at the same time, for carrying artillery pieces.

The inner bailey, built in the same material as the donjon, is set with 14
projecting square mural towers, with battered plinths all round the circuit:
entrance is via a gate to the north (the King's Gateway) and another to the
south (the Palace Gateway). Names given to various gates, it should be pointed
out, are in many cases those of later constables and do not reflect the names (if
any) used during the period under discussion. Each gate is flanked by two of the
mural towers – the earliest such usage in Britain of a twin-towered gate. The
gateways and drawbridges are of the 18th century. Each gate was protected by
a barbican, but only the northern one survives, consisting of two walls forming
a roughly triangular space, the path running at an angle to a gate with a

segmental arch (an arch that is less than a semi-circle) offset from the main gate behind it. The barbican gate has a pit to accommodate a turning bridge. Each tower was originally taller and battlemented but has been much altered and refaced over large areas. It is open-backed. Inside the inner bailey there was probably a kitchen in the south-east corner, and other domestic ranges against the curtain on these sides, now gone.

The outer walls were built by Henry II and John (later modified and cut down for artillery). From the south inner curtain a walled passage (now the 18th-century Bell Battery) ran east to the remains of Penchester Tower, before turning north. Here, on the eastern angle, the northern and eastern ditches meet, possibly echoing an Iron Age entrance: Henry strengthened a potential weak spot at this point by constructing Avranches Tower – basically a two-storey polygonal firing platform, with three arrow loops on each face. This, together with double rows on the neighbouring stretch of curtain, enabled a withering fire to be concentrated on an enemy from over 50 arrow loops, together with missiles from the battlements. From Avranches Tower, Henry's curtain running north-west is set with two rectangular mural towers. It ceases just south of the FitzWilliam Gateway, Hubert de Burgh's work to add a postern in the 1220s. Also during Henry II's reign the ditch south of the church was filled in and a bank erected across it, then cut into for the foundation of a stone wall.

The base of the square tower at Farnham, Surrey, built c. 1138, can be seen here on the left. It was protected by a motte, itself concealed behind walls raised in the late 12th century.
(Chris Gravett)

John did not initially concentrate much on Dover, and spent most on the castle after the loss of Normandy in 1204. He added domestic buildings inside the eastern side of the inner bailey, employed diggers to dig ditches and strengthened the outer curtain begun by his father, using new D-shaped mural towers in the latest design. On the northern point of the outer walls a new gatehouse with flanking towers was constructed, afterwards encased by Norfolk Towers following the damage caused by the siege of 1216, but still partially visible. The curtain running east to Henry's walls was also rebuilt following the siege. Running west and south from Norfolk Towers are Crevecoeur Tower (very cut down) and Godsfoe Tower, the latter rectangular, possibly having been used as a chamber tower to an adjacent hall, since there is a large blocked window in the wall north of it. Moreover there is a well and latrine by the Crevecoeur Tower, suggesting domestic buildings in this part of the castle. Treasurer's Tower to the south is said to have been rebuilt by Edward IV in the 15th century. Beyond it, Constable's Gateway is the new gate Hubert de Burgh built in the 1220s to replace John's obviously vulnerable gate site on the northern tip of the outer defences. It incorporates one of John's D-shaped towers, seen behind the back-to-back D-towers forming Hubert's gate. Further south lies Queen Mary's Tower, the wall from here to Peverell's Gateway an 18th-century rebuild. Peverell's Gateway is a mural tower with spurred base backing on to a gateway, on the south side of which Henry III added a semi-circular tower. The brick parapet is of the 19th century. From here a section of (now vanished) walled passage ran via the destroyed Harcourt Tower to connect by the inner bailey near the southern gate (Palace Gateway), and thence along on the south side via the now destroyed Well Tower, Armourer's Tower and Arthur's Gate, which brings you to the south-eastern corner of the inner curtain, and to where the walled passage ran east to Penchester Gate. Thus the donjon was enclosed within two circuits of walls. Finally, a section of wall running along eastwards towards the church on this side ends in Colton's Gateway, which is also rectangular. The outer curtain to the south of the work of Henry II and John is largely that of Henry III's reign, and may have had palisades before this, but possibly only the Iron Age ditch and bank.

Beyond Penchester Tower the walls ran south-east along the line of the ditch, with two further towers, Godwin and Ashford, now completely lost. Whether they were the work of Henry II, John or Henry III is not known.

Construction and Cost

Taking Britain as a test case, how were Norman castles erected? Perhaps surprisingly, little information was actually written down about the building of castles. Like any castle, a suitable site was first selected. We have already noted the use of existing Roman or Anglo-Saxon walls. Castles placed in towns might need buildings to be cleared before any construction work could begin, and this was done where necessary. At Lincoln, 166 houses were destroyed in 1068 to allow the castle to be erected where the Normans wanted it. Some castles were placed on angles of a river to command the route and use the protection of the water. Many were placed on natural hills, some on crags to benefit from the inaccessibility and from the solid rock base that deterred the use of mining. In the reign of William Rufus, for example, Robert of Bellême founded Bridgnorth in Shropshire on a hilltop site with a steep drop to deter assault, having abandoned his father's castle on the River Severn at Quatford. A rather nasty piece of work with an unhealthy interest in torture for the sake of it, he was nonetheless a fighting man with a sound knowledge of military matters.

Once the site had been selected, there might be a formal ceremony to announce the project. Building work then began, using specialist craftsmen,

augmented by the toil of native Englishmen no doubt press-ganged into helping. The Anglo-Saxon demands of burgage work (i.e. on communal defences), together with the old obligation to man the walls, could be neatly turned into demands for such labour on castles or their repair, without too obviously contravening any customs. Once a castle was built work on it could become a traditional custom, or commuted for money. The construction of ditches was the work of diggers, who made them V-shaped in cross-section, this providing for very steep sides that were sometimes revetted in timber. Some were designed to hold water and might be less steep. Timber bailey walls were laid on stone foundations.

The great donjons required the most planning, though. They were so immensely heavy that it was ill-advised to place them on an existing motte, however small the tower might be, simply because a man-made structure had not settled enough to bear such a weight, and any further settling was liable to crack the masonry. A few donjons appear to have been built upon mottes, but on closer inspection it has been discovered that in fact the tower was placed on solid ground and a mound of earth built up around it to enclose and protect the base of the tower. At Guildford in Surrey an existing motte with shell wall has been used but only the eastern side of the motte has been employed so the donjon butts up on to it, being neither on it nor actually within it.

The building of donjons was in the hands of engineers, most of whom remain unknown. However, the Pipe Rolls of Henry II's reign contain the

The remains of the north gate at Sherborne Old Castle, Dorset. Built between 1132 and 1137, this gate has a barbican formed from two long, parallel walls. (Chris Gravett)

The original 11th-century
gate at Richmond,
Yorkshire, was blocked
and turned into a donjon
in the 12th century.
(Chris Gravett)

names of several of the king's masons. Alnoth the Engineer first appears in
1158 and worked for the king for 30 years; Maurice the Mason, while working
at Dover, received a wage of 8d per day, putting him on equal footing with a
knight (his pay later increased to one shilling). Maurice worked on the donjon
at Newcastle before Dover, so it is perhaps not surprising that each castle bears
some similarity to the other. Master Elyas of Oxford appears in 1187 in Oxford
but worked in other places in southern England such as Portchester in 1192,
and three years later is referred to as 'the Engineer' rather than stone-mason or
carpenter. He had also been in charge of the royal siege engines from London
for Richard I's siege of Nottingham in 1194.

Royal castles began life as an order passed as a king's writ to the sheriff of the
county. Other sheriffs might become embroiled by way of demands for men,
materials or transport. A royal official would act as the central authority, or else
the designated constable. Royal quarries or those owned by monastic houses
were large and might be hired as a whole or a designated amount of stone
bought. Stone was cut by driving iron wedges to split away sections that were
then sawn or further split by masons. One cubic foot was a common size for

OPPOSITE
The south-west gatehouse
at Sherborne Old Castle,
seen here from the bailey,
was the main entrance
from the town. The
upper floors with square
windows are later
additions. (Chris Gravett)

The roof level of the
donjon at Richmond,
with the battlements and
the steps up to the corner
turret. (Chris Gravett)

slabs, and their faces were often smoothed by chisels in a diagonal motion. Stone was an expensive commodity, and transporting it was as expensive as the cost of the stone itself. One study has estimated that moving stone 18km (11 miles) doubled its quarried price. Many castles were built using material from the nearest quarry, or even from the neighbourhood if the stone was usable. Hence, for example, the donjon at Goodrich in Herefordshire is of the same sandstone as the rock it stands on. The main method of transport otherwise was by water rather than road. It was by sea that some of the best stone, limestone from Caen in Normandy, was shipped to England to provide smooth ashlar facings. In England, Barnack in Northamptonshire, Maidstone in Kent (for Kentish ragstone) and Quarr were close to river facilities and provided good building stone. Sometimes Norman builders reused Roman red bricks, though occasionally they actually made their own bricks.

At the site the foundations preferred were those of solid rock, since this deterred mining, and once a level surface was cut, building could commence. However, where this was not possible foundations had to be created. A trench was dug slightly larger than the size of the walls, and filled with rammed stone rubble, or else oak piles driven into the soil by a weight and pulley system. Occasionally an earlier building's foundations were commandeered, in which case a wooden raft was laid on top first.

The walls of a donjon were usually made by building a facing of ashlar blocks, and filling the gap with rougher stone, binding the whole together with mortar. Sometimes even builders' rubbish was used. When the great donjon in London was constructed it was rumoured that the blood of beasts was added to

Interior of the late-11th-century Scolland's Hall in Richmond castle, looking west. (Chris Gravett)

the mixture. Sometimes ties of metal or wood were added at intervals to help bond everything tightly. Not all castles had a smooth face, however. Some had the main walls built purely of rubble, in which case they had to be sheathed between wooden shuttering to allow the mortar to be poured and to set. Ashlar might be used at corners and around windows, to produce neat edging. As the walls of a donjon rose, square holes were left in them to allow beams to be inserted, which acted as supports for scaffolding. These putlog holes are still visible in Norman walls. On a few battlements such as Rochester, a line of holes below the crenellations indicates that the beams of wooden hoardings were fixed in them to overlook the wall base.

Many workmen would typically be employed on the building site of a major castle. Masons would be busy shaping blocks, men would burn lime and sand over fires to prepare mortar mixes, or melt lead brought from the Mendips or from Derby for roofing. Carpenters would be busy making or repairing items – the sheds to cover the craftsmen, scaffolding and floor beams, floorboards, window shutters, doors, or wooden shuttering for rubble walls or for door and window arches. Smiths would produce thousands of iron nails, hinges and handles. Tools had to be constantly resharpened. Sledges were used to pull heavy items, lighter loads being conveyed by stretcher or else in barrows or baskets.

Spiral stone vices were set into the walls using many wedge-shaped slabs of stone, each terminating at its narrow end in a circular slab, producing a sort of keyhole-shaped stone. The next step was laid on the top edge but the circular terminal was positioned over the first, like the centre point of a circle. Repeating this process formed the circular stair, whilst the stack of cylindrical slab-ends formed the vertical shaft or vice.

Once the main building was completed, the internal flooring could be added. Some castles were provided with a line of beam holes in the walls to take the floor beams; others used stone corbels (brackets) set in a line along the wall instead. The roof structure itself was usually of timber and was quite steeply angled. Wooden shingles, pottery tiles, slates or thatch covered the roof, or it might be coated in lead. Donjons with a spine wall were usually provided with two roofs, one to each room, and the top of the spine wall formed a natural gutter. Along the lower edges of the roof water runnels lined with wood or lead were usually cut through the thickness of the wall.

Waterpipes, drainpipes and spouts of lead were used. Doors were hung on iron butt-hinges. Wooden drawbars ran into holes in the adjoining wall, while two-leaved doors (i.e. with two halves) might have a pivoting bar attached. Some had locks as well. Work often stopped between Michaelmas and Easter unless it was a matter of urgency to carry on building, in which case it might also be continued at night. Expenditure on castles varied depending on their perceived importance. Henry II spent a hefty £1,144 on Newcastle upon Tyne between 1167 and 1178, but only £106 12s 9d on Norwich between 1160 and 1188 – less than was spent on Scarborough in one year (£107 6s 8d in 1160–61). Similar cost variations were experienced in Normandy itself, depending on the amount of work involved. For the building of Château-Gaillard, Richard I spent about £11,500. During his time the government of Normandy was responsible for the upkeep of about 45 castles.

The Principles of Defence

The castles built by the Normans can best be seen as defended bases. On the Seine, a main artery running through the disputed Vexin territory, castles were built by both sides to try to block the other's advance. Château-Gaillard, the greatest late-12th-century castle in this area, was but one of a number of fortresses here. At Tosny, the Isle de la Tour (Boutavant) and Le Muret were forts guarding the approaches to the château. Boutavant was a quadrangular tower (of which some parts survive) on an island 5km (3 miles) upstream, and controlled light defences in the river to bar the Seine peninsula between Tosny and Bernières. Le Muret was a ditched motte and bailey with a circular tower on it, 2km (1¼ miles) south-east of Gaillard, in the parish of Cléry. Neaufles-Saint-Martin, built below a tributary of the Epte, was a large, deeply ditched motte and bailey castle with a donjon, which reinforced the defensive line against the French castles of Trie, Courcelles, Boury and, further down, Chaumont en Vexin.

The castles contained a number of knights and other soldiers who were trained for war, meaning that it was just as likely that the garrison would be

The motte at Gisors, showing the buttressed polygonal shell wall and the donjon. (Chris Gravett)

The polygonal donjon at Gisors, built by Henry I, sits on the motte. Henry II added the top two storeys. The stair turret is a 15th-century addition. (Chris Gravett)

prepared to come out and fight if they thought the odds were in their favour. At Tillières in 1119 the Norman castellan (constable), Gilbert, had his men patrol the neighbouring paths and stalled a surprise attack on the castle by surprising the French raiders instead. When King Louis advanced against Breteuil, the Norman Ralph of Gael led his cavalry out and left all the gates open to challenge the enemy to try to get in: after bitter fighting the French withdrew. The same thing happened at Falaise when Richard of Lucy dared Geoffrey of Anjou to enter: the latter declined and went off to plunder instead. This boastful attitude backfired at Le Mans, however, when the Normans in possession of the town had to retire and failed to shut the gates against the pressure of the Count of Maine's troops: the Normans barely reached the citadel.

No matter how bold the occupants, a castle had to be suitably protected, and as we have seen location was a key factor. Where possible an imposing site was chosen, preferably a rocky outcrop that would deter mining. Falaise was built on such a promontory, perched on a sheer rock face leading down to the stream at its foot, removing the need for a ditch on this side. Mont Orgueil on Jersey was built on a rocky peak controlling the port of Gorey, though little 12th-century work remains today except the two chapels. La Roche-Guyon began life as a fortress cut into the rock face, but in the 12th century was built up in stone. The castle at Arques (Pays de Bray) is also perched high on a long ridge overlooking the town, protected by steep ditches cut in the rock. A ravine divided the ridge, and a further courtyard would be added in the 13th century beyond this gap. On the larger site was placed the main castle, with its walls overlooking steep slopes. Another example is the castle at Saint-Saveur-le-Vicomte, which towers over the valley of the Douve below. A number of castles used other natural features to their advantage, forcing an enemy to approach from one side only, which would then be cut off by a man-made ditch. Vire stands at the central point in south-west Normandy, in the centre of a network of castles and at a crossroads. The donjon (rebuilt by Henry I in 1123) is sited on a granite outcrop bordered on two sides by the River Vire, the only access being from the north where the spur joins the plateau: the town was founded here, and served to protect the castle. At this junction a deep ditch cut the castle from the town. The town walls and towers at Vire would only be added in the 13th century though. On its spur, Tancarville made use of the Seine itself to shield one side of the castle, while at Montfort-sur-Risle the River Risle similarly protects the south-west side of the castle, which covers an area of about 280m × 165m (918 × 541ft).

The curtain wall at Gisors, with one of the late-12th-century prow-shaped mural towers on the left. (Chris Gravett)

The curtain at Gisors, seen from the top of the motte. (Chris Gravett)

At Cherbourg the area of land on which the town is situated was cut off by a moat that connected with the sea at either end. At one end of this artificial island a further section was cut off to form the area on which the castle was built. The castle was strengthened in stone during the second half of the 12th century. The donjon was enclosed in a bailey approximately 120m × 100m (393 × 328ft), which was cut off by water from the rest of the castle. Other castles that stood by a town or city also often utilized the latter's defences. The castle at Avranches, with its slim square donjon, once stood against the south-east curtain wall of the town. At Bayeux the castle was situated in the western corner of the walls, which were later given 18 towers. The castle at Carentan was built in a bottleneck in the south-east corner of the city, though the city's defences were probably of wood until replaced by stone walls, possibly in the 13th century.

The first obstacle protecting any Norman castle was the ditch or moat surrounding the site. A good ditch was deep enough to make an effective obstacle, steep sided and perhaps revetted with wood to make it slippery to climb. It might be filled with stakes, not so much to impale the enemy but to slow him down and thus make him a better target. Some were flooded but most needed only a few feet of water and mud to present a real obstacle to easy movement. The earth was thrown up to form a bank on the inner lip, and often an outer bank as well. Stone bailey walls, though they rarely survive in any quantity, do not initially appear to have been too high. Those at Rochester have been estimated at about 6.7m (22ft) high and 1.4m (4ft 6in) thick at the base. At Dover the inner walls of the 1180s that form the ring around the donjon have been robbed of their battlements. Framlingham looked to the walls and tall towers for its main defence.

The stone curtain walls were the next line of defence, and were at first often devoid of mural towers. Later these became increasingly common. Most mural towers were square or rectangular in plan, with two or three floors. Those on the strong inner curtain at Dover have latterly lost their fighting tops and been cut down to line up with the curtain wall. The towers at Framlingham were open backed, this closed by wooden screening or curtain. In time of war it meant the screens could be removed, exposing the inside of the tower and thus denying shelter to an enemy who managed to gain entry. Access across the tower at wall-walk level was by wooden planking, which could be thrown down if it appeared the tower might be lost. Each tower jutted out from the wall, and was provided with arrow loops in the side, to allow archers in the tower to enfilade the wall face or those on the battlements to shoot along the parapet below. By the 1180s a new concept was being tried out, whereby the tower was made multi-angled, then round, instead of square. The polygonal experiments gave way to towers either D-shaped, so they presented a rounded front to the field, or

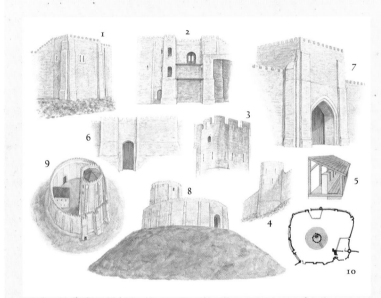

THE MAIN ELEMENTS OF DEFENCE

The elements shown in this illustration derive mainly from the frontier fortress of Gisors in the Vexin. At top left and centre are outer (1) and inner (2) views of one of the rectangular wall towers of the second half of the 12th century.

Below and to the right (3) is a semi-circular example, a late-12th-century tower liberally supplied with arrow loops, some in merlons. Below this (4) is the D-shaped Tour du Diable of 1180–90, pierced by loops. Several towers were of beaked or prow shape, with a solid stone projection

to throw off missiles and deter mining. The wooden hoardings or brattices (5) were built out from battlements to allow defenders to command the base of a wall through slots in the floor. The wood was protected by raw or wet hides. The supporting beams often passed through holes in the wall running along below the crenellations. In the middle left (6) is the Porte des Champs, a gate set in the wall and flanked by a rectangular tower on its right and a bastion to its left. At top right (7) is a gate-tower from nearby Château-sur-Epte, basically a passage through a tower. The large earth motte at Gisors was topped by a polygonal shell wall (8), the angles protected by shallow buttresses but with three large ones at one side. Inside was built a polygonal tower (9); the little chapel of St Thomas Becket can also be seen. The plan of Gisors (10) shows the large round tower on the far right added by Philip Augustus in the early-13th-century.
(Adam Hook © Osprey Publishing)

Carlisle castle, Cumbria. The main walls and towers of this large castle were built by Henry I in 1122. The donjon, seen here, is attributed to the King of Scotland (1136–57) but may have been built between 1150 and 1175. The roof was later converted for use as a gun platform. (Chris Gravett)

cylindrical. This allowed all round vision from the battlements, with no blind spots caused by angles, and provided no angles for a sapper's pickaxe to prize out stones.

At Framlingham the merlons were provided with vertical arrow loops with splayed backs. Some crenels could be protected by a wooden shutter, which pivoted on an iron bar: one end fitted into a hole in the side of a merlon, the other end into a short curved slot in the opposite end. They were presumably held open by a wooden peg, or simply lifted to allow an arrow or bolt to be loosed off.

Early gates were protected by a tower set beside them, but soon developed into the form of a square or rectangular tower pierced by a passageway. Above were one or more floors and battlements at roof level. It was late in the 12th century that a more substantial gatehouse appeared, now with twin square towers flanking a gate passage. This can be seen, for example, at Newark, whose massive recased plinths appear to be Norman, and at Dover in the inner and outer gates. At Caen the gate-tower was further supported by the proximity of the donjon. Some had a portcullis. Also new was the barbican or outwork, designed to help protect the gate, examples of which are rare. Sometimes these were of timber, as at Dover in the outer gate, here as late as 1216. However, the side walls of the late 11th-century gate at Exeter project slightly and are provided with an arch above, while at Sherborne in the 1130s a pair of parallel walls jutted forward down the bank from one of the gates. The barbicans protecting the north and south inner gates at Dover were of stone, the northern one of which survives as walls leading to a gate set off-centre from the main gate.

The castle at Carentan in the Cotentin, probably begun in about 1150 and popular with King John from 1199, has a square donjon with clasping corner buttresses on the eastern side of the castle enclosure, forming a gate-tower (with billet moulding) over the moat as well as a flanking tower. The enclosure itself was an irregular circle seemingly at that time without further mural towers. At Château-sur-Epte the bailey was surrounded in the 12th century by a stone wall with two gate-towers set with flat buttresses, with that on the plateau retaining traces of decoration. Part of the bailey was enclosed by an internal wall and connected to the motte summit by a wing wall. The internal wall has a similar gate-tower, altered in the 14th century for a drawbridge, and a second tower by the motte. This form of gate-tower became the norm until

GATE TOWERS AND GATEHOUSES: EXETER AND RICHMOND

Norman gatehouses varied in size and sophistication. Exeter's gatehouse (1) was built in the second half of the 11th century, its pointed Anglo-Saxon-style windows revealing its early date. Essentially it is a tower with a passage through it: the front walls extend forward, as can be seen in the plan view of the walls (2), and are provided with an arched top. Like the Tower of London, this castle, founded by William the Conqueror, utilized the Roman city defences to form two walls of the enclosure.

The 11th-century gate at Richmond, North Yorkshire (3), originally provided access to a large stone-walled enclosure above the River Swale (see plan view, 4). It was then turned into a donjon in the mid-12th century when a stone tower was built on top and the original gate opening blocked by stone. A new first-floor opening reached by timber stairs was added, leading to a single-room, two-storey interior over a blocked basement. The main living quarters seem to have been in Scolland's Hall at the other end of the bailey (5), so this donjon may have been the private solar tower of Duke Conan. It certainly demonstrated the lord's power, being the first impression gained of the castle from the town. There are three windows at first-floor level overlooking the town market place, one with a tympanum or filled stone space above the lintel: here the lord may have shown himself to the people via a wooden gallery. Similar arrangements survive at castles such as Newcastle and Dover, and early towers such as Oxford and Sherborne.

(Adam Hook © Osprey Publishing)

the turn of the 13th century, when the passage was itself defended by a substantial tower at either side. At Domfront the entrance is flanked by two strong polygonal towers that appear to date from the end of the 12th or beginning of the 13th centuries, probably built by the Plantagenet kings. These are the precursors of the drum or cylindrical form that would become common in the 13th century. The towers contain vaulted galleries designed to shelter archers shooting through numerous arrow loops.

A gate was accessed via the ditch and approached across a wooden bridge usually with a removable section by the door. Some of these were drawbridges, raised by means of a winch in the room over the passage, or occasionally bascule bridges, the bridge chains attached to horizontal counter-weighted beams above. A few were turning bridges, the bridge acting as a see-saw with a weighted rear end that dropped into a pit.

The donjon was probably the last point of defence, and its imposing strength meant it was very difficult to attack. Corner and side buttresses often added to its strength, and the walls were so thick that catapults usually had little impact on them. Being of stone the tower could not easily be burned unless fire could somehow be brought to the roof, but that was usually shielded behind the upper walls and battlements. The entrance was nearly always situated at first-floor level, being reached by a stair along the outside of the wall. This was often of wood, so that in an emergency, when everyone had retreated inside the tower, the stairs

The donjon at Domfront was probably built by Henry I in the early 12th century. The first-floor entrance can be seen on the right. (Chris Gravett)

Only two walls of the donjon at Domfront survive, but they stand above the rest of the fortifications in the foreground, which form part of the defended gate and possibly date from 1202–03. (Chris Gravett)

could be destroyed, presumably by burning, since it would take quite an effort to throw down a sturdy timber structure. Similarly, some stairs were interrupted by a drawbridge pit. This is seen, for example, in front of the forebuilding at Rochester, and in the approach stairs at Dover. However, it would be a hefty wooden platform that would be in use daily, and exactly how this was 'run back', as has often been written, is uncertain. Perhaps it had runners; perhaps it was simply burned away, or pushed off the edge of the entrance step by brute force.

A few late donjons (such as Château-Gaillard) were *en bec* to strengthen defence against missiles. Cylindrical towers of the late 12th and early 13th centuries, such as Neaufles-Saint-Martin (c.1180), with their better fields of fire and lack of vulnerable angles, were continued by Philip Augustus, as seen at Falaise. The best way to make an impression on a donjon was by mining, or to starve out those inside. Since most donjons were provided with a well and the basement was largely for storage, this too could prove a lengthy option.

However, the ability of the defenders to hit back was fairly limited, and it is interesting to see how gradually these great towers fell from favour during the late 12th and early 13th centuries. The battlements were often quite high and offered

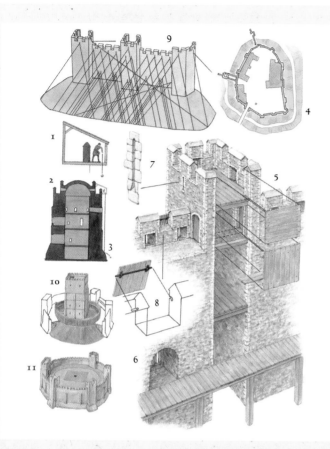

DEFENDING A CASTLE: PEMBROKE, FRAMLINGHAM, AND FARNHAM

The main (and passive) defensive quality of a donjon was its solidity: when required, though, active defence was carried out from battlement level. In a few castles holes were created below the battlements for the erection of timber galleries called hoardings (1), onto which soldiers could step unseen beyond the crenellations. They could shoot through slits in the planking or command the base of the wall through gaps in the floor. The circular donjon at Pembroke (2), built by William Marshal in about 1200, is unusual in not only possessing these, but also having a second parapet and

a stone dome, which obviously removed the danger of a timber roof being set alight or being smashed with missiles. The circular shape is seen in a number of late-12th-century towers, especially in the West. The removal of angles made it harder for enemy miners to pick out stones, and also removed blind spots from the corners of the battlements. The sloping battered plinth (3), seen on a number of donjons, thickened the wall base against attack and meant that material dropped from above bounced out at uncertain angles into the enemy.

The castle at Framlingham in Suffolk, built c. 1180, had no donjon and relied for its defence on powerful curtain walls (4) set with rectangular

towers (5). The towers were open-backed, fitted only with timber above battlement level and probably curtaining below that. The passage through each tower was spanned by wooden planking that could be removed, plus wooden doors; thus a section of curtain wall could be cut off if the enemy took it. The tower battlements were reached by ladder. The curtain walls were provided with embrasures each with twin vertical loops (6): the loops slope downwards externally, allowing plunging fire to the ground for archers. As these are now well above ground level, it seems they were reached from the first floor of a now vanished timber barrack block, though it is possible the ground level here has been lowered. On the battlements of towers and curtain wall, the merlon itself was sometimes provided with a vertical loop, internally splayed (7). Additionally, merlons were provided with a hole and slot to allow a wooden shutter to be inserted, to further protect archers on the parapet (8). The field-of-fire diagram shows the strength of the curtain walls and the fire cover provided (9).

The castle at Farnham, Surrey (10), may demonstrate the origin of the earth mound or motte. In about 1132 a square stone tower was built and its lower part enclosed in an earthen mound to protect it. However, in the later 12th century the tower was demolished until flush with the motte top, and a shell wall constructed at ground level to encase the motte (11). The gap between the wall and the curved top edge of the motte was later filled to produce a flattened surface. It may be, therefore, that mottes originated to protect the bases of timber towers in the same way. (Adam Hook © Osprey Publishing)

only long-range shooting. The donjon at White castle in Gwent was demolished when the castle underwent renovation, and defence was entrusted to strong round towers. The windows in a donjon were always quite small, though those on the upper levels might be slightly larger. Internally they were splayed to allow as much light and air to enter the room as possible. It is often thought that some of these windows also served to shoot arrows from. However, a true arrow loop needs a plunging opening to the outside to allow the archer to shoot down towards ground level. Most of these windows do not possess them; moreover, some are placed so high in a room as to make it impossible for an archer inside even to see the ground outside. Only a few, mostly late donjons possess true arrow loops, at a time when they are beginning to appear generally. They can be seen unusually early in Kenilworth (possibly c.1130), otherwise in late examples such as Skenfrith. Similarly, embrasures are built into the walls of Framlingham. The inside of the

LEFT Henry I's donjon at Falaise is perched at one end of the castle on the rock overlooking the stream. Legend says Arletta was bathing at this spot when Duke Robert spied her from his castle; William the Conqueror was the issue of their union. The *Grand Donjon* (of about 1120) stands to the left of the *Petit Donjon*, while the cylindrical tower of Philip Augustus was added in about 1200. (Chris Gravett)

BELOW LEFT The interior of the donjon at Falaise during renovation, and prior to the insertion of new floors. The top floor with its two light windows can be clearly seen. (Chris Gravett)

BELOW RIGHT The blind basement and the first floor of the donjon at Falaise. (Chris Gravett)

Falaise castle seen from the courtyard, showing the donjon's first-floor entrance, now masked by a modern forebuilding. Philip's tower is clearly visible. (Chris Gravett)

wall is cut out to form a cavity with an arched roof in the thickness of the wall behind the loophole. These are now several feet off the ground: presumably they were either reached by a platform, or else the ground level was higher than it is today. At Dover the early 13th-century Avranches Tower on the outer curtain wall is a good example of the new concept in defence, a mural tower with shallow angles rather than right angles, each facet set with three levels of arrow loops, which, with the battlements, allowed archers at three levels to pour missiles on to an approaching enemy and to command the ground below.

The base of many donjons is protected by a battered plinth. This is basically a thickening of stone at the base, angled like a flange to the base of the tower. It served two purposes: firstly, it strengthened the vulnerable base of the wall with additional masonry and secondly, it allowed any offensive material dropped from the wall head to bounce off the batter and fly into the enemy ranks at unpredictable angles. Such splayed bases were also seen on curtain walls and mural towers. By about 1200 some towers had spurs – thick, pointed masonry bases, jutting towards the field.

With arrow loops rare, and only the wall top to shoot from, defenders trapped in a donjon must have felt quite cut off: they would have to rely on the supplies stored in the ample basement and the water supply. Some internal staircases were staggered between floors, forcing anyone using them to cross the entire donjon to reach the next flight, but many did not have this refinement. Nor is it certain whether stairs spiralling upwards clockwise really were greatly beneficial to a right-handed defender backing up the stairs.

A view of the castle of
Falaise, showing the
curtain wall of the bailey
with its towers, many of
which are of 13th-century
date. (Chris Gravett)

There are few references to donjons being besieged. The most famous concerns Rochester, besieged by John in 1215, when he brought down a whole corner by use of a mine. The defenders withdrew behind the massive cross-wall and continued to resist. Some doors were guarded by a portcullis, now detectable in the vertical groove either side of the passage. Some were of wood shod with iron. Others, however, must have been purely of iron, as the groove is quite thin. At Rochester the door into the donjon from the forebuilding had a portcullis whose mechanism was situated in the entrance of the chapel above: the same applied to the main door at Orford, where its winch mechanism was also located, demonstrating the lack of concern this proximity presented to the military minds of the time. Doors were of thick planking, perhaps reinforced by metal. Drawbridges, lifted by means of chains and winches, are not detectable at the entrances to keeps, though Dover had one in the forebuilding, and a turning bridge at the barbican.

On the roof the battlements were usually raised up to a level that protected the roof from fire arrows or catapult stones. Here the main fighting platform was located, but on large donjons it might be 30m (100ft) or so above the ground. Some castles could erect wooden hoardings (brattices) out over the battlements, with the support beams using the holes provided under the battlements, thus allowing men stationed inside to command the foot of the wall below them whilst unseen from outside. However, though defenders might try and cover wooden hoardings with raw hides or clay, to snuff out flames, they were also vulnerable to catapult balls. Once inside a donjon, there was little

The mid-12th-century tower at Wolvesey Palace, Winchester, Hampshire, has provoked much debate. The walls are too thin to qualify it as a defensive tower, and it has been suggested this was a kitchen. (Chris Gravett)

chance of escape, since there would be no side door unless the tower was joined to a curtain wall, when there might be access to a wall-walk. In some castles there might be postern doors in the bailey.

Château-Gaillard is an early proto-concentric castle. As noted previously, the only practical approach was via the south side, and from here an attacker was forced to capture an outer, then a middle, then an inner courtyard, the latter including the powerful donjon. It was not a true concentric design, in which inner walls follow and protect the outer walls, since this only occurs on sections of the inner and middle walls, but it utilizes its setting to full advantage. La Roche-Guyon also shows this use of two curtains supporting each other, but they do not completely surround the donjon.

Dover is one of the earliest examples of a concentric castle. The outer walls, built by Henry II on the north side of the complex, and added to by John, complement Henry's inner ring and, within that, his great rectangular donjon, hence a triple ring of defences. Here we see a slightly irregular concentric defence, not as refined as in later castles such as Beaumaris, where the outer ring runs almost parallel to the inner, but nevertheless an extremely early version of an inner wall supporting an outer. In theory this meant that the

The walls of Berkeley castle enclose a motte. The manor was granted in 1153–56 and Henry II pledged to fortify a castle here. (Chris Gravett)

defenders possessed three rings of defence, the outer curtain, inner curtain, and donjon. However, the great donjon was already rather archaic in design. Here too we find early barbicans defending a gateway. Early Norman gatehouses basically consist of either a tower set beside a gateway set in a wall, or else a passage cut through the lower part of the tower itself.

Castles needed to have a water supply to hand. Some were supplied direct from underground streams and, like the White Tower in the Tower of London, the water was sourced via a well in the basement, so there was a supply on hand if the garrison was trapped in the donjon. At Rochester, the water could be drawn up through each floor by a shaft in the thickness of the cross-wall, a sort of watery dumb waiter. Dover had an elaborate piping system, whereby rainwater was collected in a cistern and then fed via lead pipes. Sometimes water could be brought in by pipe from a river flowing past the castle. If there was no water under the donjon itself there needed to be a well in the bailey; but if defenders were forced into the tower with no water their only drink would be the wine or beer stocks stored there, before – as we have seen – more unpleasant alternatives were considered out of desperation. Food supplies were also necessary and could be stockpiled in time of siege, since the basement of a

The latrine block at Wolvesey, showing the drainage channel. (Chris Gravett)

donjon was usually spacious and must have been given over to storage. Many are subterranean or semi-subterranean, and few have any natural lighting. Some were reached by spiral stairs but others must have been accessed by trapdoor and ladder. Presumably there was a rope and pulley system for hauling up large items. Since few donjons possessed internal kitchens there would be little hot food if the defenders were forced inside the tower, other than that which could be cooked over the wall fireplaces or braziers.

Life in a Norman Castle

As noted previously, the domestic buildings that filled the Norman castle have yet to be studied to any great degree. The hall was the largest building on the site. In general, Norman halls have been considered to be built in stone on two levels, with an undercroft on the ground floor in which food and drink were stored, and the main living area on the first floor, reached by an external stair. Anglo-Saxon and Danish halls, however, were built in timber with a single, ground-floor area of beaten earth. The roof of the hall was high-pitched, and running down its length on either side were a row of wooden pillars to help support the roof. The space between these and the outer walls provided an area for benches or beds, and spaces between pillars could be sectioned off as needed. A central hearth provided warmth, and a louvre in the roof helped remove the smoke.

Another important room in the Norman castle was the solar ('sun room'), the private withdrawing chamber for the lord, his family and guests. Anglo-Saxon and Viking social organization had usually meant the lord and his followers all bedded down together in the great hall, and modern viewers would be shocked by the lack of privacy. By the time of the Norman Conquest this state of affairs may still have existed in some castles, perhaps amongst those lords inured to war and the comradeship it engendered. Many, however, were already

On one side of the cross-wall at Castle Rising sits a kitchen on a stone vault; on the other side, seen here, there is a latrine through the left door and urinal through the right – perhaps separating the sexes? (Chris Gravett)

seeking to distance themselves from the rest of the castle, at least for part of the day. Some so-called first-floor stone manor houses, such as Boothby Pagnall in Lincolnshire, are now considered by some to be in fact private solar or chamber blocks for a missing ground-floor hall. The solar would hold the lord's bed, a four-poster with curtains not only for added privacy – the whole family and guests might be in this room, as well as a body servant or two – but also to help keep out the draughts. Other furniture would include at least one large trunk or chest for clothes, and perhaps another for armour, though rods or rails for hanging clothes might be provided. A chair would be a luxury for the lord and lady. Stools, benches or the floor were good enough for most people. The floor might be covered with fur rugs. A favourite falcon or hawk might be kept on a perch in the room, and perhaps a favourite hunting dog or a lap dog for the lady. Inside a donjon or external hall the main rooms were probably plastered and perhaps whitewashed. Some could be decorated, a common theme being painted lines to represent masonry.

Exactly what form the early halls took in Normandy itself has been a subject of much debate. Impey suggests that the domestic complexes in Normandy between 1125 and 1225 resembled those in England. The typical arrangement consisted of an independent communal great hall at ground-floor level, open to the timber roof, associated with a residential block in two stages. The development was notably coherent, the title 'Anglo-Norman' being perhaps justified by the apparent absence of this need among non-Norman continental lords. This style perhaps developed from an Anglo-Saxon tradition already formulated, which crossed to Normandy after the Conquest. At the same time an early tradition persisted, that of storied houses, the most evident being the donjon, which was brought to England in various forms.

In the 11th century, ground-floor chambers in Normandy do not tend to correspond with English models but in the early 12th century we find two-storey stone buildings at Domfront and Vatteville-la-Rue. At Vatteville the upper stage is carried by a series of partition walls, at Domfront by an alignment of three piers. The most impressive surviving hall, and the earliest, is that within the enceinte of Caen castle. The so-called Exchequer Hall (a 19th-century name) was 31m x 11m (101ft 8in x 36ft 1in) in surface area, perhaps the best preserved of its type in Europe, though it was badly damaged in 1944 and has been restored. The 11th- and 12th-century floor levels have been only partly preserved: this was probably a ground-floor hall, though some think that part of the area served as a kitchen, with a floor above being the principal hall.

Caen had a complex of buildings in close proximity, including perhaps a chamber block. Beaumont-le-Richard in Calvados has a mid-12th-century rectangular hall with a central nave. About 10m (33ft) away there is a smaller rectangular block, perhaps a solar block, consisting of a vaulted ground-floor room with a room over it, preceded by an arched antechamber. These buildings

A corner stair in Norwich was converted into a kitchen oven, utilizing the thick, solid stone of the wall to counter the risk of fire. (Chris Gravett)

are aligned on the same axis. Creully in Calvados is especially similar to a type of hall often seen in England but in Normandy only at Bricquebec, Beaumont-le-Richard and Barneville-la-Bertran. It was a huge hall some 17m (55ft 9in) high, with a series of arcades separating a side aisle with a sloping roof. The hall was reworked in the 14th and 16th centuries and now has a Renaissance facade. The hall is connected to a long residential block whose outer wall also forms the rampart wall. A two-storey building, the lower floor is vaulted throughout. The upper floor, at least, must have formed private appartments. One sees the two elements forming a coherent united structure.

Bricquebec (towards 1190) and Barneville (towards 1220) are probably the direct ancestors of the usual 13th-century dispositions, at least in England. The

A fireplace and sink in a kitchen set within a buttress at Orford. (Chris Gravett)

chamber block forms a right angle with the high end of the hall, and it is plausible that a second chamber was superimposed at the lower end. At Bricquebec the placing of the buildings is perhaps dictated by the line of the curtain wall but their disposition approaches more a right angle than a continued axis. The chamber entrance is found in the side wall and not in the gable wall (which is the case at Beaumont). Equally important is the placing of a very small chamber above the services. This construction makes a projection in the court and had a roof forming a right angle with that of the hall; it constituted one of the cross-wings, the earliest known. At Barneville the chamber block of the 13th century crossed the high end of the hall but was only accessed via an external stair. It is not known if a second chamber stood above the services at the lower end, as would become common.

Around the hall were satellite buildings. The kitchen contained at least one oven, probably with spits, tables for food preparation, shelves and hooks for storage and hanging utensils. At least one hearth was needed for large cauldrons for boiling ('seething') meat, a common form of cooking at the time. The hall of a castle was large enough to hold gatherings, and it was normal for kitchens to be a short way from the hall, whether in manor or fortress, so folk were probably used to barely warm food. Kitchens sited in the bailey would be of a suitable size to accommodate the amounts of cooked food required. Only in smaller donjons, where a limited clientele was to be catered for, might a kitchen be sited inside the tower itself. Thus Norwich has a kitchen oven added into the corner where a stairwell once stood. Castle Rising in Norfolk has a kitchen on a stone-vaulted floor at one end of the donjon, with what appears to be a pantry next door complete with cupboard areas formed in the stonework, all cut off by partition walls. The circular tower of Conisbrough in Yorkshire has a sink channel set in the wall on two floors, while perhaps the most perfect en suite facilities are to be found in Orford, the famous polygonal donjon built by Henry II in about 1165. Here the great buttress on one side is used to accommodate fireplaces (where the stone floor helps protect against fire) and sinks, though it has been suggested that one of these is a bath drain.

A few castles also boast the occasional urinal, a rare utility in a Norman donjon. Privies are much more common in donjons, set within mural chambers reached by a short passage or sometimes without one. They are sometimes formed in pairs, side by side or back to back either side of a wall section, and thus sometimes share a chute. Some are obviously designed for use by anyone in the main room, but others lead from a mural chamber and are obviously more private. Some were provided with a wooden door, probably more to block off odours than for privacy. Window openings in a privy might well have no shutter, the better to vent the room. The opening of a privy would be covered by a wooden seat, probably with a rectangular or keyhole aperture cut in it. The waste passed out through an opening on the outside of the wall face, some of these being quite elaborate: Castle Rising boasts tall arches covering the vents. If there was a convenient nearby river or moat the waste could fall into the water, but often it simply rolled down to the foot of the wall and would eventually (presumably) be removed by a gong fermer. Dover has a cess pit at the bottom of one wall with a small archway in a central buttress giving access; but the ordure still sat there until dealt with.

If the size of the castle warranted it, there might be a granary for grain and flour, probably set on short piles to guard against vermin. Otherwise dry food such as flour and bread would be kept in a pantry (the word deriving from the French word for bread, *pain*). The buttery (from the old French word *bouteul*, meaning bottle) held barrels of wine, beer and perhaps cider. Limited stocks of spirits, such as English mead or French brandy, might be held for the lord and his guests. Both these buildings would, from the late 12th century, be more frequently situated at the lower end of the hall, separated from it by the main entrance passage running across this end of the hall, the latter screened from the hall to shield against draughts.

In Normandy the 11th-century Exchequer at Caen with its gable door parallels Rufus's Westminster Hall in London. The door at Beaumont is not known but at Creully it is on the extreme south of the aisle. This allows the development of the screens passage across the end of the hall, perhaps the earliest being at Oakham castle hall in England. Bricquebec and Barneville each

The triangular urinal in the wall passage outside a mural chamber at Orford. (Chris Gravett)

have a service door, but the principal entrance has been lost. The service buildings included a kitchen with ovens and hearth. At Langueuil in Seine-Maritime are 12th-century remains of a domestic building within which was a kitchen and places for tables and stone sinks. However, at Vatteville-la-Rue (Seine-Maritime), two walls remain of a domestic building, on the ground floor of which was a kitchen, cellars, store and kitchen annex. Above was a residential floor, with a large window and a door, probably to latrines overlooking the ditch.

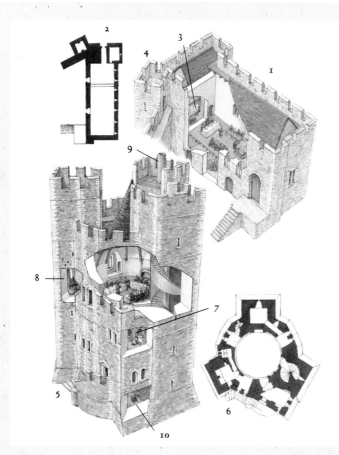

THE LIVING CASTLE: RICHMOND AND ORFORD

In many castles the main living area was a hall in the bailey, whether or not there was a donjon. Scolland's Hall in Richmond castle, North Yorkshire (1, also shown in ground-floor plan view, 2), was built in the late 11th century before the gate was transformed into a donjon in the mid-12th century. It is a first-floor hall set on an undercroft that led at its eastern end out into a barbican. On the first floor (reached by an external stone stair) this eastern end was divided off to form a withdrawing room or solar for the lord and his family (3). At the north corner was a small tower that contained the latrines (4). Cooking was carried out in a separate building outside. It was not until the 13th century that the hall was redesigned in the latest style by adding a kitchen flanked by pantry and buttery at the western end: the kitchen was reached by knocking the window through to form a doorway.

Orford in Suffolk (5), built by Henry II in about 1165, has a polygonal tower in the new experimental style. However, the large buttresses give it even squarer angles, as well as blind spots, while the numerous rooms set in the buttresses mean the walls are quite thin (see the entrance-level plan view, 6). This all suggests the tower was not designed primarily for defence. As a solar tower, however, it does contain all the conveniences for a king and his guests. There is a small chapel (7), a kitchen with fireplaces, a sink and drain on each of the two principal floors (8), garderobes, a urinal outside one of the mural chambers, and a bread oven in one of the roof turrets (9). A chamber below the entrance with a narrow entrance from above may be a prison rather than a store (10), due to the inconvenient entry. It has also been suggested that the dimensions of the building, like those of cathedrals, have symbolic meaning. (Adam Hook © Osprey Publishing)

The remains of the chapel of Saint-Symphorien, dating from the 11th or 12th century. The priory was situated within the enceinte of Domfront. (Chris Gravett)

In Italy the internal domestic arrangements of castles often include the central courtyard and sometimes a square fronting the entrance, a cistern for storing rainwater (more likely than a well), buildings for corn, oil or wine, and sometimes a chapel. Residential rooms seem to have followed the pattern of the lord on the first floor and the servants on the second floor. Underground or overhead walkways frequently connected buildings, such as that between the palace and the chapel at San Gennaro at Lucito.

Other buildings in the Norman castle might include a brewery for producing beer (in Italy and Sicily a wine press), a bakehouse for making large quantities of bread, not to mention dovecotes to provide pigeons for the table. There would also be grain silos, barns, stables and animal pens. Many of these buildings would be timber-framed with wattle and daub infills, and some might be of lean-to form. Barns contained fodder for animals, as well as farm equipment such as ploughs or harrows, for working the demesne in the nearby fields. They would also contain carts, in some royal or large castles quite a number, not just agricultural wagons but also the numerous vehicles required to carry all the equipment if the king or lord went on campaign or on a long journey. Stables were essential: not only were there knightly warhorses, but riding horses of varying quality, from good palfreys for the lord, lady and knights, to hacks for squires and perhaps mounted sergeants. Packhorses and carthorses were also needed. In some cases mules were used instead for riding, or as pack or draught animals, or oxen might be used to pull carts. All of these beasts of burden needed accommodation and food. Some lords might have kennels for a pack of hunting dogs, since hunting was almost an obsession with many Normans, not least the royal court circle. A large castle might even have a mews for keeping hunting birds.

Together with the housing for animals and equipment, there were the various workshops necessary for keeping a castle in working order. A carpenter's shop was essential since so much of even a stone castle was made from wood; the roof beams, flooring, doors and draw-bars, window shutters, some roof shingles, toilet covers, tables, benches, stools and chairs, shelves, cupboards, chests, beds, perhaps even shields and weapon staves, not to mention those domestic buildings constructed from wood. Together with this work went that of the blacksmith: he provided nails for everything, as well as hinges, door handles and bolts, iron implements of all sorts, plough shares, etc. In many castles he may have turned his hand to repairing or making simpler pieces of armour, but this was more the job of the professional armourer or mail maker, who might also produce, repair or sharpen weapons. Smiths would need a furnace, bellows, anvil and water trough or bucket for quenching. Their workshops would need to have either shuttered windows or none at all, to allow them to judge by colour when to remove metal from the fire.

All castles would require a chapel, if not in the donjon itself then a separate building in the bailey. It might be anything from small and fairly plain to attractively decorated and impressive. The personnel varied according to the size of the structure and the importance of the holder. Some chapels were incorporated into the donjon itself. Others were free-standing within the bailey, such as at Crèvecoeur-en-Auge. Some were set in the forebuilding, on the top floor or, in the case of Newcastle upon Tyne, its basement. Rochester is slightly unusual in having two chapels, one in the forebuilding and another on the top floor; however this was a bishop's castle. Orford's chapel is within a buttress and is small, plain and dignified, with the remains of a stone altar. The chapel at the Tower of London, though still exerting a quiet aura, has altered the

The 11th–12th-century chapel at the castle of Crèvecoeur-en-Auge, with the bridge to the inner courtyard on the right. (Chris Gravett)

south-east corner to include its apsidal end. The Chapel of St John has an arcade of pillars (as do several others such as the one in Durham castle) supporting a barrel vault, and a gallery running around it. In the forebuilding at Dover the main chapel has a private entrance from the royal suite so the monarch could enter without passing through the main rooms. There also appears to be a lower chapel. Perhaps the most famous surviving English chapel is the delightful, circular 12th-century example at Ludlow in Shropshire: internally the walls are decorated with blind arcading.

At Condé-sur-Huisne in the canton of Rémalard, the castle has a chapel 9m × 7m (29ft 6in × 22ft 11in) in area, connected to a large room 15m × 9m (49ft 2in × 29ft 6in) via a door in the north-east wall. This room also gave access to a partly subterranean crypt, with four groined vaults radiating from a central pillar, holding up the main chapel above. This crypt may have been used

The interior of the circular, free-standing chapel at Ludlow castle, Shropshire, probably built in the mid-12th century. (Chris Gravett)

as a second chapel. At Gisors Henry II built the chapel of St Thomas next to the shell wall on the motte.

A priest had an important role in a castle. Since the whole community was Catholic, religious services were attended, despite the behaviour of those such as Henry II, who might be found stitching a glove while a sermon was read. However, if a man was seriously wounded, or simply old or dying of disease, a priest was needed to confess and shrive him before his end. In some castles a priest or his clerks might be the only people able to read, and this was a necessary skill if messages arrived from the duke or king. Such men might also teach young pages or squires reading skills. Though many would probably never lift a pen, it may be worth remembering Orderic's record of conversations about scripture he held with young knights in the cloisters of his monastery at Saint-Évroul. Not all knights were ignorant.

The size of population living in a castle varied greatly. Royal castles might only see the king occasionally and therefore be run on a skeleton staff. Some lords of modest means simply could not afford a large staff. The lord had to maintain the fabric, to make sure the garrison was at its correct strength and that those liable to perform service did so at the required time and for the required period. Noble youths sent from the households of other lords were under his tutelage and were assigned to knights for training as pages or squires. He and his lady also toured the estates held by them, to check with their stewards on the produce being farmed. The lady of the castle also usually oversaw the domestic routine of the castle, including the daily menu and the ordering of supplies. It was routinely her task to oversee the reception and

The building in the inner courtyard at Crèvecoeur-en-Auge may contain a foundation of Romanesque masonry. (Chris Gravett)

entertainment of guests. A lady might well have a number of ladies-in-waiting, themselves sometimes the wives or sisters of knights, and families were often quite large, with numerous sons and daughters. Babies required wet nurses or ordinary nurses to look after them. The lady was ultimately responsible for the training of girls from noble households who were learning to be ladies. She nominally ran the castle if her lord was absent, or indeed if she were a widow. This might well include supervising its defence during a siege.

Other people might live in a castle, and their numbers varied depending on the size and importance of the fortress. A seneschal or a steward might look after the household, taking orders directly from the lord or lady. A marshal might see to the defences and the training and equipment for the soldiers. He also had responsibility for the horses, for buying or selling as necessary, and to direct the grooms who tended the beasts. Servants were necessary to tend the daily needs of the richer members of the castle community. Washerwomen and serving girls would also be seen. For the lord's pleasure falconers took care of his birds and dog-keepers cared for the hunting dogs sometimes housed in kennels within a castle. Such people might well travel with the lord as he moved about the country. A butler might be employed to run the kitchens and would be responsible for supplies of wine and beer. At least one cook was needed, with kitchen servants to assist and servers to take the dishes to the tables. In royal castles entertainment might be lavish: King John ordered ovens to be built at Marlborough and Ludgershall large enough to take two or three oxen. Castles were also places for celebrations. Indeed, it appears that the donjon at Hedingham in Essex was designed largely to mark the elevation of John de Vere to the earldom of Oxford.

Castle Rising, Norfolk, was built by William de Albini in the late 1130s, based on Norwich. The forebuilding has stately decoration. (Chris Gravett)

Kings and great lords held a number of castles and were in any case often on the road, overseeing royal or feudal justice, attending courts, meeting with peers or vassals, visiting estates or towns, or travelling with an army. In Britain, when such men were absent (and some fortresses might rarely see their lords) a castle was held by a representative, the constable or castellan, who basically carried out his master's duties for him. Crucially, if the castle was liable to be attacked he must know what his master's intention would be, and if not, then find out. It would not do to surrender to an enemy if his lord had expressly forbidden it.

In early Normandy (at least before about 1035) the dukes were aware of the dangers of losing control of castles and were careful to place *comtes* and *vicomtes*

The impressive entrance stairs to first-floor level within the forebuilding at Castle Rising. (Chris Gravett)

in charge of them. William the Bastard tended to choose family members as a safeguard against treachery, but this did not always work, as the revolt of his uncle, Count William of Arques, in 1052–53 bears out. Henry I placed his own household knights in his castles under chosen leaders to protect the surrounding areas against raiders, as at the castle at Conches in 1135. Rarely was a castle held by anyone else, except occasionally by one of the higher magnates, and these tended to be situated in areas probably less under ducal control, such as Laigle, or Échauffour. Indeed, one result of the accession of the young William the Bastard had been the revolt of western *vicomtes* who held important castles. Such men, together with certain magnates, took the

Scarborough, Yorkshire; the castle walls and tower were built between 1127 and 1177. The donjon, shown here, dates from between 1157 and 1169, though. (Chris Gravett)

opportunity to build castles, until William regained control at the battle of Val-ès-Dunes in 1047. Orderic implies that Henry I used paid troops, especially in frontier areas of the duchy.

The most important contingent of a castle's inhabitants was its fighting men. In Britain, the knights and serjeants who formed its garrison were, in the years immediately following the Conquest, often household men brought in with the lord who lived in the castle and were ready for instant action. Increasingly, as the country settled down, knights were given portions of land to settle and in return performed service. At the time of King Stephen this seems to be have been two months per year in time of war and usually 40 days in time of peace. This latter service could be basically broken down into two parts, castle guard and escort duty. Castle guard was performed at one or more of a lord's castles. Thus castles were defended by a rota of a lord's men, serving as garrison soldiers. This service, useful after the Conquest, meant that large numbers of men were called up for duty when not really needed in time of peace, and it became more difficult to enforce castle-guard service. From the time of Henry II lords began to bargain with tenants to enable them to commute the service for money, as much as the lord could squeeze from them, though usually not enough to hire a substitute. With this he could employ smaller garrisons of mercenaries, topped up by feudal troops in time of war. Gradually it became more difficult to enforce such service, which fell into decay when feudalism itself declined. King John was notorious for employing large numbers of foreign crossbowmen, something that helped alienate the weapon in England. In time of war the size of a garrison might alter as feudal fee holders were called in to reinforce a garrison or to form part of a larger body of men using the castle as a barracks whilst awaiting orders to move out on campaign. Equally castles in Marcher areas needed men to be ready for action.

In pre-Conquest Normandy feudal obligations were far less clearly developed than they would become in England after 1066. It is difficult to know exactly how early castles were garrisoned in Normandy. It may be that many had a number of household knights that lived with their lord and were ready at a moment's notice, similar to post-Conquest England. Also in Normandy the existence of allodial land meant these private family estates owed no service.

A similar system was employed in southern Italy and Sicily, the knights usually being present in multiples of five or ten. Not surprisingly, the early settlers brought the feudal customs of their homeland with them, until they had settled down in their new country. In about 1040 the Byzantine *theme* (provincial) armies of southern Italy were disbanded and defence was left to local urban militias (mostly Greek though some were Lombard), some of whom then went over to the Normans after their arrival. A similar reliance on urban militias was prevalent in Lombard areas, such as Capua and Benevento, while in the countryside garrisons were formed by the stronghold's owner. Some cities such as Naples had wealthy citizens who would be made knights under the Normans. Certain cities put up such an impressive defensive show that the Normans allowed the citizens to continue to man their fortresses or gates. In Sicily the existing Muslim *iqta* was a form of fief that probably provided the model for smaller Sicilian feudal fees. In western Sicily the *jund* system of recruiting regional militias was continued under the Norman conquerors. On the island Lombard, Greek or Muslim villeins were expected to perform garrison service, since theoretically the Normans could summon all able-bodied men in southern Italy. Local militias gradually declined, though, especially in well-organized areas such as Sicily and Calabria. In Sicily a landed Muslim

Bungay in Suffolk once boasted a large donjon, but following the siege of 1174 a mine was driven under one corner to destroy it, though the threat was never carried. This may be the entrance to the mine. (Chris Gravett)

aristocracy survived until the 13th century, holding on to a number of smaller castles, and provided both horse and foot throughout the period. Elsewhere the Normans gave paid employment to Muslims, and in return offered religious toleration. Muslim archers were valued for their rate of fire as well as for their agility. Equally the Muslims would provide skilled siege engineers for the reduction of obstinate fortresses or towns. Mercenaries were generally employed in all Norman areas, sometimes as part of a garrison; such men seem to have included Muslims and Lombards.

In time of war, if a castle was besieged, it was the garrison's duty to bear the brunt of the fighting. However, all hands might be called upon to assist in its defence, even if it only meant hurling stones from the battlements or helping tip a pan of boiling water over the heads of attackers. If the walls were breached, the enemy would think little of butchering anyone they found inside, and would delight in raping women or girls. Thus a spirited defence was advisable.

Castles were, of course, centres for controlling the surrounding area. Since armoured knights could comfortably ride out perhaps 16km (10 miles) or more and back in a day, each castle effectively controlled the area within a radius of at least that distance. In times of unrest castles could become a real liability. If their holders defied royal authority the troops within could become a menace to the surrounding area.

The notion of the robber baron, seizing innocent victims to torture in his dungeons to reveal their wealth, is rather overdone. No doubt it did happen on

The donjon and walls of Carrickfergus, Antrim, were built in the late 12th century. (Topfoto/ Woodmansterne)

occasion, and no doubt a castle was sometimes viewed by those outside with suspicion, but it was still a part of the scene. It was not simply an imposing set of barracks for housing men. Often a lord would use the most important of his fortresses, the 'chief' of his honor, as the centre for his court and, following from that, the centre for the administration of his estates. If a nobleman had been appointed high sheriff of a county, the castle within the main town was usually the seat of his power.

Together with administration came the dispensation of justice. In Britain by the time of Richard I judges were sent round the country to hear cases and represent the king. For a lord in his castle justice meant hearing complaints in the manorial court, but it was also the scene for feudal courts to deal with matters of honorial dispute between vassals or tenants. A castle was a convenient place to hold suspects, perhaps those caught poaching deer, but they were not generally designed for use as prisons, and men were held until a hearing was arranged, when the king, sheriff, judge or lord, depending on the case, was in the area. Once a case had been heard, a person found guilty was punished by fine, mutilation or execution. Usually only in church courts was imprisonment imposed as a punishment, though those captured in battle, either awaiting ransom or royal justice, would usually be penned up.

The Castles at War

Britain

Numerous Norman castles were besieged in Britain in the period from the Conquest to the death of King John. Some sieges were very swift, lasting but a few days. Others, mainly those of important strongholds, dragged on for two or three months. There were several periods when siege warfare was marked in England. The first was during the turbulent period directly after the Norman Conquest, but much of this was against towns and cities held largely by Anglo-Danish inhabitants, such as Exeter which was taken when William drove a mine under the walls, or York which he visited three times in three years. Their defences comprised surviving Roman and Saxon works, and fall outside the scope of this book. The second period was during the civil wars of Stephen's reign. A number of these sieges were also against towns, or against earth and timber castles. In 1173–74 came the determined attack from Scotland on the north of England, resulting in numerous sieges. Finally, civil war broke out in 1215 against King John, only ending with his death the following year. This last period saw the greatest set-piece sieges of the time.

During the civil wars of Stephen's reign, the king learned that the Empress Matilda had taken refuge in Oxford castle. The royalist troops arrived on the banks of the River Thames in September 1142 to find the Angevin garrison on the other side manning the battlements and shooting arrows at them across the

The small, rather bleak tower at Clun, probably erected in the mid-12th century, sits within earthworks in the heart of the Welsh Marches. (Chris Gravett)

river. Wasting no time, Stephen moved to a fording place in the river that nevertheless required swimming, and plunged in to lead his men across. Angevin soldiers outside the gates were pushed back as the royalist troops surged forward. They forced the gates of the city and charged in, torching the houses and setting fire to the city. Then, arriving in front of the castle, they settled down to a siege. Matilda was trapped.

Oxford castle was considered a tough nut to crack. It comprises an oval enclosure, ditched and banked, beside the river. This was originally topped with stone curtain walls rather than palisades. On the far side stands a motte: it was partly cased in clay to prevent slippage, and topped with two decagonal shell walls, some 17.6m (58ft) and 6.7m (22ft) in diameter. Simple square towers were set along the curtain, one of which, the stepped St George's Tower, may be the 'very tall tower' mentioned in the *Gesta Stephani*. It is built of coursed limestone rubble with a diagonally set stair turret.

The donjon at Newcastle upon Tyne was probably built between 1168 and 1178. The battlements have been rebuilt. The chapel is housed in the lower part of the forebuilding. (Chris Gravett)

Stephen built a siege-work to the north of the castle, and settled down to wait for the defenders to starve. He posted sentries all around to prevent escape, and then brought up siege engines, more to lower morale than to effect a breach. Brian FitzCount organized a force at Wallingford to try and rescue the empress, but refused to attack the royalist siege lines. Robert of Gloucester threatened Wareham, allowing the commander to send a message to Stephen that he would surrender if the king did not come to their aid within a certain time. He hoped this would draw Stephen away from Oxford, but Stephen obstinately refused to leave. Meanwhile Wareham surrendered and Robert went on to capture Portland and Lulworth castles.

Just before Christmas, one of the most famous incidents in siege warfare occurred. Supplies were running low in Oxford castle, and the Angevins inside were getting desperate. It was cold: deep snow covered the ground and the Thames was now frozen over. One night Matilda, covered in a white sheet for camouflage, succeeded in slipping out of the castle and away. She may have shinned down a rope or simply crept out of a postern gate, the latter being the more likely suggestion of William of Malmesbury. The sentries were evidently not asleep, for we are told there were trumpet calls and shouts, but nobody spotted her as she crossed the ice with three or four knights to escort her, and made her escape to Abingdon. At Oxford the garrison now surrendered and were treated honourably by the king. It is interesting to note that Oxford castle, considered strong enough with its walls and towers, was not even assaulted by Stephen, who was content to endure a long siege to starve out his prey, even though the winter conditions would be horrible for his own men. There was no large donjon to intimidate the besiegers with a show of impregnability, and St George's Tower, while strong, is not an especially large building by comparison to others.

Interesting details of siege warfare against castles with stone defences and donjons emerge during the Scottish invasion of England in 1173–74. King William of Scotland came south to claim back Northumbria with a powerful army that included many Flemish mercenaries, and in so doing laid siege to a number of castles in the north of England. In 1174 his troops spent three months besieging the strong fortress of Carlisle in Cumbria. The castle is triangular in shape, with a donjon in the inner bailey in the eastern corner and a large outer bailey. The donjon was erected by about 1175 and the Scots threatened to throw the castellan, Robert de Vaux, from the top of the tower if they captured him. Carlisle did not fall, and when the Scots tried to bribe de Vaux instead with gold and silver, he replied that the garrison was loyal to him and that they had plenty of wheat and wine. In the event the besiegers finally withdrew on hearing of the capture of King William at Alnwick in Northumberland. Before this, while some of his troops were at Carlisle, William himself had marched on Appleby-in-Westmorland, a modest castle with a small donjon and which, the chronicler Jordan Fantosme states, was

The small donjon at Appleby in Cumbria was probably erected in the third quarter of the 12th century. The battlements appear to have been raised a little at a later date. (Chris Gravett)

undefended and offered no resistance at all. Its elderly constable was later fined a hefty 500 marks by Henry II for his dismal performance. The Scots then occupied the donjon in high spirits.

The Scottish army then attacked Brough castle in Cumbria, which was defended by six knights. Brough was basically an enclosure defended by walls erected in about 1100, with a square donjon at one end, against which the curtain terminated. The Scots laid siege to the castle on all sides and, after a hard fight, they managed to take possession of the outer walls the same day. The defenders pulled back and sought refuge in the tower. Temporarily foiled, the Scots brought up combustibles and set fire to the tower. This would suggest it was made of wood, but the foundations of that tower survive, showing it was of stone, built on the remains of Roman barracks, with a huge foundation of herringbone masonry. As the fire and smoke took hold, the garrison surrendered, and all appeared to be over. However, as Jordan relates, a newly arrived knight would have none of it. Remaining in the donjon he took two shields, climbed to the roof and hung them over the battlements. He threw three javelins down on the Scots, killing a man with each. Then he seized sharp stakes and hurled them, shouting 'You shall all be vanquished!' Once the shields had been consumed by fire, he decided he had done enough and surrendered. Jordan relates that 'the better part of the tower' was overthrown, suggesting that after the siege the Flemish soldiers assisted in its demise with pickaxes. Once again a donjon had revealed its weakness. The respite for the hard-pressed garrison had been only temporary. The enemy had not gone away but continued with their efforts to take the whole castle, successfully in this case. Only from the battlements could the defenders fight back. Nevertheless, in the late 12th or early 13th century a second stone tower was erected on the foundations of the first at Brough, set on a raft of timbers, which survives to this day. Clearly it was felt that these donjons were still worth erecting.

After a blooding while attempting to seize the motte and bailey at Wark, the Scots moved on to Prudhoe. This was a walled enclosure with a square stone gatehouse, and a small donjon at one end, complete with forebuilding. Its lord, Odinel, rode out on hearing of King William's demand for surrender, leaving a determined garrison while he reluctantly went off in search of additional troops. When the Scots arrived they tried to assault the outer walls but the garrison stood its ground and beat off all attempts. The besiegers nonetheless did much damage to the surrounding land and gardens, destroying crops. Finally, King William decided to withdraw from the siege, and the castle was never taken. However, in a reversal of political fortune, Prudhoe surrendered to King John in 1212.

The siege of Rochester in 1215 is one of the great set-piece sieges of a donjon in Britain. King John had encountered problems concerning who should hold the castle, namely the Archbishop of Canterbury or a constable. After John's agreement to and, soon afterwards, repudiation of Magna Carta in June 1215, Rochester was restored to Archbishop Stephen Langton, but in August letters patent transferred it to a friend of the king, Peter des Roches, Archbishop of Winchester. At the end of September a group of rebels entered the castle and said they were holding it with the consent of its constable, Reginald de Cornhill. This move helped block the route to London, where the rebels had their headquarters, since John was at Dover. The rebel leader, William de Albini, realized that the castle was low on supplies and did his best to provision it. The garrison appears to have consisted of sergeants, crossbowmen and others, a total of between 95 and 140 men.

Unfortunately for William, John wasted no time in confronting him. The king had been busy recruiting mercenaries, but already it seems some of his troops had arrived at Rochester from the direction of Malling. The royalists massed on the banks of the River Medway and the bridge over it was broken down to stop any

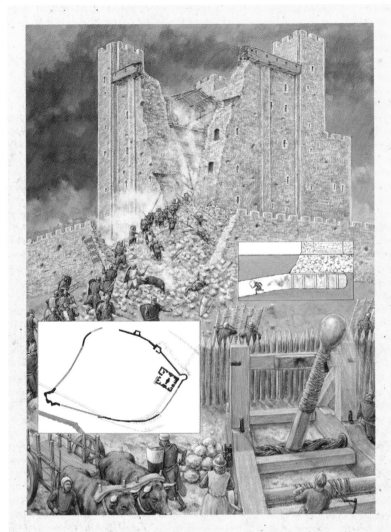

THE SIEGE OF ROCHESTER,
LATE 1215
King John besieged the rebels in
Rochester on 11 October 1215.
His assault began by breaching the
curtain wall (see inset plan view),
probably by means of a mine though
one chronicler says catapults were
used (a torsion catapult can be seen
in the lower right of the illustration).
However, the great donjon was
impervious to such missiles and the
sappers set to work to undermine
the corner. When work was done,
the props in the tunnel were set
alight (see inset); pig's fat was used
for fuel. Having burned through,
the mine collapsed and brought
the entire corner section down. The
main illustration shows royalist
troops surging forward, as the
defenders withdraw behind the
cross-wall of the donjon. Here they
continued to resist, until starvation
forced them to surrender. Note the
timber hoardings on the battlements
and the large forebuilding on the
right-hand side of the castle,
guarding the entrance.
(Adam Hook © Osprey Publishing)

advance by relief forces from London. Ralph of Coggeshall says the first royalist attack on the bridge was beaten off but the king's men persisted and on 11 October managed to enter the city itself in a surprise attack. The castle was now put under siege, and John himself now appeared on Monday, 13 October.

The king probably set up his camp on Boley Hill, and lost no time in erecting five catapults to harass the defenders. The bombardment became a relentless pounding both day and night, backed up by missiles from archers and crossbowmen, one contingent relieving another to keep up the pressure. Those inside reciprocated with vigour, their crossbowmen inflicting a number of casualties. At one point (according to a possibly apocryphal report) a crossbowman noticed that King John, busily inspecting the castle for weak spots, had come within range, and asked William de Albini for permission to shoot. The reply came that it was not up to ordinary people to kill God's anointed, and John passed unscathed. The limited time that the rebels had enjoyed to prepare for the siege began to be felt, as provisions ran dangerously low; men resorted to eating horseflesh, even their precious war horses, and drank water, both of which activities, we are told, were quite alien to men of rank. Roger of Wendover says that the catapults actually achieved very little, apart from being a nuisance, but the Barnwell chronicler recounts that the engines finally breached the walls of the bailey. However, Wendover attributes this to the work of miners, who dug a tunnel under the walls and brought down a section of the defences. A writ dated 14 October demands that the reeve of Canterbury oversee the manufacture of as many picks as possible, to be sent speedily to the king. A possible mining trench has been discovered north of the most northerly of the two mural towers on the east side of the castle.

On 26 October rebel leaders in London approached with a relief force of 700 cavalry but changed their minds on reaching Dartford, probably because John was marching to meet them and, says the Barnwell chronicler, they lacked foot soldiers. As the bailey wall was breached, the rebels inside the castle retired into the massive bulk of the donjon. It was safe from catapults but not safe from the king. John now ordered a mine to be dug under the south-east corner, the only option left to him – short of starvation – that might result in the castle's capture. On 25 November he despatched a writ to his justiciar, Hubert de Burgh, with instructions 'to send to us with all speed by day and night forty of the fattest pigs of the sort least good for eating to bring fire beneath the tower'.

Launceston in Cornwall has a motte (slightly distorted through later modification) on which lies a 12th-century shell keep with wing walls. The circular tower inside was added in the 13th century. (Chris Gravett)

The great round tower at Pembroke was built in about 1200. (Chris Gravett)

With the mine dug and shored up with wooden props, and wood piled below the stone seating, the whole was smeared with pig fat and set alight. As the fire increased and the props burned away, the gaping hole left by the miners below the angle took its toll. With nothing to hold it up, the corner cracked and collapsed, exposing the inside of the donjon itself.

Yet the defenders still defied the king, now withdrawing behind the cross-wall to continue their resistance. Although the attackers could command the south-west of the two main rooms, their only access through the cross-wall on the ground and first floor was via two narrow doorways, easily defended and probably barred. Presumably the defenders did not attempt to hold the principal floor above, since here the cross-wall was represented by arches. Moreover, the corner stairwell was now in the hands of the royalists, who could use the gallery running round the principal level. Here too they could access the stair in the opposite corner and descend to emerge into the room held by the rebels. We do not know if this was tried, whether any struggles took place as John's men attempted to force a way from the stair doorways. What is known is that the garrison was not beaten by direct assault, but by failing supplies of food and water.

Still hopeful of a relief force, the rebels refused to lose heart. The first casualties were those of least value, pushed out to be seized by the royalists,

213

who it is said cut off the hands and feet of many. Soon, inevitably, the rest were captured, and the castle passed into John's hands on 30 November. John, in a fury, was all for hanging every one of the nobles taken, and since the castle was taken by force he was quite within his right to do so. However, Savaric de Mauléon, a royalist captain, managed to sway him from this course of action, since, he pointed out, it would cause retaliations against royalist garrisons in the same position and cause them to surrender to avoid a similar fate. In the event, John hanged only a crossbowman turned traitor whom he had taken care of since boyhood, while most of the men of rank were packed off to Corfe and other royal castles for safekeeping. John left with much of his army but on 8 December sent a writ from Malling ordering money for his half-brother, William Longespée, Earl of Salisbury, so that he might leave Rochester with suitable honor. The damaged donjon was still considered important and was rebuilt with a rounded corner in Poitevin style, which remains to this day.

The siege shows the strengths and weaknesses of the donjon. Once the bailey wall had been breached, the defenders, faced with a powerful royalist army, had no option but to take refuge in the great tower, but here they could do little to fight back. Though very difficult to damage significantly with missiles, the donjon was, like any castle wall, vulnerable to the deadly mine. Whether the defenders could have held out beyond the cross-wall if provisions had been sufficient is debatable. The siege was the greatest to date in England: the Barnwell chronicler makes the telling comment that 'after it few cared to put their trust in castles'. An interesting footnote is that the following year Prince Louis of France, the new rebel leader, arrived before Rochester and took the castle: unfortunately no details of how this was done have survived. At Easter 1264 the castle was again attacked

The interior of the donjon at Rochester of c. 1130, showing the arcaded spine wall on the left incorporating the well shaft with its access doorway. (Chris Gravett)

and again the defenders (royalists of Henry III this time) withdrew into the donjon. Various reports mention a mine and bombardment but the tower was never taken because the siege was raised in two weeks.

Not long after Prince Louis attacked Rochester he launched a major assault against another tough castle, this time at Dover. Having landed in Thanet, Kent, in May, Louis had caught John by surprise, and the king just had time to provision Dover and place the justiciar, Hubert de Burgh, inside it, supported by 140 knights, while he rode for Winchester. In the autumn Louis settled himself in Dover Priory to direct the siege, setting his camp north-east of the castle itself. The French saw that the castle lay below the crest of the hill, and resolved to use it to their advantage. They fixed their efforts on the main northern outer gate, newly built by John. In front was a ditched outwork or barbican, but its walls were of timber, presumably a late attempt by the royalists to defend the gate. Amongst other engines placed in the besiegers' camp was a great *petrarie*, or stone-thrower (probably a counterweight trebuchet), nicknamed *Malvoisin* ('Bad Neighbour'), which pounded the walls. A huge siege tower or belfry was begun, protected by hurdles and with a covered bridge to stretch on to the battlements of the wall tops. Meanwhile miners quietly began to undermine the outwork. During this time the energetic garrison made several sorties to damage engines or kill enemy troops. However, the French miners did their work: the outwork was undermined and a charge by the French captured it, the garrison withdrawing behind the main walls. Now Louis's miners got to work once more, digging another mine below the gate itself, aiming it at the eastern of the two towers flanking the passage. Several surviving short tunnels begun within the castle suggest that these are countermines dug in the vain hope of breaking into the enemy tunnel, and that either Hubert guessed that a second mine was approaching or Louis made no attempt to hide the entrance, hoping to break the morale of the defenders with this most dangerous of siege weapons.

The mine was successful, and the tower was brought down. However, all did not go as hoped for the rebels. Hubert and his men offered desperate resistance against the incursion of the rebel soldiers. His audacity paid off: perhaps the narrowness of the breach also worked in his favour, for the French were driven back and forced to quit it. Hubert then managed to block the breach with solid timber baulks and crossbeams, and the gate was never taken. The garrison made temporary repairs to the walls, while Louis found his supply trains being attacked by guerrillas from the Weald. A truce was called in the autumn, to allow fresh orders to be received from the king, but in October John died at Newark castle, to be succeeded by his infant son, Henry III. With the truce extended, Hubert marched out. Louis passed Dover by sea the following April, to see his camp burned by the men from the Weald. He returned the following May to resume the siege, needing to protect his supply route. He now had little alternative but to use a direct assault to bring about a swift conclusion, but the French were defeated at Lincoln three days later and the war was effectively over. Louis withdrew to France, and Dover remained bloodied but unbowed. The present Norfolk Towers were built over the damaged gate, which was permanently blocked up, but evidence of the damaged original gate remains concealed behind. Hubert's spirited resistance shows that, despite a three-line defence, he did not retire to the inner bailey and certainly not the donjon, preferring to present an aggressive front even in what might appear a hopeless

BELOW LEFT
The circular tower at Skenfrith, Gwent, dates to the early 13th century. (Chris Gravett)

BELOW RIGHT
Tretower is a small circular tower erected between 1174 and 1220. (Chris Gravett)

defensive position on the outer wall. The new concentric style of defence now beginning to make its appearance had not prevented a near disaster, unless firepower from the inner walls contributed to the discomfiture of the rebel attack. His defence also reveals that the outwork protecting the gate could not stop a determined foe. Events also swayed the siege. If the French had not been beaten in battle, would an assault on Dover have worked? We shall never know.

Roger Bigod II, the man who rebuilt Framlingham castle, refused to support King John and, not surprisingly, he found himself under siege there in 1216 by royal foreign mercenaries. Inside the walls were 26 knights, 20 sergeants and seven crossbowmen, plus a chaplain and three other persons. Despite its powerful towers that cut off sections of wall, its loopholes and shuttered battlements, the castle surrendered after two days. So again a major factor in the holding of a castle was the quality of the defenders. Some were tough and bloody-minded men, but the commander's word was final. On rare occasions, his word was not enough: at Bridgnorth, in 1102, the mercenaries in the garrison had to be locked up because they refused to agree to the surrender terms that the rest of the garrison were willing to accept from Henry I. Another factor was the size of a garrison. Strong walls with cunningly conceived loopholes are of little benefit if there are only seven crossbowmen to man them; and crossbows had a relatively slow rate of fire, though not as slow as later when mechanical winders became common to draw back more powerful bows. Seven men could not hope to stop an assault pressed with determination. A castle may hold off a larger force with ladders, since only one attacker can reach the wall top at a time, but a lack of archers can be fatal.

One factor that emerges from a number of sieges, both great and small, during the Norman/Angevin period, is that few castles could stand up to a prolonged siege when the king himself was determined to capture them. Even a great castle such as Rochester could not easily withstand John when the full might of royal power was brought to bear, despite members of the baronage being in revolt. Similarly a donjon was not necessarily a deterrent.

Normandy

Given the turbulent history of the duchy of Normandy, it is not surprising that castles figure prominently in the struggles between the dukes and their subjects, and arising from external threats, notably from the counts of Anjou and the French kings. One of the periods of siege warfare that was to test the quality of early castles occurred after the death of Robert the Magnificent in 1035, during the first years of the rule of Duke William the Bastard, when a number of powerful nobles opposed him and set off the struggle for power that would only end when William had effectively neutralized all potential rivals. Many unauthorized castles were built, no doubt often earth and timber structures. The first milestone in his success came, with major assistance from the king of France, at the battle of Val-ès-Dunes in 1047, which effectively broke the power of the western rebels. However, William was still not fully secure, and a number of sieges were required before he would have effective control of the duchy. Despite the persistence of several rebels, his position was now so much improved that he was able to demolish all unlicensed castles. He could now demand that no castle be erected without a licence, and expect baronial fortresses to be opened to him when required, a situation that endured for the rest of his reign.

Following the rebels' defeat, one of William's chief rivals, Guy of Burgundy, had withdrawn to his citadel of Brionne, where he continued to defy the new duke. William must have surveyed the deep ditches and ramparts of the castle, which, says his panegyrist William of Poitiers, had a stone hall that served as a donjon. William decided he was not going to risk losing men in a costly assault, but equally was not going to have his whole army tied down in one area. He ordered siege castles to be built on both sides of the River Risle, extensive earthworks within which stood wooden towers. In these defences he placed his troops, protected, as William of Poitiers notes, from sorties by the garrison. Having thus pinned down the rebel garrison he left his men to watch Brionne, and withdrew with the rest of his troops. Even so, Guy held out obstinately, his men making daily forays, and it was not until late 1049 or early 1050 that Brionne finally surrendered.

William was faced with a further threat in late summer or early autumn of 1051, when Count Geoffrey of Anjou invaded the duchy and seized Domfront and Alençon in a bid to expand his power. William reacted by marching towards Domfront and then beat off Geoffrey who had confronted him. With the count sent packing back to Anjou, William built four siege castles in front of Domfront and paused. However, with no external threat now imminent, he led part of his force away one night and rode fast to reach Alençon by morning. Then, possibly insulted by the garrison's reference to the hides hanging over the ramparts and to William as the son of a tanner (his mother's family), he launched a violent assault on the town and made a breach. He then ordered retribution, the public severing of the hands and feet of those he captured. Perhaps not surprisingly, the remaining defenders wasted little time in negotiating a surrender. By the time William returned to Domfront the news had reached the garrison and they hurriedly made peace.

In the summer of 1052 Count William of Arques tried his luck and broke out in rebellion. Duke William was in the Cotentin and galloped towards the castle with a small body of men. On the way he picked up more troops from Rouen, who had tried without success to prevent Arques from being provisioned. On arriving at the castle the garrison attacked his own force but were pushed back and driven inside again. With the gates closed, the castle on its ridge presented too great an obstacle to be taken by storm, and so William resolved to build a wooden siege castle and filled this tower with men under Walter Giffard to watch the castle. William then set out to block any attempt to relieve the rebel garrison. In this his plan proved wise, for the French king, now his enemy, pushed up towards Arques, only to be ambushed by some of William's men. Despite this he managed to ferry some men and supplies in before being forced to withdraw: the count was left to starve slowly inside the walls. Late in 1053 he surrendered on condition his men could leave unharmed.

FIRE-ARROWS AT BRIONNE, 1092

In 1092 a besieging force under Robert, Duke of Normandy, came to Brionne. The castle was apparently not the one that now stands on the ridge, but the earlier fortress built in the valley. When dealing with the previous siege of 1047 by Duke William, the chronicler William of Poitiers notes that Brionne possessed a stone hall, or *aula lapidea*, which served the defenders as an *arx*, or donjon, in time of trouble. This leads us to suppose that most of the buildings inside the bailey were of wood. Robert ordered the construction of a forge, and then had his archers heat arrowheads in it. The archers then aimed at the dry wooden shingles of the roof. Usually an incendiary-arrow was made by wrapping some form of cloth or tow around the shaft and setting light to it, the tell-tale smoke trails marking the progress of the missile. Now, however, the heated heads left no trail and, once lodged within the wood, they set fire to it. The defenders realized too late, and the flames took hold. Orderic was obviously impressed by this shrewd use of incendiary materials, calling it 'ingenious', which may indicate that the outer defences were also of stone, as shown here. It is also possible that they consisted of wooden palisades covered by raw or wet hides, or clay, or were plastered, since there is no reference to fire being brought to them.

(Adam Hook © Osprey Publishing)

219

The three sieges by William give an interesting insight into his methods. He was cautious in assaulting a powerfully sited castle with (at least in the cases of Brionne and Arques and probably at Domfront) some stone defences. Nevertheless he was swift to seize the opportunity for a surprise move, as at Alençon. His vigorous investment of the city may, if the stories are true, have been the result of loss of temper at insults aired, but he may have decided that the defences could be breached, and the story of the hides may possibly have been invented to cover up a sudden fit of blood lust, for hides were used as a protection against fire. Whatever the truth, William quickly learned from the reactions of the men at Domfront that a brief demonstration of cruelty was worth months of passive siege. His actions at Alençon had marked him as a man to be respected, and a reputation thus achieved could only prove useful in the future. Respect was always a valuable commodity in siege warfare. Henry I built up a similar reputation as a man not to be crossed, and Orderic tells us that castellans would hurriedly give up their keys when they heard that the royal army was approaching.

The three sieges do demonstrate, however, that the strength of the defences count for nothing when the enemy is determined and the supplies within the castle are limited. Notice also how the garrison of Brionne continued to launch daily attacks, while those at both Domfront and Arques rode out initially to confront William's forces; despite a strong castle they had decided to try their luck in the open. This helps to place castles in perspective and to emphasize the fact that, to a knight, honor counted for much; it could override prudence on occasion. Perhaps it was a similar scenario that allowed Geoffrey to seize Domfront so quickly, while William had chosen to starve out the Angevin intruders.

The anarchy on William's death in 1087 saw the new duke, Robert Curthose, ignored as ducal castellans were expelled by barons who took over the castles. The new king of England, Robert's brother William Rufus, was astute enough to use bribery to win over strongholds. Thus he took Aumale, Eu and Gournai on the Norman frontiers, and by this means was soon in control of much of Upper Normandy. A popular rising within Rouen in favour of Rufus was only put down after much street fighting. When he came over in person in 1090 he soon reduced Robert to a treaty and they turned on their younger brother, Henry, and besieged him in his stronghold at Mont-Saint-Michel, forcing him to leave the Cotentin. Thus the castles had largely been won not by brute strength but by a cunning reading of the venal desires of the Norman barons. After Rufus's death Henry conquered the duchy in three expeditions. In 1104 he came to Domfront, which he had held for years, and placed royal garrisons in the castles whose owners he had corrupted. In 1105 he did the same in the Cotentin, but also attacked Bayeux, which he burned, and Caen, which surrendered peacefully. In 1106 he came for the third time, besieged Tinchebrai castle and was then brought to battle there by the advance of his brother, Robert, who was defeated. Once more many castles had been taken by diplomacy rather than force. But Henry also used siege castles

Henry I's donjon at Vire, built around 1123, survives as two walls. The rock base can be seen. (Chris Gravett)

on occasion. Orderic mentions one at the siege of Vatteville-la-Rue in 1123–24 against Galeran de Meulan, to prevent foraging in the forest.

The conquest of Normandy by Geoffrey of Anjou between 1135 and 1145 was a matter of siege warfare rather than any major battles. In four invasions between 1135 and 1138 his fortunes see-sawed. He failed to take Le Sap in 1135, his army caught dysentery in 1137 and went home (leaving 'a trail of filth' as we are picturesquely informed), and he decided to withdraw from Falaise in 1138. However, he was able to win Fontanei in 1140, and in 1141 changed from raiding and plundering in the duchy to a methodical advance.

Geoffrey's advance against Carentan and Bayeux saw the capitulation of both without a fight. He then came to Saint Lô, which had been fortified by the

Le Mont-Saint-Michel, perched on its tidal island, is a monastic fortress. Parts of the rampart on the south-west and south sides date from the 11th century, as do some western building walls and areas of the church; some buildings below the south ramparts have 12th-century work. Henry, youngest son of William the Conqueror, fled here after his father's death in 1087 to escape his brothers.
(Chris Gravett)

Bishop of Coutances and held 200 soldiers. The latter came out to confront the Angevins but were driven back inside the defences by the first enemy attack. On the third day the defenders surrendered, and opened the gates, keen to swear homage to the count. When Geoffrey moved on the city of Coutances he entered without opposition for, says John of Marmoutier intriguingly, the bishop was away. Presumably the defenders decided they would make up their own minds when faced with a sizeable army. Geoffrey put his own garrison inside, filled the city with provisions, and called the barons of the Cotentin to do homage. One, Ralph, refused and fortified his castles while his brother, Richard de la Haye, prepared Cherbourg and installed 200 or more troops. Geoffrey in true feudal style ravaged the lands of Ralph to deny him supplies and deal out a symbolic personal insult, then took his castles and captured Ralph into the bargain. Geoffrey now marched on Cherbourg, and readied his siege engines. The walls and towers were a sight that the chronicler Marmoutier attributed to Julius Caesar; moreover he says that Richard de la Haye had filled it not only with knights, squires and retainers but plenty of provisions. For his part, Richard now ordered his men to fight well, and set off by ship to England to get help from King Stephen. Meanwhile his garrison held out stoutly and the walls and towers proved a tough nut, as missiles flew on both sides. Unfortunately Richard's ship was seized by pirates and he was taken away. When the news reached his men they were severely shaken, and though they had plenty of supplies (and access to ships, presumably) they decided to ask for terms before things got any worse. Geoffrey accepted their oaths of fealty, the place was handed over and, with winter approaching, the count disbanded his forces. He moved east in January 1144, crossed the Seine and

The donjon of the
11th-century castle of
Saint-Saveur-le-Vicomte
may contain elements of
12th-century work; but it
may also be wholly 14th
century following archaic
style. (Chris Gravett)

advanced on Rouen. The city opened its gates but the castle held out for three
months before capitulating. The last castle to be taken was Arques. Geoffrey
was now duke of Normandy as well as count of Anjou. His invasion had, on the
whole, been fairly bloodless and many castles offered little or no resistence to
him, namely Avranches and Coutances in 1141, Verneuil and Vaudreuil in
1143, Rouen in 1144, and Arques in 1145. All these latter castles, no matter
how advanced their defences, did not stand up to a siege by an army on a
winning run, and with King Stephen and other leading men busy with civil wars
in England, anarchy had reigned in Normandy.

The donjon at Chambois was built by William de Mandeville, a vassal of Henry II, before 1189. It is 25m x 15m (82ft x 49ft) in surface area and almost 26m (85ft 4in) tall. Note the two-light windows, marking the two principal floors. The machicolated parapets were probably added in the 15th century, when the turrets were raised. (Chris Gravett)

Between 1173 and 1174 came a major rebellion against Geoffrey's son, Henry II, that also involved England and other areas under Angevin control. The king made sure, either in person or through his lieutenants, that castles were defensible and as safe as could be expected. In 1173 the 'Young King', together with Count Philip of Flanders, and his brother, Matthew, Count of Boulogne, attacked and swiftly took Aumâle. Next he moved on Drincourt, which was stormed successfully despite being well fortified, partly through an act of treachery. He then proceeded towards Arques. In 1174 the 'Young King' and others attacked the city of Sées but were successfully held off by the citizens, despite there being no leaders present. That same year, with Louis VII of France and Count Philip, he came before Rouen on 22 July, with the Seine on their left. The outer walls were attacked in formation with siege engines but the defenders, despite being few compared to the large besieging army, forced them back by hurling square stones, sharp stakes and long pieces of wood. In order to keep up the pressure the French and Flemish took it in turn to try to undermine the walls and keep the defenders busy. This went on for several days but, says Ralph of Diceto, the Normans inside were confident they would win: their numbers were growing and food was plentiful, while men were slipping

The interior of the donjon at Chambois. The timber floor beams were carried on stone corbels, visible along the walls. (Chris Gravett)

away from the siege lines for fear of starvation. Presumably surrounding lands had been torched. The final straw came with rumours that Henry II had invaded and was approaching, for Louis feared he would by-pass Rouen, invade the lands of France and attack Paris. After discussions, the besiegers burned their engines, pulled down their tents, fired their huts and other temporary buildings, and retreated from Rouen on 14 August, despite the fact that the rumours had died down. People from the border country then advanced on the furthest part of the fortification and plundered weapons and equipment.

The struggle for power between Richard I and Philip II was given a twist when Richard was captured returning from the Third Crusade. However, French barons refused to support an attack on the lands of an absent crusader. This did not stop Philip. In 1193 he invaded Normandy and seized a number of border strongholds. He advanced on Gisors, which gave up through the treachery of its castellan. He overran the Vexin and Neaufles also fell. He besieged Rouen, but the city held out because of the command of Robert, Earl of Leicester, and Philip withdrew. This partial success was to prove a false dawn, however. Richard was released in 1194 and two months after his return to England was back in France. He made for the castle of Verneuil, which Philip

was besieging. According to Diceto, Philip had used catapults, other siege-engines and mining to try to break into the castle, but all to little effect. Richard pushed his men into the castle, then led more men around the French rear. This was enough for Philip, and he withdrew swiftly, abandoning his siege engines in his bid to extricate himself. He took out his anger by ignoring Rouen (which he held in healthy respect) and instead besieging a small town nearby called Fontaine, which held four knights and 20 men. On the fourth day he attacked the gate, broke in and destroyed everything.

Their wariness of unpredictable open battles caused commanders to withdraw and lose a siege rather than risk all by staying to confront a relief force. Thus at the siege of Fréteval in 1194 and at Gisors in 1198, Philip Augustus abandoned the sieges rather than risk an encounter with Richard I. John was a different proposition, though his victory at Mirabeau in 1202 and capture of Arthur of Brittany led Philip to withdraw from Arques, when he was close to capturing it.

John, however, did not maintain his record; he upset a number of barons and tended to be lethargic. Philip judged his man. When he moved to seize Normandy, Anjou and Poitou from John, he fought a small river battle near Château-Gaillard but no further battles. The greatest siege of the age came in late 1203, when Philip Augustus, determined to break the rule of the English kings in Normandy once and for all, advanced against the toughest nut in the Norman duchy, Château-Gaillard. The castellan, Roger of Lacy, perhaps against his better judgement, had allowed people from the surrounding area to take refuge within the walls. Philip advanced his forces against Petit Andely and seized it, but the castle loomed over this small triumph. The king knew the only means of

OPPOSITE
The square residential tower at the eastern corner of Tancarville castle was built in the 12th century, but the windows were altered and enlarged in 1360. (Chris Gravett)

The gate at Tancarville is Romanesque, but the large flanking towers were added in 1473–78. (Chris Gravett)

approach was from the south-east, and here he was opposed by the outer courtyard with its cylindrical towers, cut off by deep ditches, just as Richard had planned. A relief force arrived but was beaten off. Then Philip organized the digging of two ditches stretching from the Seine to the Gambon, to cut off the castle on the landward side and safeguard his own siege lines. He set wooden towers at intervals along the lines. Then he settled down to wait. Lacy's earlier leniency began to work in Philip's favour. As the supplies began to run low, Lacy decided there was no alternative but to turn out all those who were not necessary for the castle's defence. The 'useless mouths' were forced out of the castle to take their chances with the besiegers. At first the French complied, and we are told the first 1,000 were allowed through. Then the attitude hardened, and the route to freedom was sealed. Those who remained tried to get back inside the castle but the gates remained shut. With no prospect of immediate succour, the wretched folk were forced to huddle in the ditches through the harsh winter months, dying where they lay, tormenting the minds of those within the walls. Finally, in early 1204 Philip came up to review the situation and ordered the survivors to be allowed through and to be given food and drink. For many it was too late: on trying to digest food they succumbed.

With the coming of spring the king ordered the first direct attack on the castle. A siege tower was manoeuvred into position on the ground beyond the outer courtyard, from where French archers and crossbowmen could overlook the battlements and pin down the garrison. Catapults were brought up to pound the walls, though it is not certain whether they were torsion machines or trebuchets. Mantlets, shields of wood or wicker, were set up to protect archers and crossbowmen, while a wooden penthouse, known variously as a sow, cat or mouse, was slowly pushed forward across the ditch as men threw stones, earth and rubbish into the yawning gap to provide a causeway to allow the shed to reach the walls to protect sappers. The work was slow, and eventually the latter used ladders to descend into the ditch and up the other side to excavate a breach by the large tower. A hole was made, the inserted wooden props burned through, and a section of wall collapsed. Men swarmed across to seize the outer courtyard. The first section of the castle had fallen but there were two more courtyards and a formidable donjon still to confront. One day a soldier reconnoitering came upon the exit of an old latrine chute on the south side of the curtain of the middle courtyard. Above was a chapel butted against the wall. He managed to climb the noisome passage, emerging in the latrine below a window. Standing on a companion's shoulders he then managed to gain the window and pull some others up by rope. Once inside they made so much noise that the garrison panicked and fled, believing a large force had broken in. As they ran they fired the building. The Frenchmen opened the gates to allow their companions into the middle bailey. Next, however, they faced the corrugated inner wall. A mine was dug under it but Lacy ordered a countermine, which managed to break into the French works.

However, the digging had weakened the walls and a catapult made a breach. The garrison fought on but were overwhelmed. The donjon does not appear to have been used, or perhaps the garrison was overtaken before they could retreat inside. However, it is possible that the battlements were unfinished.

The siege of Château-Gaillard was a salutary lesson that, no matter how powerful and well garrisoned a castle may appear, it is down to the skills and willpower of the men inside and outside, and perhaps to a modicum of luck. Strong walls may hold off an attacker, but food and water will run out, especially when the local population is allowed inside for protection. As in other sieges, the mine was to prove lethal, and more effective than catapults. By good fortune the French found the unguarded latrine shaft, and this weak spot was used to full advantage. A slight oversight in checking the defences had cost the garrison dear. For all the ingenious design of corrugated walls and a donjon *en bec*, the French still managed to move incessantly forward and the garrison was forced to give up. The style of defence, with successive baileys and one direction of approach, might have stopped a less relentless foe, but in the end it did not save the Normans.

At Easter 1204 Philip gathered an army and attacked Falaise, which he took without resistance. The citizens of Caen similarly yielded 'for they had no-one who might defend them', states Coggeshall. Philip then took the whole province up to Barfleur, Cherbourg and Domfront. The citizens of Rouen and Verneuil and the garrison of Arques asked for 40 days in order to send messages to King John. No help came, for John feared treachery at home, and these places submitted. Normandy was lost forever.

Château-sur-Epte is a motte and bailey castle in the Vexin, which was fortified in stone in the early 12th century. The gate-tower had drawbridge beam slots added in the 14th century. The cylindrical donjon on the motte rising behind the chemise was probably built by Henry II in 1184. (Chris Gravett)

The donjon at Arques, built by Henry I probably after 1123, sits at the far end of the spur on which the castle is built. The deep ditches can clearly be seen. The donjon has deep buttresses. (Chris Gravett)

Southern Italy and Sicily

The Norman incursions into Italy and Sicily saw periods of similar turmoil as these northern adventurers carved out territories for themselves and then attempted to hold them. In 1035 the Normans managed to gain Melfi when their leader, the Lombard Ardoin, with his Norman followers simply persuaded the defenders to open the gates. From this already fortified mountain stronghold the Normans were able to command the country around. Many sieges were directed against native strongholds, such as Guiscard's attack on the Byzantine city of Bari in 1068, whose final capture in 1071 broke the power of the eastern emperor in southern Italy. Similarly, in Sicily sieges were initially directed at existing fortifications, for example the capture of Messina by Guiscard and his younger brother, Roger, in 1061. Roger, the 'Great Count', besieged Cosenza (1091), Castrovillari (1094), Amalfi (1096) and Capua (1098). It was not long before the new Norman rulers faced revolts. Robert Guiscard was opposed by feudal factions in Apulia in 1074, 1078 and 1082. He led a swift campaign in the winter of 1078/79 to quell revolt in Calabria and Apulia, his wife Sichelgaita besieging Trani while he was dealing with Taranto. In 1084 Jordan, Count Roger's son, rebelled and took San Marco d'Alunzio, the first Norman castle on Sicilian soil. When Guiscard died in 1084 his sons and brother fought over his inheritance.

   In the summer of 1062 the Greeks in Sicily rose up against the Normans. As soon as Count Roger was safely out of the way they attacked Troina, where he had spent about two weeks putting the fortifications in order and garrisoning the place. The townspeople tried to capture his lover, Judith, but the garrison

beat them off in day-long street fighting, and managed to send out a messenger to Roger, who was besieging Nicosia. He came racing back, only to find that about 1,000 Muslims had joined the Greeks. Roger ordered a retreat to the citadel and the nearby streets, and barricaded the approaches. Lookouts were posted, and the siege was set. There they remained for four months, while bitter winter weather set in, all the more noticeable because of Troina's elevated position. Supplies were running dangerously low, and clothing and blankets wholly inadequate. The chronicler Malaterra says that the Normans feigned hilarity to try and keep up morale, but by early in the year 1063 Roger knew things were becoming desperate. Then the lookouts discovered that the enemy was increasingly imbibing local red wine, which helped them to keep out the cold. The Normans sized up the situation and, one night when they were reasonably sure their enemies were sleeping from the effects, seized their chance. Moving silently on the thick snow, they were able to overpower the sentries, surprise the besiegers and capture their siege lines. The ringleaders were summarily hanged, though Malaterra glosses over the fate of others.

Roger II of Sicily managed to ride the revolt against him by avoiding battle and holding his castles securely. When Guiscard's grandson, William of Apulia, died in 1127 Roger was then able to take the mainland areas as well.

When the German emperor Henry VI came down into southern Italy in 1191, Tancred spent time strengthening the defences of Sicily, the heel of Apulia and larger towns where locals preferred him to an emperor. Further north the strongholds, including Capua, hurriedly opened their gates; Salerno surrendered before Henry even arrived. Despite a pounding, Naples held out,

The small castle at Pirou is a simple enclosure with no donjon. The walls are probably of late-12th-century date. A single polygonal turret survives, carried on large buttresses. Where these buttresses meet the wall, a triangular machicolation is formed. One can be seen on the far right of this picture. (Chris Gravett)

The Norman palace building of La Cuba, in Palermo, Sicily. It once formed part of a large park in the city. (David Nicolle)

Sicilian ships harrying his fleet and restocking the besieged citizens, until the heat forced the Germans to withdraw. Henry returned in 1194, and with Tancred now dead, Naples simply gave up. Salerno, which had given up Henry's wife (left there for safe-keeping) to her enemies as soon as he had gone home, now slammed its gates in terror but was stormed by the irate emperor; many were slaughtered, the town looted and the walls razed. As with William the Conqueror and Henry I, this lesson encouraged most other places to quickly surrender. Spinazzola and Policoro refused and suffered the same fate. Sicily was invaded and its towns and castles yielded quickly. The young heir was sent to the castle of Caltabellotta near Sciacca but the garrison lost its nerve and surrendered. On 20 November 1194 Norman rule in Sicily ended.

Appendices

Museums

It should be noted that those wishing to study actual Norman arms and equipment are rather poorly served. Even museums which provide fairly extensive displays of items of the period cannot but give a flavour since so many pieces of arms and armour must be studied in the context of comparable pieces rather than as actual 'Norman' items of the 10th to early 13th centuries. Examples of armour are extremely rare; only four helmets survive of 'Norman' type and only one of these, in the Metropolitan Museum of Art in New York, appears to be from northern France or England. Even then there is no proof that it dates from the period under discussion.

The other surviving helmets are from eastern Europe. That supposedly of the 10th-century St Wenceslas is held by Prague Cathedral along with a mail coat which has never been fully studied but which may be from the 10th or 11th century. The Hofjagd-und Rüstkammer in Vienna holds the conical helmet forged in one piece. While this is a major museum of arms and armour, items of the period are rare and not from a Norman context.

The Royal Armouries in Leeds displays the segmented conical helmet on loan from Liverpool Museum. Swords, maces, spears and spurs of the time can also be seen. A 14th-century mailcoat gives an idea of the appearance of this form of armour. The Armouries' Education Centre in the Tower of London has replicas of a conical helmet, kite-shaped shield and sword which are used as teaching aids. The British Museum has a large collection of swords, spears, axes, knives, shield bosses and spurs dating from the migration period up to the 11th century, many of which are held in store.

The British Library is useful for studying manuscript representations of warriors, although many will, of necessity, be included in folios kept in store. The Centre Guillaume le Conquérant in the Rue de Nesmond, Bayeux, houses the Bayeux Tapestry and provides an introductory display, exhibition and film show as well as the actual embroidery itself. The Musée des Antiquités at Rouen possesses some artefacts from Viking settlements in Normandy.

The north door and west front of the church of San Nicola, Bari, the ceiling of the Cappella Palatina in Palermo and the cloisters of Monreale Cathedral just outside Palermo, are all sources of pictorial representations of Norman knights and their mixed followings. Manuscript pictures and sculptures are also scattered throughout museums, churches and cathedrals of Europe.

Visiting the Castles Today

The following is a guide to the key fortified Norman sites in France, Italy and Britain. The list does not claim to be comprehensive; rather it makes a selection of those most worthy of attention. The following abbreviations refer to the locations of sites, towns and cities mentioned in the following treatment.

dép. *département* ('department', a French administrative district)
rég. *région* ('region', a French administrative area comprising several *départements*)
prov. *provincia* ('province', an Italian administrative district)
reg. *regione* ('region', an Italian administrative area comprising several *province*)
CADW acronym of the Welsh Historic Monuments organization

Normandy

Arques-la-Bataille (dép. Seine-Maritime, rég. Haute-Normandie)
About 9km (5 ¹/₂ miles) south-east of Dieppe. Part of the donjon has survived. The gatehouses and some foundations in the bailey are later work, as is the outer courtyard. It was subsequently rebuilt and then destroyed in the 18th century.

Bayeux (dép. Calvados, rég. Basse-Normandie)
About 26km (16 miles) north-west of Caen. Now a ruin, with a donjon in the north-west corner: much of the city wall and its 18 towers are also lost. A visit to the Bayeux Tapestry is a must, as it provides examples of contemporary castles and palaces in Normandy and Brittany.

Beaumont-le-Richard (dép. Calvados, rég. Basse-Normandie)
About 20km (12 ¹/₂ miles) north-west of Bayeux. In the south-west of the castle a mid-12th century rectangular great hall and residential block survive.

Bonneville-sur-Touques (dép. Calvados, rég. Basse-Normandie)
At Touques, about 2km (1 ¹/₃ mile) south of Trouville-sur-Mer. Documents date it to between 1059 and 1063, and it was favoured by the dukes until 1204. An oval enclosure, it lies halfway up the valley: some parts of the ramparts reveal earlier masonry, but most of what now survives is of the 13th century. There is little evidence for a donjon.

Brionne (dép. Eure, rég. Haute-Normandie)
About 31km (19 miles) south-west of Rouen. The original castle in the valley was replaced by the present hill fortress (perhaps originally a siege castle). The castle is now ruinous: only two sides of the donjon survive. Earthworks to the north may be the remains of another of Duke William's siege castles.

Bricquebec (dép. Manche, rég. Basse-Normandie)
13km (8 miles) west of Valognes. Begun in about 1000 by the Bertrand family, this was a motte and bailey castle controlling a forest road from Valognes to the east coast. A 14th-century polygonal donjon may contain some 12th-century work, but a 12th-century hall complex survives.

Caen (dép. Calvados, rég. Basse-Normandie)
About 14km (9 miles) south of the ferry port of Ouistreham. The large enclosure has an impressive curtain wall set with 12th–13th-century towers, though the battlements were removed in the 17th century. Much of the original castle interior has been destroyed, including the donjon, of which only the foundations remain, set within the ditch of Philip Augustus. However, the impressive 12th-century Exchequer Hall survives. Also worth viewing is the 14th-century gatehouse.

Chambois (dép. Orne, rég. Basse-Normandie)
About 25km (15 ½ miles) south-east of Falaise. The donjon is one of the best-preserved 12th-century examples in Normandy, though it is now a shell, lacking its internal floors.

Château-Gaillard (dép. Eure, rég. Haute-Normandie)
Some 40km (25 miles) south-east of Rouen. This huge fortress is now sadly much damaged, though it is still a very impressive ruin, particularly the ditches. The climb from Les Andelys provides good views, and there is a car park close to the castle.

Château-sur-Epte (dép. Eure, rég. Haute-Normandie)
About 50km (31 miles) south-east of Rouen. A delightful surviving motte crowned with a chemise and round tower, and good examples of gate-towers. The castle is now a private residence, but the interior can be seen from the gate.

Conches-en-Ouche (dép. Eure, rég. Haute-Normandie)
18km (11 miles) south-west of Evreux. Flanking towers were added to the exterior wall in the reign of Philip Augustus. Another D-shaped tower is a 13th- or 14th-century addition.

Condé-sur-Huisne (dép. Orne, rég. Basse-Normandie)
About 10km (6 miles) north of Nogent-le-Rotrou. Originally an 11th-century motte and bailey castle, a 12m (39ft) wide stone donjon plus other buildings were added in the 12th century. All of these were destroyed in 1428 except for the chapel in the north-west area.

Courcy (dép. Calvados, rég. Basse-Normandie)
About 16km (10 miles) north-east of Falaise. Much of the castle known to Orderic Vitalis has been reinforced, so that the stone enceinte now has 13th-century mural towers and gates. It remains a charming little stronghold set in quiet country, but is now a private farm.

Creully (dép. Calvados, rég. Bass-Normandie)
About 12km (7 ½ miles) east of Bayeux. It dominates the Seulles valley. The oldest part dates from around 1060. There are remains of a 12th-century hall and a long residential building.

Crèvecoeur-en-Auge (dép. Calvados, rég. Basse-Normandie)
17km (10 ½ miles) west of Lisieux. A delightful enclosure containing a number of half-timbered medieval buildings, including a 12th-century chapel. Elements of the stone tower probably remain in the later building work.

Dangu (dép. Eure, rég. Haute-Normandie)

About 8km (5 miles) west of Gisors. Two castles were built in the 12th century: little remains of one. The other was built on a hill west of the town, opposing the French castles of Courcelles and Boury. It features a motte surrounded by an enclosure, with a donjon built on the enclosure wall; a bailey has an enclosure wall too.

Domfront (dép. Orne, rég. Basse-Normandie)

21km (13 miles) south of Flers. The castle sits on a hill overlooking the town. The donjon was dismantled in about 1610 by order of the French king Henri IV. A double-aisled building once stood 20m (65ft 7in) west of the donjon, which perhaps was a reception *aula*. The gatehouse of c. 1200 has impressive defences. Much of the castle is ruinous, including the donjon, and is overlaid by later work, but the town's defences (of mixed date) remain and make for a pleasant walk, as some towers now form part of private houses.

Falaise (dép. Calvados, rég. Basse-Normandie)

34km (21 miles) south-east of Caen. The birthplace of William the Conqueror, the castle was abandoned in 1617 and damaged in 1944. The rectangular donjon of Henry I has been renovated, floored and roofed, but the strange excesses (seen at the entrance especially) are wholly a matter of personal taste. Some parts of the town wall also survive.

Gisors (dép. Eure, rég. Haute-Normandie)

About 34km (21 miles) south-west of Beauvais. The castle is set on one side of the town, with parking next to the walls. The motte gives a good view of the rest of the castle. The walls, with their 12th-century towers of varying shapes, are an important survival though some parts are the work of Philip Augustus.

Hacqueville (dép. Eure, rég. Haute-Normandie)

About 16km (10 miles) north-east of Les Andelys. One of the best-preserved shell keeps in Normandy. The summit had a 12th-century wall, remains of which are included in the present farmhouse.

Ivry-la-Bataille (dép. Eure, rég. Haute-Normandie)

About 22km (13 ½ miles) north of Dreux, across the River Eure. The important remains of the early donjon survive amid later work.

La Haye-du-Puits (dép. Manche, rég. Basse-Normandie)

24km (15 miles) west of Carentan. The castle comprises a slender quadrangular tower, with remains of a circular or polygonal wall, set on a motte. It probably dates from the 12th century, perhaps from the period of Henry I.

La Roche-Guyon (dép. Eure, rég. Haute-Normandie)

About 11km (7 miles) east of Vernon. It was built on the eastern bank of the Seine (between Vétheuil and Giverny) on a vertical rock set with holes. The late 12th-century cylindrical donjon *en bec* is attributed to Guy of La Roche: there are two curtain walls around it. The current entrance was built in 1780. The new fortification was connected to the old cave fortress by a subterranean stairway cut in the rock.

Le Plessis-Grimoult (dép. Calvados, rég. Basse-Normandie)

About 8km (5 miles) south of Aunay-sur-Orne. This site features an early earthwork and enceinte.

Lillebonne (dép. Seine-Maritime, rég. Haute-Normandie)
About 8km (5 miles) south-east of Bolbec. The now-destroyed hall of the castle hosted William the Conqueror's attempt to persuade his barons to invade England. The impressive cylindrical donjon is of 13th-century date.

Longueville-sur-Scie (dép. Seine-Maritime, rég. Haute-Normandie)
About 20km (12 ½ miles) south of Dieppe. Lying at the bottom of the Scie valley near the town, the castle was rebuilt in the late 11th/early 12th century on top of a hill on the site of Saint-Foy priory. It was a large oval enceinte with walls but no mural towers. A wall of the gate-tower survives behind a facing wall, but there is no trace of a donjon.

Maulévrier-Sainte-Gertrude (dép. Seine-Maritime, rég. Haute-Normandie)
About 5km (3 miles) south of Yvetot. Known locally as 'Le Butte au Diable', the remains are to be found at the northern edge of the Caudebec forest. Probably of 11th–12th-century build, it consists of a motte encircled by a solid, levelled wall, perhaps the remains of a quadrangular donjon. The motte has a semi-circular bailey with curtain wall. A well and traces of ruined buildings survive. On the village side there is additionally an arc-shaped outer bailey whose walls cross the ditch at each end to join those of the inner bailey.

Mont-Saint-Michel (dép. Manche, rég. Basse-Normandie)
About 22km (13 ½ miles) south-west of Avranches. This is a must to visit, because it is a unique fortress-monastery whose defences and buildings accumulated over the centuries. Visitors must check the tide times when crossing the causeway. It is also worth making the effort to arrive early, for the site is full of narrow streets and with many guided tours it soon becomes extremely busy.

Montfort-sur-Risle (dép. Eure, rég. Haute-Normandie)
About 14km (9 miles) south-east of Pont-Audemer. Built between 1035 and 1054, the donjon, whose remains lie in the south-west corner, was probably built in 1123 by Hugh IV of Montfort, but was later confiscated by Henry I. King John dismantled parts of it, and it then fell to Philip Augustus in 1204. The castle, c. 280m × 165m (919 × 541ft) in area, sits on the banks of the Risle, and has a ruinous, thick-ditched, polygonal wall set with six towers of various types. The chapel of Saint Nicolas is set against the western wall of the donjon.

Neaufles-Saint-Martin (dép. Eure, rég. Haute-Normandie)
About 4km (2 ½ miles) west of Gisors, Neaufles is a large, deeply ditched motte and bailey castle. The motte carries the remains of a cylindrical donjon built in the 1180s by Henry II, though the chemise wall has vanished. The donjon is 20m (65ft 7in) high and 14m (45ft 11in) in diameter, with three floors on corbels, the top floor with bonded *oculi* (circular openings). The castle was dismantled in the 17th century.

Pirou (dép. Manche, rég. Basse-Normandie)
About 27km (17 miles) north-west of Coutances. Pirou is a moated enceinte without a donjon. Its surviving walls and polygonal turret probably date from the late 12th century. It was rebuilt in the 14th century.

Saint-Saveur-le-Vicomte (dép. Manche, rég. Basse-Normandie)
15km (9 miles) south-west of Valognes, and 24km (15 miles) north-west of Carentan. The castle now consists of a higher court and a lower court to the south. The higher

court is in the form of a lop-sided square, with a square donjon attached to, and jutting from, the south-east corner. This appears to be of 14th-century date but may be an altered 12th-century original. All the mural towers along the walls of the high court are round and of the 13th century, while only a few remnants of the lower-court defences remain.

Tancarville (dép. Seine-Maritime, rég. Haute-Normandie)

About 12km (7 ¹/₂ miles) south of Bolbec. The 12th-century Norman tower remains at the south corner of this long triangular castle enclosure overlooking the Seine. A smaller square tower, flanking the ramp leading to a huge beaked 15th-century tower, may also be of 12th-century date.

Valmont (dép. Seine-Maritime, rég. Haute-Normandie)

About 11km (7 miles) south-east of Fécamp. The early square donjon is now amalgamated into the later château but is clearly visible at one corner. The castle is relatively compact and follows the line of the original layout, though one half is largely missing. There is also extensive parkland.

Vatteville-la-Rue (dép. Seine-Maritime, rég. Haute-Normandie)

About 15km (9 miles) south-east of Lillebonne, across the Seine. The castle consists of a motte with remains of a polygonal shell-keep on top. Across the ditch, to the east, is a crescent-shaped bank with remains: excavation has shown this to be a residential building. The motte south of Vatteville on Route 65 is perhaps the siege castle built by Henry I in 1123–24.

Vire (dép. Calvados, rég. Basse-Normandie)

54km (33 ¹/₂ miles) south-west of Caen, and 26km (16 miles) west of Condé-Sur-Noireau. The castle is easily reached from the town, with the donjon rearing up on its rocky base. It was dismantled by Richelieu in 1630 and collapsed in 1802.

Southern Italy

Bovino (prov. Foggia, reg. Apulia)

Bovino stands south of the River Fortore. It was built either by the Norman Drogone, or by the counts of Loritello, on Roman remains.

Campobasso (provincial capital, reg. Molise)

Located on a high spur over the town, the castle was erected by the Normans on the site of a Lombard tower, which contains remains of Samnite walls beneath. The castle was four-sided, with a donjon situated between the northern and western sides. Four circular corner towers were added later.

Castel d'Arechi (prov. Salerno, reg. Campania)

Situated at an elevation of 300m (984ft) on Mt Bonadies, the site was developed and fortified by Arechi II, a Lombard prince. In 1077, following a lengthy Norman siege, the castle was taken from Gisulfo II, the last Lombard prince of Salerno. The site was much altered in the 16th century, and abandoned in the 19th century.

Castel Bagnoli del Trigno (prov. Isernia, reg. Molise)

A four-sided Langobard castle on a rocky spur overlooking the Trigno river valley. The Normans raised escarped walls, with three sides slightly overhanging: the wall with the entrance overhangs more prominently. Internal arrangements against the inner walls have decayed and what appear to be cannon loops have been inserted in the remains.

Castel dell'Ovo (prov. Naples, reg. Campania)

The Normans chose the site for their base in the 12th century, and commissioned the architect Buono to expand and improve the existing shore fortifications. The 'Normandy' tower dates from this period. The site was altered once more under the Swabians.

Castropignano (prov. Campobasso, reg. Molise)

Castropignano lies about 20km (12 ½ miles) from the regional and provincial capital, Campobasso. The four-sided castle itself sits on a rocky ridge and was originally a Langobard fortress, which the Normans rebuilt to include a donjon and towers.

Conversano (prov. Bari, reg. Apulia)

The town is about 18km (11 miles) from Monopoli. The castle was built on a preceding Byzantine structure. It is of trapezoid form and three of the 12th-century square towers survive, together with a cylindrical 14th-century example. It was restructured by Frederick II in 1230. There is an archaeological museum within the castle.

Deliceto (prov. Foggia, reg. Apulia)

Deliceto is located 50km (31 miles) from Foggia, and the town sits on a hill at an elevation of 550m (1,804ft). The castle was erected in 1073 by the Norman Tristainus.

Dragonara (prov. Foggia, reg. Apulia)

The castle was built, probably on Roman remains, by Drogone Count of Apulia, the second son of Tancredi, from whom it derives its name.

Fiorentino (prov. Foggia, reg. Apulia)

The city is famous for being the place where the emperor Frederick II died on 13 December 1250. The Normans expanded the city considerably, adding a suburb called the 'Carunculum', and erected a small castle on the highest point of the hill. The castle was later altered by Frederick II.

Longano (prov. Isernia, reg. Molise)

Located about 10km (6 miles) from Isernia, in the Matese highlands. The castle overlooks an elongated township. Little remains of the enceinte, much of the stone having been pillaged for urban construction, and controversy exists over the precise date of foundation.

Melfi (prov. Potenza, reg. Basilicata)

The town of Melfi was taken by the Normans in 1041 and was their first capital in southern Italy. Remains of a Norman rectangular donjon are visible, though the castle was heavily rebuilt in 1281 and badly damaged in an earthquake in 1851.

Monteroduni (prov. Isernia, reg. Molise)

The castle is located on the slopes of Mount Altone, near the River Volturno. The Langobard defences were overlaid in later centuries. In 1064 it was taken over by the counts of Molise on the deaths of Bernardo I and his sons in battle against the Normans.

Very probably in the Norman period, the small courtyard enceinte was given four corner towers, but much of the castle was heavily altered in the centuries that followed.

Mount Sant'Angelo (prov. Foggia, reg. Apulia)

The castle lies to the west of the town itself, and is now in a ruinous state. The pentagonal Tower of Giants was erected by Robert Guiscard.

Nicotera (prov. Cosenza, reg. Calabria)

The castle was built in 1065 by Robert Guiscard, but was destroyed in 1074. Count Roger, having been granted Nicotera in a will, rebuilt it and transferred his *domus regia* and *praedia regis* there. However, it was destroyed again in 1085. It was rebuilt again in 1122 by the young Count Roger, but suffered an earthquake in 1184. It was much altered by Frederick II and rebuilt in the 18th century. The castle contains several museums.

Pesche (prov. Isernia, reg. Molise)

A fortified burgh on Mount San Bernardo. The village is surrounded by a curtain set with cylindrical corner and middle towers, making the buildings an initial obstacle to attack. Behind rises the castle, with a redoubt like a small donjon on an escarped base. This enceinte and redoubt are more like Abruzzi castle forms, and are not common in the Molise region.

Pescolanciano (prov. Isernia, reg. Molise)

Situated on a rocky spur, the castle has a trapezoid floor plan and features a four-sided donjon (possibly Norman). Frederick II removed much early work, as he did in other Molisian castles. Much rebuilding has taken place at the site.

Riccia (prov. Campobasso, reg. Molise)

The town is some 32km (20 miles) from Campobasso. The castle is located on the eastern side of two hills, overlooking the valley formed between them. It has an irregular enceinte with three circular towers (one almost vanished) and a cylindrical donjon of basement and three storeys.

Roccamandolfi (prov. Isernia, reg. Molise)

Located some 23km (14 miles) from Isernia, the castle (originally called Rocca Maginulfi) sits on a hilltop overlooking the town. It was destroyed by Frederick II, and only ruins remain. The enceinte, featuring somewhat later cylindrical and D-shaped mural towers, follows the irregular hillside and on two sides incorporates a four-sided structure, possibly a donjon.

Rotello (prov. Campobasso, reg. Molise)

Founded by Robert of Loritello (grandson of Robert Guiscard) from whom it derived its name: the castle currently goes under the name of Palazzo Colavecchio, and is situated in the centre of the village. Although it has been much altered, its structurally dissimilar elements seem to indicate an earlier Norman building.

San Marco Argentano (prov. Cosenza, reg. Calabria)

Located some 50km (31 miles) from Cosenza, the castle was built by Robert Guiscard in 1051, including a stone donjon, and rises to dominate the whole valley. Interestingly, the so-called 'Norman tower' was in fact built in the late Swabian period, or may indeed date to the 14th century.

Scribla (prov. Cosenza, reg. Calabria)

The site lies in northern Calabria, a few kilometres south-east of the city of Castrovillari. Built by Robert Guiscard, probably between 1044 and 1048 (the first date is provided by Lupus Protospadarius, while the second is by Goffredo Malaterra). Archaeological research has indicated that the site was abandoned for a period of ten years, before being reoccupied. It featured a trapezoid wall with a tower on its east side.

Termoli (prov. Campobasso, reg. Molise)

In the Norman period the Langobard tower was rebuilt and incorporated into an expanded defence system. There was probably an enceinte and possibly a donjon before Frederick II rebuilt the place. Within the city is the palatium of the Loritellos, where Tancred finalized an agreement against Henry VI in 1191.

Tremiti Islands (prov. Foggia, reg. Apulia)

The fortress here features a long ramp leading up to a gate, and high escarped walls on bedrock. The Tower of St Nicholas protected the artificial ditch that separated the citadel from the north-eastern side of the island.

Tufara (prov. Campobasso, reg. Molise)

A castle in the county of Civitate, it owed the king the service of a soldier. In the mid-12th century it belonged to Drumanus. Traces of piling from the original wooden defences have been discovered. The shape is elongated and kinked, the length probably due to successive building. During the Norman period there seems to have been reworking on the south-east side, where it overlooked the Celano–Foggia route and the River Fortore. The creation of the block that houses the armoury can probably also be traced back to Norman rebuilding work.

Venafro (prov. Isernia, reg. Molise)

The castle stands on the edge of the town on the hill of Sant'Angelo. Its cylindrical donjon was built over the course of several centuries on top of a pre-Roman structure.

Sicily

Aci Castello (prov. Catania)

The castle, of black lavastone, sits on a spur overlooking the sea on a site that had been fortified since the Roman period. It was rebuilt by Tancred in 1189.

Adrano (prov. Catania)

This is an early, square donjon surrounded by a later low chemise wall with circular corner towers. Other elements of the castle complex are of later date.

Caccamo (prov. Palermo)

The castle is perched high on a ridge of Mount Calogero, about 14km (9 miles) from Termini Imerese, south-west of Cefalù. It was built by a rich Norman called Matthew Bonnellus. The castle has been much rebuilt and restored.

Calascibetta (prov. Enna)

The town is some 6km (4 miles) to the north of Enna, and lies at a quota of 691m (2,267ft) in the Erei mountains. The town's name is of Arabic origin (*Kalat-Scibet*), and means 'the castle on the summit'. In 1062 Count Roger built a castle and church here.

Caltabellotta (prov. Agrigento)

The site has a single Norman tower surviving which stands on a hill at an altitude of 950m (3,116ft). The castle was built on the site of a former Arab castle. It was here in 1194 that the widow Sybil took refuge together with her son William III from the pursuit of the Swabian emperor Henry VI.

Lentini (prov. Siracusa)

The town lies at a height of 56m (183ft), and is some 45km (28 miles) from the provincial capital Siracusa. The Arabs fortified the town, before it fell to the Normans. The town suffered earthquakes in 1140 and 1169, which destroyed many buildings of the period. The site of the castle was overlaid by Frederick II.

Mazara del Vallo (prov. Trapani)

The town is on the west coast of Sicily, some 40km (25 miles) south of Trapani. The site was fortified by Roger I in 1072–73, to protect against the Saracen invasions. The first Sicilian parliament was held here soon after. Only its double-arched entrance remains, near Piazza Makara.

Milazzo (prov. Messina)

The city lies 40km (25 miles) west of Messina. The oldest part of the site is the 'Mastio', which is known as the 'Saracen Tower'. The castle was heavily reworked in 1240 by Richard of Lentini for Frederick II.

Palermo: Castellaccio

Perched on Monte Caputo, and built in the second half of the 12th century, the site forms a large irregular rectangle, with rectangular towers. The ground plan of a square donjon with a dividing wall still exists.

Palermo: La Cuba

This palace-tower was built by King William II in 1180, and was set in a large park, which also contained another building, 'La Cubula' (see below). It now stands in the grounds of the Villa di Napoli, on Corso Calatafimi, through which access is gained.

Palermo: La Cubula

The building is located on Corso Calatafimi, near to La Cuba: once again, access is via Villa di Napoli.

Palermo: La Ziza

La Ziza lies in the north-west part of the Sicilian capital in Piazza Guglielmo il Buono, near Porta Nuova. It was begun by William I in about 1162, and was completed by his son, William II. Today it contains a museum of Islamic art.

Palermo: Palazzo Conte Federico

Via dei Biscottari. Arab-Norman work survives in the tower of this palazzo, called the 'Scrigno Tower': it is now a private building.

Paternò (prov. Catania)

Located 13km (8 miles) from Catania, the lavastone castle, which dominates the town, was built by Roger I in 1073 and rebuilt in the 14th century. It has been much restored in recent years. The castle is open to visitors daily.

Termini Imerese (prov. Palermo)

The castle lies in the upper part of this thermal spa town, which is 36km (22 miles) from Palermo. The site is an ancient one, stretching back to classical times, and its use was continued by the Normans following their takeover in the 13th century. The castle was overlaid by Frederick II.

Trapani (provincial capital)

The castle lies on an ancient site on the summit of Mt Erice, and provides excellent views over the city. In the 12th century the Normans used materials from existing structures to build a castle and curtain wall. The original site was more extensive than today's remains indicate and contained an outer ditch with three towers in advanced positions.

Great Britain

Appleby-in-Westmorland, Cumbria (private, but open to the public)

From the A66, continue into the town on the B6260: the castle stands on a hill above the town centre, within a loop of the River Eden. It has a well-preserved donjon.

Arundel, West Sussex (the seat of the Duke of Norfolk, open to the public)

Off the A27 between Chichester and Worthing. The castle has been much restored, having been in constant occupation since the 11th century. The village is also worth visiting.

Bamburgh, Northumberland (private, but open to the public)

The castle is situated on a cliff and can be accessed from the village on the B1341, turning off the A1. The most majestic view, made famous by films and calendars, is from the beach below. The donjon has been much altered and furnished inside, making it difficult to trace the original parts.

Barnard castle, Co. Durham (English Heritage)

On the A67, the castle has a cylindrical tower dating to about 1200, with other medieval buildings. The Bowes Museum is nearby.

Berkeley, Gloucestershire (private, but open to the public)

Berkeley is on the B4509, reached via the A38 or M5. The castle consists of a motte with two baileys, the motte concealed within Norman walls. There is a 14th-century domestic range in the eastern bailey.

Carlisle, Cumbria (English Heritage)

Approached from the A595, this castle lies on the northern outskirts of the medieval walled town. It was occupied until the 19th century and therefore contains buildings of several periods. The castle consists of an inner and outer bailey, and the Norman remains include the donjon and parts of the curtain walls. The original door into the donjon has been blocked and a ground floor entrance is now used. One side of the donjon has been thinned and covered by a new wall.

Carrickfergus, Co. Antrim (Environment & Heritage Service: Built Heritage)

13km (8 miles) north-east of Belfast on the A2. One of the largest Irish castles, Carrickfergus is a long, narrow castle on a peninsula. It was host to King John in 1210.

Castle Acre, Norfolk (English Heritage)
Castle Acre (the town and castle share the same name) is reached via the A1065: the castle and town gate lie at the north end of the town. From the castle, an easy walk through the town brings you to the Norman priory ruins, with a superb west front.

Castle Hedingham, Essex (private, but open to the public)
The village is reached via the B1058; the castle lies just to the north of it. The tower is well worth a visit, though only earthworks survive otherwise.

Castle Rising, Norfolk (English Heritage)
Best reached by car, 9km (5 ½ miles) north-west of King's Lynn on the A149.

Colchester, Essex (borough council)
Situated on the A12, the castle stands just north of the high street in the town. It now houses the Colchester and Essex Museum.

Conisbrough, Yorkshire (English Heritage)
On the A630 between Sheffield and Doncaster, the castle stands in the centre of the town, and is largely a 12th-century ruin.

Corfe castle, Dorset (English Heritage)
Situated on the A351, but the preserved Dorset Light Railway also has a station in the village. Best reached by parking in the car parks on the village outskirts and walking to the castle ruins through the village, which is charming. The castle perches on a ridge above the village.

Dover, Kent (English Heritage)
Dover is situated on a height on the eastern outskirts of the town, off the A2. If using a car, be prepared for traffic approaching the town and port, especially during holiday periods. From Dover Priory railway station in the town the castle can be reached by taxi, or the more energetic can hike. Parking is within the earthworks, and most of the castle can be explored, though there are numerous later additions, especially dating from the Napoleonic and Victorian periods. There is a restaurant within the inner bailey that gives a good view of the wall fabric. Most of the battlements have either been renewed or lost when towers were cut in size. The donjon windows are mainly of Edward IV's time, as are other internal insertions, while barrel vaults on the top floor and other insertions date from the 1700s.

Framlingham, Suffolk (English Heritage)
Located north of Ipswich on the B1120, the castle is in the centre of the village in Christchurch Park. The castle shop offers free hire of an audio tour pack for the wall walk.

Grosmont, Gwent (CADW)
This castle forms part of the 'Three Castles' given to Hubert de Burgh in 1201, together with Skenfrith and White castle. It lies on the B4347 some 3km (2 miles) from Pontrilas. There is a first-floor stone hall of about 1150 within a towered enclosure.

Helmsley, North Yorkshire (English Heritage)
The castle is in the town centre, some 32km (20 miles) north of York on the A170. It is set on a curtain wall, and a Tudor range stands in the enclosure.

Kenilworth, Warwickshire
Reached from the A46 south-west of Coventry. The impressive donjon in red sandstone was poorly altered by Robert Dudley, Earl of Leicester, and slighted in the 17th century.

Dudley also built a complex of buildings, and the castle was the scene of a lavish visit by Elizabeth I. The 14th-century hall of John of Gaunt also survives.

Launceston, Cornwall (English Heritage)
Launceston lies off the A30, west of Exeter. It is largely intact, apart from later interference with the motte on which the shell keep and 13th-century tower sit.

Ludlow, Shropshire (borough council)
Reached via the A49 or A4117, the town of Ludlow contains a number of interesting old buildings. As well as the Norman donjon on the old gate and the circular chapel, the castle has a 14th-century hall complex and Mortimer's Tower.

Middleham, North Yorkshire (English Heritage)
Reached via the A6108 from Leyburn: the large donjon is set closely within a fortified enclosure of the 13th and 14th centuries. One of its famous owners was the Earl of Warwick, 'the Kingmaker'. The original motte and bailey can be seen to the south-west.

Newcastle upon Tyne, Tyne and Wear (City of Newcastle)
In the centre of the city, off the A69: the castle can also be seen from the train that passes remarkably close to its walls. An impressive donjon with basement chapel; there is a bagpipe museum in the gatehouse.

Norham, Northumberland (English Heritage)
On the A698 and B6470 from Berwick-upon-Tweed. There are defences of all periods from the 12th to 16th centuries. The donjon was altered in the 15th century.

Norwich, Norfolk (City of Norwich)
The castle on its hill stands in the middle of the city: if arriving by car it is best to use the park-and-ride facilities. Much of the donjon was refaced in the 19th century, though following the original layout. It now houses displays from Norwich Museum.

Orford, Suffolk (English Heritage)
Best reached by car, it lies 13km (8 miles) east of Woodbridge on the B1084. Go through the village to the site car park. The remains are of the donjon set within its earthworks.

Pembroke, Dyfed (CADW)
Reached via the A4139 or the A4075, the castle is perched above the river to the north-west of the city centre. The donjon sits within a large enclosure surrounded by 13th-century defences.

Portchester, Hampshire (English Heritage)
Portchester is situated on the south coast, 6km (4 miles) east of Fareham, off the A27. It stands in the corner of a Roman fort, with a 12th-century Augustinian priory in the opposite corner. The donjon was given an additional two storeys some time before 1250.

Restormel, Cornwall (English Heritage)
Reached from the B3268 south of Bodmin or the A390 from Lostwithiel: Restormel castle is set on a low mound on the west bank of the Fowey. The 12th-century shell keep contains the remains of 13th-century domestic buildings inside.

Richmond, Yorkshire (English Heritage)
On the A6136, west of the A1, the castle stands in the centre of Richmond, just off the market place: it gives good views over the River Swale below.

Rochester, Kent (English Heritage)

Rochester castle lies on the river in the centre of Rochester: the city can be accessed by train, or by car via the A2. The castle site is large, but much of the Norman curtain and mural towers have been overbuilt or destroyed. A visit to the donjon is well worth it, though the window openings have suffered. There is no replacement flooring internally, and those with no head for heights may find the views from the window embrasures unsettling. The rebuilt rounded corner is perhaps best viewed from the road outside the castle. The Norman cathedral is only a short walk from the castle too.

Scarborough, Yorkshire (English Heritage)

The A170 or the coastal A165 lead to Scarborough. The ruins are perched on a headland on the east side of the town but can be reached on foot if necessary.

Sherborne Old Castle, Dorset (English Heritage)

Reached via the A30 or the A352, the Norman castle is not to be confused with the new (Tudor) castle next door. The old castle lies on the eastern outskirts of the town, and there is ample parking. Sherborne Abbey is also worth visiting in the town itself.

Skenfrith, Gwent (CADW)

Situated on the B4521, the castle is relatively unspoiled.

Tower of London (Historic Royal Palaces)

There are no visitor parking facilities except for a nearby multi-storey paying car park, so it is best to arrive by the Underground (Tower Hill on the Circle and District Line is the closest stop) or by bus or taxi. Small sections of the Roman city wall are still visible, but the Conqueror's ditch is filled in. The White Tower houses displays by the Royal Armouries. The Crown Jewels are, of course, also displayed in the Tower. On the north side additional entrances have latterly been inserted. All the windows were enlarged in about 1700 except for a small pair above the entrance, and a blocked pair beside them that lit the passage. The top floor was inserted in the 1490s, so the floor below does not look as it did during Norman times. Outside is the stump of the 12th-century Wardrobe Tower, on the line of the Roman city wall. The late 12th-century polygonal Bell Tower is normally closed but can be viewed from the outside. There is a restaurant in the New Armouries building, though the castle can become very busy during the summer months.

Trim, Co. Meath

Situated 37km (23 miles) north-west of Dublin on the L3 off the N3. The donjon is sited in a triangular bailey with curtain wall and towers.

White castle, Gwent (CADW)

The castle is on the B4233, 10km (6 miles) east of Abergavenny. The 12th-century walls, which remain in good condition, have 13th-century towers and a gatehouse.

Windsor, Surrey (Historic Royal Palaces)

Reached by train or via the B3022, the castle lies in the centre of town. It consists of two very large baileys with a motte between. The shell keep was rebuilt by Edward III, and was raised and restored by George IV in the 19th century. Much of the original castle is built over but offers plenty of interest, notably the royal tombs in the 15th-century St George's Chapel, home of the Knights of the Garter.

Bibliography

Allen Brown, R., *English Castles*, 2nd edition (London, 1976)

Allen Brown, R. (ed.), *Castles: A History and Guide* (London, 1980)

Allen Brown, R., *The Architecture of Castles* (London, 1984)

Allen Brown, R., *Castles from the Air* (Cambridge, 1989)

Anderson, W. F. D., *Castles of Europe* (London, 1970)

Anglo-Norman Studies (originally *Proceedings of the Battle Conference in Anglo-Norman Studies*); first published in 1978, this journal is essential reading for any student of Norman military history.

Armitage, E., *Early Norman Castles of the British Isles* (London, 1912)

Baylé, M. (ed.), *L'Architecture Normand au Moyen Age*, 2 vols (Caen, 2001)

Beck, Bernard, *Châteaux Forts de Normandie* (Rennes, 1986)

Bennett, M., 'La Règle du Temple as a Military Manual or How to Deliver a Cavalry Charge', *Studies in Medieval History Presented to R. Allen Brown*, pp.7–19, (1989)

Bennett, M., 'The Status of the Squire, the Northern Evidence', *The Ideals and Practice of Medieval Knighthood* (1986)

Bennett, M., 'Wace and Warfare', *Anglo-Norman Studies*, Vol. XI, pp.37–57 (1989)

de Boüard, M., *Le Château de Caen* (Caen, 1979)

de Boüard, M., *Les Châteaux Normands de Guillaume le Conquérant à Richard Coeur de Lion*, exposition, Musée de Normandie (Caen, 1987)

Bradbury, J., 'Battles in England and Normandy', *Anglo-Norman Studies*, Vol. VI, pp.1–12 (1984)

Bradbury, J., *The Medieval Siege* (Woodbridge, 1992)

Brown, R. A., *The Normans and the Norman Conquest* (London, 1969)

Brown, R. A., 'The Status of the Norman Knight', *War and Government in the Middle Ages*, ed. Holt and Gillingham, pp.18–32 (1984)

Cahen, C., *La Syrie du Nord a l'époque des Croisades* (Paris, 1940)

Coad, J., *Book of Dover Castle* (London, 1995)

Coad, J. G. and Streeten, A. D. F., 'Excavations at Castle Acre Castle, Norfolk 1972–77: Country House and Castle of the Norman Earls of Surrey', *Archaeological Journal*, Vol. CXXXIX, pp.138–302 (1982)

Caronia, G., *La Ziza di Palermo: storia e restauro* (Bari, 1982)

Caronia, G. and Noto, V., *La Cuba di Palermo: Arabi e Normanni nel XII° secolo* (Palermo, 1988)

Châtelain, André, *Donjons romans des Pays d'Ouest* (Paris, 1973)

Châtelain, André, *Châteaux Forts, Images de Pierre des Guerres Médiévales* (Paris, 1995)

Chibnall, Marjorie, 'Feudal Society in Orderic Vitalis', *Proceedings of the Battle Abbey Conference, 1978*, pp.35–48 (1979)

Clapham, A. W., *Romanesque Architecture in Western Europe* (Oxford, 1936)

Colvin, H. M., Allen Brown, R. and Taylor, A. J., *The History of the King's Works, The Middle Ages*, 2 vols (London, 1963)

Coulson, C. 'Peaceable Power in Norman Castles', *Anglo-Norman Studies*, Vol. XXIII, pp.69–95 (2001)

Counihan, J. M., 'Mrs Ella Armitage, John Horace Round, G. T. Clark and Early Norman Castles', *Anglo-Norman Studies*, Vol. VIII, pp.73–87 (1986)

Cruden, S., *The Scottish Castle*, 3rd edition (Edinburgh, 1981)

Davis, R. H. C., 'The Warhorses of the Normans', *Anglo-Norman Studies*, Vol. X, pp.67–82 (1988)

Davison, B. K., 'The Origins of the Castle in England', *Archaeological Journal*, Vol. CXXIV, pp.202–11 (1967)

Dixon, P., 'The Myth of the Keep', *The Seigneurial Residence in Western Europe AD c800–1600*, BAR International Series 1088, pp.9–13 (Oxford, 2002)

Douglas, D., *William the Conqueror* (London, 1964)

Douglas, D., *The Norman Achievement* (London, 1969)

Gies, Joseph and Gies, Frances, *Life in a Medieval Castle* (London, 1975)

Gillingham, John, 'Richard I and the Science of War in the Middle Ages', *War and Government in the Middle Ages*, ed. Holt and Gillingham, pp.78–91 (1984)

Goodall, J. 'Dover Castle and the Siege of 1216', *Château Gaillard*, Vol. XIX, pp.91–202 (2000)

Gravett, C., *Hastings, 1066* (London, 1992)

Gravett, C., 'Kitchens and Keeps: Domestic Arrangements in Norman Castles', *Royal Armouries Yearbook*, Vol. III, pp.168–75 (1998)

Gravett, C., 'Siege Warfare in Orderic Vitalis', *Royal Armouries Journal*, Vol. V, pp.139–47 (2000)

Gravett, C., *The History of Castles* (Guilford, CT, 2001)

Guy, John, *Kent Castles* (Gillingham, 1980)

Heath, Ian, *Armies of the Dark Ages*, Wargames Research Group (1977)

Heath, Ian, *Armies of Feudal Europe*, Wargames Research Group (1978)

Hill, Rosalind, 'Crusading Warfare: A Campfollower's View 1097–1120', *Proceedings of the Battle Abbey Conference 1978*, pp.75–83 (1979)

Holland, P. 'The Anglo-Normans and their Castles in County Galway', *Galway: History and Society*, eds. G. Moran and R. Gillespie, p.126 (Dublin, 1996)

Holland, P. 'The Anglo-Norman Landscape in County Galway: Landholding, Castles and Settlements', *Journal of the Galway Archaeological and Historical Society*, Vol. XLIX, pp.159–93 (1997)

Impey, Edward, 'The Seigneurial Residence in Normandy, 1125–1225: an Anglo-Norman Tradition?', *Medieval Archaeology*, Vol. XLIII (1999)

Kenyon, J. R., *Medieval Fortifications* (Leicester, 1990)

Leask, H. G., *Irish Castles and Castellated Houses*, 3rd edition (Dundalk, 1977)

Le Patourel, *The Norman Empire* (Oxford, 1976)

Lindsay, M., *The Castles of Scotland* (London, 1986)

Marshall, Pamela, 'The Great Tower as Residence', *The Seigneurial Residence in Western Europe AD c800-1600*, BAR International Series 1088, pp.27-44 (Oxford, 2002)

McNeill, Tom, *Castles* (London, 1992)

Mesqui, J., *Châteaux et Enceintes de la France Médiéval*, 2 vols (Paris, 1992-93)

Mesqui, J., *Châteaux Forts et Fortifications en France* (Paris, 2002)

Moore, J., 'Anglo-Norman Garrisons', *Anglo-Norman Studies*, Vol. XXII (2000)

Morillo, S., *Warfare under the Anglo-Norman Kings, 1066-1135* (Woodbridge, 1994)

Norman, Vesey, *The Medieval Soldier* (London, 1971)

Norwich, J. J., *The Normans in the South, 1016-1130* (London, 1967)

Norwich, J. J., *The Kingdom in the Sun* (London, 1970)

Parnell, Geoffrey, *The Tower of London* (London, 1993)

Paterson, Linda M., 'Military Surgery: Knights, Sergeants, and Raimon of Avignon's Version of the Chirurgia of Roger of Salerno (1180-1209)', *The Ideals and Practice of Medieval Knighthood II*, pp.117-146 (1988)

Pettifer, Adrian, *English Castles: a Guide by Counties* (Woodbridge, 1995)

Pettifer, Adrian, *Welsh Castles: a Guide by Counties* (Woodbridge, 2000)

Phillips, G., *Scottish Castles* (Glasgow, 1987)

Platt, C., *The Castle in Medieval England and Wales* (London, 1982)

Renn, Derek, *Norman Castles in Britain* (London, 1968)

Renoux, A., 'Châteaux et résidences fortifiées des ducs de Normandie aux Xe et XIe s.', *Les Mondes Normandes (VIIIe-XIIe s.): actes du IIe congrès international d'archéologie médiévale*, pp.113-124 (Caen, 1989)

Rowley, Trevor, *The Norman Heritage, 1066-1200* (London, 1983)

Saunders, A. D. (co-ord.), *Five Castle Excavations* (RAI, London, 1978)

Stenton, F., *The Bayeux Tapestry*, 2nd edition (London, 1965)

Tabraham, Christopher, *Scottish Castles and Fortifications* (HMSO, Edinburgh, 1986)

Thompson, M. W., *The Rise of the Castle* (Cambridge, 1991)

Thompson, M. W., 'The Military Interpretation of Castles', *Archaeological Journal*, Vol. CLI, pp.439-45 (1994)

Toy, S., *Castles: Their Construction and History* (London, 1939)

Tuulse, A., *Castles of the Western World* (London, 1958)

White, P., 'Castle Gateways During the Reign of Henry II', *Antiquaries Journal*, Vol. LXXVI, pp.241-7 (1996)

Wilson, D., *The Bayeux Tapestry* (London, 1985)

Wood, M. E., *The English Medieval House* (London, 1965)

Yewdale, R. B., *Bohemond I, Prince of Antioch* (Princeton, 1924)

Yver, J., 'Les Châteaux-Forts en Normandie jusqu'au Milieu de XIIe Siècle', *Bulletin Soc. Des Antiquaires de Normandie*, Vol. LIII (1955-6)

Zadora-Rio, E., 'L'Enceinte Fortifié du Plessis-Grimoult, Résidence Seigneuriale du XIe Siècle', *Château-Gaillard*, Vol. V (1970)

Glossary

Aketon	A padded garment, quilted to keep the stuffing in place, worn under or instead of armour. First mentioned in the 12th century.
Apse	A rounded end.
Arçon	The saddle bow and cantle.
Ashlar	Smooth, flat masonry blocks.
Bailey	Courtyard of a castle.
Baldric	Belt slung across the right shoulder, occasionally used to suspend the sword in the 10th and early 11th century.
Ballista	Projectile engine resembling a giant crossbow, utilizing the tension of a bow or the torsion of two arms. Usually shot large arrows or bolts.
Bar hole	A hole in a wall into which a drawbar slides.
Barbican	An outwork that protects a gate.
Barrel vault	A cylindrical plain stone vault.
Batter	The base of a wall thickened with a sloping front.
Belfry	A wooden tower, often mobile, used to overlook a wall or transfer troops on to it.
Berm	The space between a wall and ditch.
Boss	Metal hand-guard on circular shield; decorative on kite-shaped shields.
Braies	Linen drawers.
Brases	Straps for holding a shield.
Brattice	Wooden hoarding built out from battlement to command the base of a wall.
Buttress	Stone support built against a wall to reinforce it.
Cantle	The rear projection of a saddle.
Caparison	Cloth covering for a horse, introduced in the later 12th century.
Chape	Guard fitted to end of scabbard.
Chausses	Leggings of cloth or mail.
Chemise	A wall closely surrounding a donjon.
Coif	Headwear of cloth, usually quilted for military use; a mail hood.
Conroi	Squadron of horsemen, usually 25 or 50 in number.
Corbel	A supporting stone bracket.
Countermine	A tunnel dug from a castle aimed at breaking into an enemy mineshaft.
Counterscarp	The outer slope of a ditch.
Crenel	The open section of a battlement.
Crenellation	Battlement.
Cross-vault	A vault in which two barrel vaults intersect.

Curb	Bit with long levers to which the rein is attached.
Curtain	A length of wall surrounding a castle enclosure.
Destrier	The warhorse.
Donjon	A great tower, but it can also mean an upper bailey or lord's private area.
Drawbar	A wooden beam for securing the inside of a door.
Embrasure	An internal opening in a wall, sometimes for the use of archers.
Enarmes	See 'Brases'.
Enceinte	The area enclosed by the castle walls.
Forebuilding	A stone building erected against the donjon to cover the entrance.
Fuller	Groove running down a sword blade to lighten it.
Gambeson	See 'Aketon'.
Gonfalon	Penon carried by a baron.
Great tower	A keep.
Groined vault	A cross-vault whose edges are sharply defined.
Guige	Strap supporting shield round the neck, or for hanging it up.
Hauberk	Originally a neck-guard. Usually used to refer to the body armour.
Helm	Helmet enclosing the whole head.
Hilt	The cross-guard, grip and pommel of a sword.
Hoarding	See 'Brattice'.
Housing	See 'Caparison'.
Infulae	Pair of cloth strips worn on the rear of the helmet by men of rank.
Jamb	The side of an opening through a wall.
Joggled	Keyed together by overlapping joints.
Keep	The word used in England from the 16th century to describe a donjon or great tower.
Kettle Hat	Open helmet so-called from its likeness to an upturned cauldron.
Lamellar	Armour composed of small metal strips laced together. Uncommon in north-western Europe.
Locket	Metal, ivory or bone guard for the mouth of the scabbard.
Loop	A narrow opening in a wall that splays out internally, designed either to admit light or for shooting through.
Machicolation	Battlement brought forward on corbels to allow soldiers to command the base of a wall.
Mail	Armour composed of many interlinked iron rings.
Mangonel	Variously used to describe a torsion catapult utilizing a skein of cord as a spring, or a trebuchet, often the type utilizing manpower.
Merlon	The solid section of a battlement.
Mine	A tunnel dug under a wall to weaken the foundations and bring it down.
Moat	A ditch, either wet or dry.
Motte	Earthen mound, usually artificial.
Muffler	Mail mitten formed by extending the sleeve.
Mural chamber	A vaulted chamber formed in the thickness of a wall.

Mural passage	A vaulted passage formed in the thickness of a wall.
Mural tower	A tower set along a curtain wall.
Nasal	Nose-guard.
Palfrey	A good riding horse.
Parados	A low, inner wall of a wall-walk.
Parapet	The outer wall of a wall-walk.
Pattern-welded	Method of making a sword blade by twisted rods of iron and carburized iron. Less common after c. 900.
Petrary	A stone-throwing catapult.
Pilaster	A shallow pier built against a wall to buttress it.
Pommel	The weighted end of a hilt; the knob on a saddle bow.
Portcullis	Lattice made of wood clad in iron, or iron alone, dropped to block a gate.
Postern	A small rear door.
Pourpoint	See 'Aketon'.
Prick Spur	One with a pointed terminal.
Rampart	An earthen bank.
Revetment	The side of a ditch, bank or motte faced with wood, stone or brick.
Ring-work	A circular or oval earthwork with bank and ditch.
Rouncy	An ordinary riding horse.
Scale	Armour composed of overlapping metal, bone, horn or leather scales.
Scarp	The side of a ditch.
Scutage	The commuting of knight service by a money payment introduced in the 12th century.
Shell keep	A motte where the timber palisade on the summit is replaced by a stone wall.
Snaffle	Ring bit.
Spur	A solid, pointed stone reinforcement at the base of a tower.
Sumpter	A pack horse.
Surcoat	Cloth garment worn over armour.
Testier	Padded head defence for a horse.
Trapper	See 'Caparison'.
Trebuchet	A catapult whose throwing arm utilizes the principle of counterbalance.
Tree	The wooden framework of a saddle.
Turning bridge	A bridge like a see-saw, the rear half falling into a pit as the front section is raised.
Turret	A small tower.
Vault	A curved ceiling of stone.
Ventail	Flap of mail laced up to protect the throat and lower part of the face.
Vice	A spiral stair.
Wall-walk	A passage along the top of a wall.
Ward	See 'Bailey'.
Wing-wall	A wall descending the slope of a motte.

Index

maps:
Normandy – 130.
Sicily – 134
England – 141

Despite the small geographic extent of Normandy, its people played a crucial role in the history of the medieval world. Throughout the 11th and 12th centuries the Norman knight was possibly the most feared warrior in Western Europe. Their military prowess was renowned throughout the known world and resulted in the Normans conquering Sicily in 1060 and England in 1066, as well as playing a major part in the First Crusade. They built strongholds in important towns such as London and many of their great castles, including the Tower of London, still stand today as a testament to their building skill. This beautifully illustrated book not only looks at the world of the Normans, but also at the life of a typical Norman knight and discusses in detail the inspirational castles that they built to protect their hard-won territory.

Christopher Gravett is a former Senior Curator at the Royal Armouries, Tower of London, and a recognized authority on the arms, armour and warfare of the medieval world. He has worked as an advisor for numerous TV and film productions, and has written a number of books. He currently works as a curator at Woburn Abbey, Bedfordshire.

David Nicolle worked in the BBC's Arabic service for a number of years before gaining an MA from the School of Oriental and African Studies, London, and a doctorate from Edinburgh University. He has written numerous books and articles on medieval and Islamic warfare.

Sep

ganges

eufrates
e theodo
eupka

aspa minor

f. carm

p. hircania

aldaa

spar tan
albania superioz

armeni

amazones
hircanie
albama ibrroz

o. urbam
clasfia

vethe
cozoza
im tov

arealsi an du

xenon

nohinor

selueni
ar oz
eidenia
trileito

grecia

macedo
nia

farma
etea

lantsa
athe

citia
olens

alma
aca

roma

dambul

co tour

bingu

tollo

parilinf